FLORENCE NIGHTINGALE
CASSANDRA
SUGGESTIONS FOR THOUGHT

FLORENCE NIGHTINGALE

CASSANDRA

AND OTHER SELECTIONS FROM

SUGGESTIONS FOR THOUGHT

Edited by

MARY POOVEY

PICKERING & CHATTO

1991

Published by Pickering & Chatto (Publishers) Limited
17 Pall Mall, London SW1Y 5NB

British Library Cataloguing in Publication Data
Nightingale, Florence, *1820–1910*
   Cassandra and, Suggestions for thought. –
   (Pickering Women's Classics)
   I. Title   II. Poovey, Mary   III. Series
   305.42

   ISBN 1–85196–022–8

Printed and bound in Great Britain by
Billing & Sons Limited
Worcester

CONTENTS

INTRODUCTION

Most modern readers associate Florence Nightingale with one of two nineteeth-century campaigns – the creation of modern nursing or the feminist protest against the enforced idleness of middle-class women. Nightingale's reform of nursing (and, perhaps even more significantly, of military hospitals) and her personal demonstration that women could work were undoubtedly her most visible accomplishments, but Nightingale's own reflections on this work reveal that all of her activities were expressions of a complex and unorthodox religious philosophy, which was largely developed before Nightingale left for the East in 1854. *Suggestions for Thought to the Searchers after Truth Among the Artizans of England*, which is published here for the first time, contains Nightingale's most sustained treatment of religious ideas.[1] A major contribution to the religious controversies of the 1850s, *Suggestions for Thought* also explains the reconceptualization of power that underwrote Nightingale's own emotional and intellectual transformation from a frustrated upper-class daughter to the indomitable heroine of a foreign war. As a meditation on the relationship between individual frustrations and the working out of a divine plan, it constitutes Nightingale's contribution to understanding – and resisting – the place that women were alloted in mid nineteenth-century Britain.

The heart of the three-volume, 829-page *Suggestions for Thought* was probably composed between 1850 and 1852. Nightingale's first mention of what she variously called the 'Works' and the 'Stuff' appears in a letter to her father composed on her thirty-second birthday (12 May, 1852). Sir Edward Cook, Nightingale's first modern biographer, describes the 'works' as consisting of two manuscript books – one entitled 'Religion', the

other 'Novel'.[2] Cook argues that the novel format was abandoned after 1852, although traces of this genre remain in the
section of Volume II entitled 'Cassandra'. Scholars agree that the
manuscript book entitled 'Religion' was elaborated and enlarged
sometime between Nightingale's return from the Crimea in
1856 and its printing in 1860. Nightingale sought responses to
her religious doctrine as early as 1852, when she asked the
liberal MP and family friend Richard Monckton Milnes to 'look
over certain things which I have written for the working-men
on the subject of belief' (Cook I, 121). Not until it was privately
printed in 1860, however, did the expanded *Suggestions* receive
more than a few readings. In that year Nightingale sent copies to
six readers including, most notably, the philosopher John Stuart
Mill and the Regius Professor of Greek at Oxford, Benjamin
Jowett.[3] While neither recommended publishing *Suggestions*
without considerable revision, both men were impressed and
annotated their copies extensively. 'I have seldom felt less
inclined to criticize than in reading this book', Mill wrote. 'It
seemed to me as if I had received the impress of a new mind',
Jowett declared (Cook I, 471).

   At the time that she began writing *Suggestions for Thought*,
Florence Nightingale was thirty years old. Born in the city for
which she was named on 12 May, 1820, Florence was the
second daughter of a wealthy, politically liberal family. Her
father, William Edward Shore, had taken the name of Nightingale upon coming of age, in recognition of Peter Nightingale, the
uncle from whom Edward inherited the Lea estate in Derby-
shire. In 1825, Edward Nightingale purchased a second estate,
Embly Park in Hampshire. Frances Nightingale, Florence's
mother, insisted that the family embrace Anglicanism, because
she considered the Established Church more fitting for the
landed gentry than Unitarianism, the sect in which both Edward
and Frances had been raised. Despite the family's adopted
conformity, Florence's childhood was strongly influenced by the
political liberalism and humanitarianism with which Unitarians
were associated and in which her family had always participated.
Florence's maternal grandfather, William Smith, had used his

position in the House of Commons to fight slavery and religious discrimination, and Edward Nightingale had endorsed both parliamentary reform and Bentham's utilitarian moralism.

Florence's mother aspired to give her two daughters not only every advantage that money could buy but also the social graces necessary to shine in high society. Edward, by contrast, was intent upon developing his daughters' intellectual talents. Unable to locate a suitable governess, he personally supervised their rigorous education in Latin, German, Italian, French, history, composition, and philosophy. Each parent found a disciple. Like her mother, Florence's older sister Parthenope (also called Parthe or Pop) embraced the refinements of society – drawing, genteel conversation, and visiting. Like her father, Florence (or Flo) was drawn to abstract speculation, intellectual discipline, and moralizing. While she suffered exquisite pain from her mother's and Parthe's failure to approve her schemes, Florence generated numerous philanthropic plans to spring herself from the gilded cage of upper-class respectability. In 1837, she confided to her diary that God had called her to His service, although she could not determine the nature of His intended work. In 1844, Florence became intent upon studying nursing, but her mother adamantly rebuffed the plan. Between 1844 and 1850, as Florence divided her time between the family's English estates and two long continental tours, she was tormented by the discrepancy between her conviction that God intended her to work and the constraints imposed upon her by a combination of her mother's and sister's conventionality and her own craving for approval. Contrasting Parthe and herself, Florence struggled with her confusion. 'She [Parthe] wants no other religion, no other occupation, no other training than what she has – she is in unison with her age, her position, her country. She has never had a difficulty, except with me – she is a child playing in God's garden & delighting in the happiness of all His works, knowing nothing of human life but the English drawing room, nothing of struggle in her own unselfish nature – nothing of want of power in her own Element. And I, what a murderer I am to disturb this happiness ... What am I that I am not in harmony with all this, that their life is not good enough for me? oh God, what am I?', (Vicinus and Nergaard, 47).

In July 1850, on her way back to England from a tour of Egypt and Greece, Nightingale finally realized her long-held dream of visiting the Institution of Kaiserswerth on the Rhine. In the hospital, penitentiary, and orphanage at Kaiserswerth, working-class women were given rudimentary training in nursing under the direction of Pastor Fliedner and the Lutheran deaconesses. For Nightingale, who had first heard about this institution in 1842, Kaiserswerth promised training by which she could realize God's command to serve. She left Kaiserswerth on 13 August, emboldened with a renewed determination to study nursing. But Nightingale had not reckoned on the strength of her mother's disapproval. Frances still refused to allow her daughter to take up what was widely considered a sordid, morally suspect occupation. Plummeted into depression, Nightingale despaired of ever escaping the monotonous round of aimless leisure. 'In my 31st year I see nothing desirable but death', she wrote in 1851. 'Oh weary days. On evenings that seem never to end – for how many long years I have watched that drawing room clock & thought it never would reach the ten & for 20 or so more years to do this .... This is the sting of death. Why do I wish to leave this world? God knows I do not expect a heaven beyond – but that He will set me down in St. Giles' [a notorious London slum parish] at a Kaiserswerth, there to find my work & my salvation in my work, that I think will be the way, if I could but die' [Vicinus and Nergaard, 44–45).

By thirty-one, Nightingale was approaching the age at which even her mother might cease to expect her to marry. Having rejected the proposals of at least two suitors, Nightingale justified her celibacy by a characteristic marshalling of God's authority. 'I think He has as clearly marked out some to be single women as He has others to be wives', she declared in 1846 (Vicinus and Nergaard, 41). If God did not ordain marriage, He presumably had some plan that Nightingale had to fulfill. With the excuse of accompanying the ailing Parthe to the spa at Carlsbad, Nightingale received permission to visit Kaisers-

werth again from June through October 1851, where she probably received less nursing instruction than moral support.
Finally, with the help of her diplomatic Aunt Mai, Nightingale
got her mother to agree that 'at some future specified age'
Florence would be free to follow the example of earlier lady
philanthropists, like Elizabeth Fry, the prison reformer, and
Catharine Cappe, who worked to admit women visitors to
public and private charitable institutions.[4] While looking for a
suitable philanthropic institution and with the encouragement
of the recently converted Henry Manning, Nightingale set out to
study nursing in Paris with the Catholic Sisters of Charity. In
February 1853, Nightingale joined the Maison de la Providence
in the Faubourg St. Germain, but she was soon recalled to
England to the more socially acceptable task of nursing her
dying grandmother. While in England, Nightingale was recommended by Mrs Sidney Herbert for the superintendency of a
philanthropic organization devoted to impoverished gentlewomen, the Institution for the Care of Sick Gentlewomen in
Distressed Circumstances. Despite her mother's continued pro-
tests, Nightingale was able to accept this position because her
father agreed to give her an allowance of £500 per year – a sum
large enough to enable Nightingale to direct the Institution
without pay. After a brief return to Paris, Nightingale assumed
residence at the Institution on 12 August, 1853.

Florence Nightingale's life of service had therefore barely
begun when international events intervened. On 20 September,
1854 British and French troops landed on the Crimean Penin-
sula, in an attempt to defend the major trade routes to India
from the invading Russians. On 9 October, the first reports
from William Howard Russell, war correspondent for the *Times*,
revealed the terrible suffering inflicted on British troops by the
lack of adequate medical care. Five days later another correspondent crystallized the need in his poignant query, 'Why
have we no Sisters of Charity?' By that date, Nightingale had
begun to enquire about organizing a corps of nurses for the
Crimea, and on 15 October Sidney Herbert, the Secretary for
War, wrote asking if she would be willing to go to the East.

Nightingale was selected for this mission not simply because she asked to go or because of her rudimentary nursing training, but because of her family's political and social connections. Overcoming her parents' resistance by appealing to national duty, Herbert issued official orders to Nightingale on 19 October. Two days later, on 21 October, Nightingale and her hastily assembled band of thirty-eight nurses left London. They arrived at the Barrack Hospital in Scutari on 4 November, 1854.

In the insanitary and inadequately provisioned Barrack Hospital, Nightingale was both heroine and nemesis – heroine to the common soldiers whose pain she relieved, nemesis to the doctors and bureaucrats whose authority she challenged. More of an administrator than a nurse, Nightingale learned from her experience in the Crimea how to negotiate both institutional and individual impediments to her efforts to provision the men. If she was not quite the angel of mercy English journalists deified, Nightingale was nevertheless efficient, determined, and brave. Her service in the Crimea also finally identified for Nightingale a project worthy of her energies and God's approval, the reform of military hospitals. After her return to England in August 1856, Nightingale began her campaigns for the establishment of an Army Medical School and for the appointment of a Royal Commission on the health of the army. Although she was afflicted with an undiagnosable illness that kept her largely confined to her rooms or her couch, Nightingale was able to motivate statesmen like Sidney Herbert and Lord Panmure, the Minister for War, and to compose detailed reports on the administration of the army hospitals and the rate of mortality in army barracks. By 1860, the Royal Commission had produced its report and Nightingale had completed and circulated the work she called 'God's Revenge Upon Murder' – her richly diagrammed *Mortality of the British Army*. That same year she had the three-volume *Suggestions for Thought* set in print.

RELIGIOUS CONTROVERSY IN THE 1850S

The significance of *Suggestions for Thought* is incomprehensible without some understanding of the place that religion occupied in English society in the 1850s. So crucial was religion assumed to be for the well-being of the nation that contemporaries wanted an accurate profile of religious faith to set alongside their statistical measurements of crime, disease, and poverty. The first (and only) statistical analysis of England's faithful, which was published in 1854, disclosed that on 30 March, 1851 5,292,551 people attended the Church of England; 383,630 worshipped at a Roman Catholic Church; and 4,536,264 people attended one of the main protestant dissenting churches. Since the total population of England and Wales, according to the 1851 Census, was 17,927,609, the compiler of the religious census, Horace Mann, concluded that over five and a quarter million people who ought to have attended some place of worship on that Sabbath did not. The majority of the non-attendants, he asserted, were poor or working class.

The problem revealed by the religious census was interpreted differently by different sects: Anglicans were dismayed at the strength of Roman Catholics and dissenters; Catholics were elated at the surge in their numbers; dissenters were appalled at the scarcity of urban ministries. Whatever one's response, however, the census described a new religious landscape – one in which the Church of England no longer represented the majority and where the faithful wealthy were threatened by a growing number of godless poor. Because of the connection that middle-class Englishmen assumed between religious observance and morality, this last revelation was especially disturbing. In large measure it reflects the failure of all organized churches to keep pace with the dramatic demographic and social changes of the first half of the century.

Between 1801 and 1851, the population of England and
Wales is estimated to have doubled (from almost nine million to
just under eighteen million people). More to the point, perhaps,
during the first half of the century this population became
increasingly concentrated in the industrial cities of the north
and in London.[5] Because these demographic changes were rapid
and completely unregulated, the mushrooming urban centres
were utterly inadequate to the influx of new populations. The
capacity of cities like London and Manchester to supply the
requisite housing, sanitation, and water was soon exceeded, and
by the 1840s, slum neighbourhoods, which were often char-
acterized by overcrowded, back-to-back houses and the most
rudimentary sanitary facilities, huddled just off the main thor-
oughfares of prosperous towns. As living conditions in the worst
neighbourhoods deteriorated, so did spiritual facilities. Whereas
local tithes had previously been adequate to support parish
churches in cities as in the countryside, the simultaneous over-
population and impoverishment of some urban parishes, such as
London's St. Giles, meant that churches fell into disrepair and
some parish livings went unfilled. The failure of the Anglican
Church to respond to these changes was exacerbated by three
further factors: the challenge posed to the Church of England by
Methodists beginning in the eighteenth century; the further
challenge posed by the influx of Catholics, especially poor
Catholics, during the 1840s; and the Anglican Church's own
history of corruption and worldliness. By 1850, then, many
residents of urban slums would have found it difficult to attend
any church, even if they had wanted to, and for many, attending
an Anglican Church would have been nearly impossible. This
deplorable state of affairs worried Florence Nightingale as it did
many of her contemporaries. Beginning in 1851, Nightingale
occasionally accompanied her friend Mrs Edward Truelove, wife
of the radical publisher, to the working men's institution in John
Street, London. In the course of conversations with poor workers, she discovered what Horace Mann was also observing, that
even 'the most thinking and conscientious of the artizans have
no religion at all' (Cook I, 120). It was partly to rectify this

situation, to give 'a new religion to the Tailors', that Nightingale began formulating *Suggestions for Thought*.[6]

If Nightingale originally imagined that *Suggestions for Thought* would provide a religion for the artisans, she soon abandoned that scheme and began to address instead the religious and social concerns of her own class. These concerns were also necessarily political, for religion was an intensely politicized arena of public as well as private life at mid-century. While the institution of an Established Church and a concomitant history of religious discrimination provided the obvious bases for religion's political dimension, the political and doctrinal disputes that erupted in the 1840s and 1850s did not always pit Anglicans against their traditional foes, the Catholics and the dissenters. Indeed, many of the religious controversies that Nightingale specifically addresses in *Suggestions for Thought* exploded within the Anglican Church, although they sometimes threatened to catapult their participants out of Anglicanism altogether. One such controversy, which may well have been a precipitating cause for Nightingale's turn away from the artisans, was the so-called Gorham controversy. This dispute, which began in the mid-forties as a disagreement over the significance of infant baptism, had become by 1849 a bitter contest over whether the state had the authority to adjudicate Church matters. By 1850, when the specific issue of a clerical appointment was finally resolved, three prominent Anglicans – Viscount Fielding, T. W. Allies, and Henry Wilberforce – had converted in anger to the Church of Rome.

The Gorham controversy – along with the flurry of Catholic activity (the Papal Aggression) that coincided with its settlement – exposed to contemporaries the bitterness of the religious differences that the 1851 Religious Census tabulated. Because Florence Nightingale addresses these differences at such length in *Suggestions for Thought*, it is important to remind modern readers of some of the doctrinal and practical concerns that distinguished the various sects at mid-century. Within the Established Church, there were essentially two groups by the mid-forties – the evangelicals and the high churchmen. For evangelicals, sacraments like baptism and communion might symbolize divine grace, but such formal rituals were less important than direct inspiration, which was considered necessary for salvation. For high churchmen, who had organized themselves in the 1830s partly in reaction to what was perceived as the dangerous laxity of evangelicals, sacraments and other rites of the ancient Church were central. While evangelicals had traditionally been committed both to individual moral improvement and to social reform, the high churchmen (who were also called Tractarians, Puseyites, and members of the Oxford Movement), stressed personal discipline, the authority of the ancient Church, and tradition over good works or inspiration. Upholding the doctrine of apostolic succession, they aspired to make the English Church Anglo-Catholic.

On the one side, then, the Established Church shaded off into the main protestant dissenting sects, which also bore strong traces of evangelicalism, while on the other side it threatened to merge with Roman Catholicism. Florence Nightingale's own religious experience had brought her into contact with all of these religious groups, and, just as the energy with which she addressed these doctrinal disputes reflects the stakes involved in such sectarian disagreements, so the philosophy she developed reveals the tensions this range of influences created for her. The earliest ideas of Nightingale's religious thought were inspired by her grandparents' Unitarianism and her mother's adopted Anglicanism, and during the mid-1840s, Florence came more directly under the influence of evangelicalism through her aunt Anne's sister-in-law Hannah Nicholson. By 1850, however, Nightingale had come to distrust the evangelicals' emphasis on 'personal judgment'. 'These words are dangerous', she decided, 'because they seem to imply that one person may judge one way, and another another, according to their "private" view of things ... whereas it is the truth, as it were, which *judges* for us' (*ST* II, 294). Drawn during the next few years to the discipline and exactness of the Church of Rome – it was the only church, she maintained, that made a serious 'attempt to organize life so as to enable men to act out their belief' (*ST* II, 118) – Nightingale considered converting during the summer and autumn of 1852, shortly before her visit to Paris. Ultimately, Nightingale decided to retain her official commitment to the Church of England – not because she felt any sympathy for Anglican tolerance but because she could no more submit to Catholicism's demand for unquestioning obedience than she could sanction evangelicalism's laxness. 'My heart belongs as much to the Catholic Ch. as to that of England – oh, how much more', she wrote to Father Manning. 'The only difference is that the former insists peremptorily upon my believing what I cannot believe, while the latter is too careless & indifferent to know whether I believe it or not' (Vicinus and Nergaard, 59–60). 'The Church of England is expected to be an over-idle mother, who lets her children entirely alone,' Nightingale explained, 'because those made her who had found the Church of Rome an over-busy mother. She imprisoned us; she read our letters; she penetrated our thoughts; she regulated what we were to do every hour; she asked us what we had been doing and thinking; she burnt us if we had been thinking wrong. We found her an over active mother, and we made the Church of England, which does not "interfere" with her children at all' (*ST* II, 96–97).

By 1860, then, Nightingale had decided both that the 'artizans' were not the only audience who needed religious instruction and that contemporary doctrinal disputes, including the Gorham controversy, were not simply religious disagreements but also struggles over the terms in which social action should be undertaken. While *Suggestions for Thought* partakes of and contributes to these religious contests, it is as important for its reconfiguration of power as for its doctrinal positions. The reconceptualization of power that underwrote Nightingale's remarkable career was one effect of her attempt to address in religious and practical terms what most of her contemporaries thought of as two incompatible topics – work and women.

THE WOMAN QUESTION

One of the reasons Nightingale was attracted to the Church of Rome was because, of all formal religions, only the Catholic Church had a history of providing organized training for women. By 1850, Tractarians within the Anglican Church had established four Anglican sisterhoods in England, but, in general, Nightingale argued, the Church of England offered nothing to women who wanted to serve. 'The Church of England has for men bishoprics, archbishoprics, and a little work.... She has for women – what? ... They would give her their heads, their hearts, their hands. She does not know what to do with them' (*ST* II, 102). Nightingale formulated her quest for work in terms of religious training not only because the institutions at Kaiserswerth and in Paris where she had sought nursing instruction were religious organizations but also because the question of what middle-class women could or should do with their lives was as thoroughly a religious as a secular concern at mid-century. As long as contemporaries believed that God assigned human beings 'natures' according to their sexes, women were expected to fulfill God's plan by marrying, bearing children, and caring for a home. By contrast, working outside the home – especially for pay – seemed to undermine God's plan – not to mention subverting the money-getting role that was argued to be as natural to men as childbearing was to women.

Despite numerous celebrations of the domestic nature of woman, the 1851 census painted a picture of a society in which God's plan was in danger of going unrealized. According to the census, the proportion of women to men within the marriageable age-group of fifteen to forty-nine years of age was 107 per cent, and this, especially when added to the disproportionate numbers of men who emigrated and the tendency across the population for men to defer marriage to a later age, meant that an increasing number of women seemed fated to remain single for at least part of their marriageable years. One response to this situation was increased public concern about those women of all classes who already worked outside the home. Another response to the so-called problem of redundant women was the formulation of programs to send unmarried women to the colonies. A third response – and the one most germane to Florence Nightingale – involved the establishment of schemes to train women of all classes – but particularly middle-class women – for work.

At one extreme, training plans for women took the form of Anglican sisterhoods. The first of these establishments was the Sisterhood of the Holy Cross, founded in Park Village West, London, in 1845. Like the other early sisterhoods – the Community of St Mary the Virgin (1848), the Society of the Most Holy Trinity (1848), and the Community of Nursing Sisters of St. John the Divine (1848) – the Holy Cross Sisterhood was intended to serve two purposes: to enhance Tractarians' desire to give a higher, more Catholic tone to the Anglican Church and to give a 'holy employment to many who yearn for something' (Anson 222). While many of the women who joined these sisterhoods contributed substantially to the spiritual and domestic improvement of urban neighbourhoods and to the general level of expertise within nursing in particular, Anglican sisterhoods were received with suspicion by many of the English middle class, both because the spectre of convent-like communities was threatening to many Anglicans and because the idea of any community of women obeying a female superior instead of a husband smacked of subordination gone awry, of 'unnatural' manipulation while more obvious duties went unfulfilled.

At the other extreme, training projects for unmarried women were organized in the second half of the 1850s by a group of women without a specifically religious agenda. Led by Bessie Rayner Parkes and Barbara Leigh Smith Bodichon, the ladies of Langham Place wanted both to expand the number of jobs available to women and to address the economic inequality perpetuated by the failure of the Married Women's Property

Bill in 1857. In that same year, Bodichon published the influential *Women and Work* and in 1858 the Langham Place group founded the *English Woman's Journal*. By 1859, in response to the demand by lower middle-class women who wanted work, Bodichon and Parkes had established the Society for the Promotion of the Employment of Women. With the help of another early feminist, Jessie Boucherett, the group opened a business school for girls. The schemes established by the Langham Place group were in keeping with other, less specifically feminist educational institutions founded for women during the 1840s and 1850s. Queen's College and Bedford College were founded in 1848, and these training schools were soon followed by the North London Collegiate School for Women (1850) and the Ladies' College at Cheltenham (1850).

To a certain extent, Nightingale was sympathetic to both of these projects to expand work opportunities for women. As we have seen, Nightingale was attracted to the discipline that a sisterhood could provide, but, partly as a result of her experience in the Crimea, she became deeply suspicious of 'the evils which experience has shown to arise in religious orders' (*ST* II, 330). By the time she founded the Nightingale Nursing School at St. Thomas's Hospital (1860), Nightingale was also committed to professionalized training for women and to women working for pay. Although she shared many of the principles advocated by the ladies of Langham Place, however, she remained hostile to 'strong-minded women' as a group and opposed to women entering certain kinds of work, including medicine. *Suggestions for Thought* helps clarify Nightingale's position on women. Specifically, Volume II reveals how Nightingale's formulation of the problem of women and work in religious terms helped her chart a middle course between the 'superstitious' sister and the 'strong-minded' woman. On the one hand, as *Suggestions for Thought* makes clear, objections formulated in religious terms had to be countered before any respectable lady could substitute other work for the duty she owed her family. On the other hand, religious formulations of a 'higher calling' had already been used to authorize other women's escapes from the confines of domesticity. Nightingale's solution to the problem of women and work, then, was to represent a woman's immediate family as a microcosm of a much larger kinship system. To *this* family – the family headed by God – a woman owes the duty she fulfils by working in the world, even if that work removes her from the little family into which she was born. 'We would not destroy the family, but make it larger', Nightingale explains. 'We would not prevent people from having the ties of blood, but we would secure all that the family promises, by enlarging it' (*ST* II, 319).

Nightingale's solution to the problem of women and work could therefore pass as an extension of woman's God-given duties into the larger family of society. Following this logic, Nightingale referred to the soldiers buried in the Crimea as her 'sons' and to herself as their devoted 'mother'. Especially as it was realized in her own life, however, this solution could also underwrite a reconceptualization of social relations, which, in practice if not in theory, constituted a reconfiguration of power. After she returned from the Crimea, Florence Nightingale devoted herself to administrative and nursing reform, not just for the domestic sphere but for military hospitals and India as well. Her power was always exercised indirectly, as a woman's influence should be, but the letters and reports by which she pursued her goals were so effective that Queen Victoria wished her in the War Office. So great was her own sense of mission that Nightingale depicted herself not only as a mother but as another Christ, come to save the world that was her larger family. Viewed from the perspective of any orthodox creed, this could seem an arrogant, even blasphemous, appropriation of power. In terms of Nightingale's religious philosophy, however, her claims sought simply to realize God's perfect plan.

Suggestions for Thought to the Searchers after Truth Among the Artizans of England fills three volumes, only the first of which is directed to 'artizans'. Each volume is prefaced by an extensive digest, which summarizes the volume's contents, and the text throughout contains printed marginal commentaries and summary page headers. Volume I sets out Nightingale's religious philosophy in greatest detail. Volume II is devoted to the 'practical implications' of her creed. This volume contains two long sections on women – 'Theory of Daughters' and 'Cassandra'. Volume III summarizes Nightingale's argument, paying particular attention to two of her central tenets – the law and moral right.

Despite the organizational flaws that early readers identified – the text is both repetitive and digressive – *Suggestions for Thought* contains a complex and compelling argument that takes up most of the theological and many of the practical controversies of the 1850s. Nightingale's explicit goal in these volumes is to 'satisfy the craving of a moral nature to believe that *what is, ought to be* – in other words, that what *is, is satisfactory to a moral nature*' (III, 34). Since this is patently not the case, since 'the actual history of human existence' is a numbing chronicle of suffering and evil, Nightingale suggests that we must understand this history as partial. The 'temporary and immediate' results of God's plan, she explains – what we know as human history and everyday life – are only parts of the true '*character and tendency of Law*'. The law, she continues, reveals that God is both righteous and powerful; from this law we can therefore infer that human existence is connected to a further realization of God's nature – 'by which connexion [sic] the desire for moral right is satisfied' (III, 1).

Nightingale's solution to the problems of suffering and evil therefore combines a theory of natural law with a developmental narrative. This helps explain why Volume I opens with a discussion of different civilizations, for like many other Victorians, Nightingale is arguing that different civilizations embody different stages of human development. The difference between an 'undeveloped' society like Australia and a relatively developed society like England tells the story of human progress – not only in terms of cultural amenities but in relation to religious truth. 'The highest state of belief . . .' she proclaims, 'must be the result of the highest state of development' (I, 6).

Given this premise, Nightingale undertakes two tasks: to explain how we can transcend the imperfect state of our own civilization to know God's law; and to demonstrate the ways in which humans can contribute to the social progress that enacts this law. The first task initially entails distinguishing between what humans cannot know – 'God the Father as the spirit of perfection' – and what we can know – the 'tendencies' that point to 'the perfect purpose of God' (I, 9, 11). While Nightingale's conviction that a perfect, if unknowable, God exists depends as much on her desire for such perfection as upon any proof, her argument about 'tendencies' is founded on empirical observation: what we see in the world, she claims, reveals that God's law exists, for what we see is consistent. This consistency, which can be scientifically measured and statistically tabulated, justifies Nightingale's belief in God. Only by supposing a God, she argues, can we account for 'consistency in all existence, concerning which we know anything. . . . This consistency is found only in supposing a perfect thought, sentiment, purpose, to exist, – in supposing the nature of this existence to be perfect goodness, benevolence, wisdom, righteousness' (I, 63).

The consistency that modern science is confirming in material phenomena dispenses with the need for miracles to prove that God exists. Thus science, and statistics as an instrument of scientific inquiry, become handmaidens to religious certainty, not threats to belief. Through science we come to know law; knowing law, we understand ourselves to be parts of some greater, more perfect plan. Placing law and consistency at the heart of her doctrine, however, potentially challenges the idea of free will. Nightingale resolves this potential contradiction by distinguishing between the universal law and specific 'decrees.'

> The proposition that the smallest circumstance comes to us from the will of God is true in this sense. A man is and does what he is and does, because it is the will of God that certain definite propositions, thoughts, emotions, volitions, shall succeed or co-exist with certain organizations and circumstances. It is not true in the sense that each particular perception, thought, emotion, volition is caused directly by the decree of God that so it shall be. In the former sense, it is our business to discover, to desire and to attain the circumstances and organizations which produce the right volitions, etc., that is, those which are one with God's. This discovery we are intended to make by experience, not our own individual experience alone, but the collective experience of all mankind (I, 75).

This formulation suggests how Nightingale pursues the second crucial task of *Suggestions for Thought*. Human beings contribute to the realization of God's law, she argues, through work – work that is designed to develop individual capabilities and to enhance society as a whole. In Nightingale's scheme, work takes precedence over prayer, just as scientific investigation takes precedence over reading the Bible or awaiting miracles. As the only means to human happiness, work must be as demanding and capacious as human energy: 'a man will be really religious in feeling and act', Nightingale explains, '. . . in proportion as *all* his capabilities are rightly exercized' (I, 25). As the agent of change and the proof that God's will can be made visible, work is worship in this world. 'Not one instant does any state of sinfulness or sorrow continue which is not its development into righteousness by the only road, through which the only progress, which is perfect righteousness – viz., through the will, the work of God's servants, His children' (III, 93).

The spiritual and ethical importance Nightingale assigns to work reveals why she feels that the life of an upper- or middle-class daughter to be so cruel. 'In this life', she explains, 'human nature is not exercized to anything like the degree which it is capable of' (II, 98). Suffering what feels like tyranny from her parents, deprived of both desire and training, the young woman languishes in captivity, thereby squandering her chance to do God's work or advance His plan. Nightingale's extensive comments on the plight of wealthy daughters in Volume II are often bitter ('Very few people live such an impoverishing and confusing and weakening life as the women of the richer classes', II, 233), but she struggles to derive even from this some basis for hope. Paradoxically, the hope that Nightingale salvages is derived from suffering. Suffering, she explains, sometimes provides a motivation as keen as desire, for suffering makes one cry out for change. Like error and failure, therefore, suffering can help fulfil God's plan. 'A few of peculiar nature, are urged', Nightingale explains, 'either by suffering from the trammels of conventional life, or by feeling the want of opportunity to learn what they would do, if they could, to wish for something springing from a truer foundation than conventional life. It is for these sufferers to lead the way, if they can. It is not necessary for *all* to suffer. Some through suffering must find out the truth; but, when found, its loveliness will attract others' (II, 265).

Nightingale's theory of suffering is related to one of her most controversial doctrines, her notion that there can and must be modern-day saviours. 'There must be saviours from social, from moral error', she writes (II, 202); 'may we all be Saviours in some way to humanity!' (II, 90). A man – even a woman, as she asserts in 'Cassandra' – can be a saviour like Christ, because Christ was no more (or less) divine than any other human. Christ was a good man who made beautiful pronouncements, Nightingale claims, but sometimes he spoke 'absently' or falsely (II, 165). Nightingale insists that truth does not come to human beings through any kind of 'miraculous light' – whether this is manifested in Christ or miracles or the Bible – but only through human work, suffering, and error. 'May we not look to see the possibility of a religious society, the religion of which shall not profess to be other than the discoveries of mankind through the nature God has given to man, and through the teachings of God in His universe *to* that nature?' (II, 191).

Viewed in the context of more orthodox nineteenth-century

creeds, many of Nightingale's doctrines sound as heretical as her denunciations of Christ's divinity. In Volume III she details her departures from Anglican and Catholic orthodoxy: human beings have no innate responsibility; God's nature is not the only nature that exists; prayers are worthless; the Bible is neither the word of God nor a reliable guide to truth; human beings are not innately evil. Boldly, Nightingale embraces the heterodoxy of her audacious claims. 'There have been three parties', she declaims, '– those who have said that there was a revelation through the book; those who have said that there was a revelation through the Church, or through the book and the Church; and those who have said that there was no revelation at all. Now we say that there is a revelation to every one, through the exercise of his own nature – that God is always revealing Himself' (II, 94–95).

Nightingale's doctrines were not wholly original, of course. In addition to the evangelical and Catholic influences already mentioned, Nightingale herself acknowledges several 'philanthropical political economists [and] enlightened educationalists' whose work she read and approved. These include the Edinburgh lawyer and phrenologist George Combe; the mathematician R. L. Ellis; Richard Owen, the comparative anatomist; the French cosmologist and philosopher August Comte; H. T. Buckle, the English historian; and the Belgian statistician August Quetelet (I, 56, 239–40). What united these otherwise quite different thinkers was the importance they all assigned to the regularities of the natural world and to the systematic organization of knowledge about this world. Nightingale's life-long interest in statistics and her extensive knowledge about contemporary geological and astronomical theories are testimony to her commitment to those branches of Victorian science most devoted to recording the laws of the natural world.

Doctrines similar to those Nightingale held had also begun to be formulated within the Church of England as early as the 1830s. Partly in response to Charles Lyell's *Principles of Geology* (1830–33), scientifically minded clergymen like Baden Powell, the Savilian professor of geometry at Oxford, had endorsed the scientific doctrine of 'final causes' and argued that the non-scientific parts of the Bible were merely 'poetical imagery'. In the 1850s, the so-called broad church movement attempted to make some of the high church principles endorsed by the Tractarians accommodate not only the findings of the new science but also German philosophy, the troubling implications of which were evident in David Friedrich Strauss's *Life of Jesus* (translated into English in 1846 by Marian Evans [George Eliot]). The broad church movement included, in addition to Baden Powell,[7] Benjamin Jowett, F. D. Maurice, and Arthur Stanley. The fact that Nightingale engaged in a long correspondence with Jowett suggests that she recognized the affinities between this group's efforts to reconcile religion and science and her own.

Despite the protestations of humility that punctuate *Suggestions for Thought*, Florence Nightingale obviously seemed uncompromising and imperious to many of her contemporaries. Nightingale's infamous tendency to lecture the men who served her after she returned from war was matched by her lifelong lack of consideration for her women friends and relatives. In 1852, Florence's sister complained bitterly about Nightingale's instrumental treatment of others. 'I believe she has little or none of what is called charity or philanthropy', Parthe wrote to Madame Mohl, 'she is ambitious – very, and would like well enough to regenerate the world with a grand *coup de main* or some fine institution. . . . She has no *esprit de conduite* in the practical sense. When she nursed me, everything which intellect and kind intention could do was done, but she was a shocking nurse. . . . Whereas her influence upon people's minds and her curiosity in getting into the varieties of mind is insatiable. After she has got inside, they generally cease to have any interest for her' (Vicinus and Nergaard, 56–57).

Parthe was clearly a prejudiced witness, but no one disputes that, especially in social relations, Florence Nightingale could be difficult, to say the very least. While the doctrine set out in

Suggestions for Thought cannot justify the ruthlessness with which Nightingale sometimes used other people, it does help explain both the anger she turned against the life her mother designed for her and the ceaseless energy by which she pushed herself and others to work. For Florence Nightingale, every moment spent in a drawing room was a lost opportunity to do God's work, every diversion from the appointed task betrayed those who had already given their lives for the cause. With the perfection of humanity hanging in the balance, Nightingale felt herself not only called but driven.

Baltimore   MARY POOVEY

NOTES

[1] Copies of the privately printed *Suggestions for Thought* are held by the British Museum Library, the London Library, the New York Public Library, and the Yale Medical School Library. The only portion of this text that has been published in a modern edition is the segment of Volume II entitled 'Cassandra'. 'Cassandra' was published by Ray Strachey as an appendix to *The Cause: A Short History of the Women's Movement in Great Britain* (London, G. Bell & Sons, 1928). It was reprinted, with an introduction by Myra Stark, in 1979 (Old Westbury, Feminist Press, 1979).

[2] See Sir Edward Cook, *The Life of Florence Nightingale*, vol. I (London, Macmillan & Co., 1913), p. 119.

[3] See Vincent Quinn and John Prest, eds., *Dear Miss Nightingale: A Selection of Benjamin Jowett's Letters to Florence Nightingale* (Oxford, Clarendon Press, 1987), pp. xii–xiii. The six recipients of *Suggestions for Thought* were Nightingale's father, her uncle Sam Smith, Monckton Milnes, Sir John McNeill (who had worked on the commission of inquiry into the commissariat in the Crimea), Benjamin Jowett, and John Stuart Mill.

[4] For a discussion of lady philanthropists in the early nineteenth century, see F. K. Proschaska, *Women and Philanthropy in Nineteenth-Century England* (Oxford, Clarendon Press, 1980), chapter 5.

[5] See Eric E. Lampard, 'The Urbanizing World', in H. J. Dyos and Michael Wolff, *The Victorian City: Images and Realities* (London and Boston, Routledge & Kegan Paul, 1973), vol. I, pp. 3–57.

[6] Cook explains Nightingale's references to 'tailors' as an allusion to the hero of Kingsley's *Alton Locke*, which was published in 1850. See Cook, *The Life*, vol. I, p. 119.

[7] For a discussion of Baden Powell and other scientific clergymen, see Michael Ruse, 'The Relationship between Science and Religion in Britain, 1830–1870', *Church History* 44 (December 1975), 505–22.

WORKS CITED

Anson, Peter F. *The Call of the Cloister: Religious Communities and Kindred Bodies in the Anglican Communion* (London, S. P. C. K., 1955).

Chadwick, Owen. *The Victorian Church, Part One: 1829–1859* (1966; rpt. London, SCM Press, 1987).

Cook, Sir Edward. *The Life of Florence Nightingale*, 2 vols. (London, Macmillan & Co., 1913).

Nightingale, Florence. *Suggestions for Thought to the Searchers after Truth Among the Artizans of England*, 3 vols. (London, George E. Eyre and William Spottiswoode, 1860).

Vicinus, Martha and Bea Nergaard (ed.). *Ever Yours, Florence Nightingale: Selected Letters* (Cambridge, Mass., Harvard University Press, 1990).

NOTE ON THIS EDITION

In preparing this edition of *Suggestions for Thought*, I have included the sections that set out Nightingale's religious philosophy and her thoughts on the position of women. In almost every case, I have chosen to provide entire sections of the text rather than edit out the repetitiousness or digressions within sections. I have included a larger selection from Volume II than from either of the other volumes because Nightingale's 'Practical Deductions' are generally more accessible and interesting than the more abstract theorizing contained in Volumes I and III. Almost without exception, the themes Nightingale advances abstractly in these volumes receive more concrete and extended treatment in Volume II.

The original volume, part and section numbers have been retained. Part numbers are referred to as chapters in volume III of the original text, but are referred to as parts in this edition for consistency with other volumes. Where a part is not reproduced in full this is indicated by a dotted line under the last section reprinted.

CHRONOLOGY OF
FLORENCE NIGHTINGALE'S LIFE

12 May 1820	Born – Florence, Italy
1849–50	Tour of Egypt, Greece and Germany. Two-week stay at Kaiserswerth
July–September	Returns to Kaiserswerth
1850	Begins *Suggestions for Thought*
Aug1853–Oct 1854	Superintendent of Harley Street Hospital for Gentlewomen
Oct 1854–July 1856	Superintendent of the English Hospitals in the East during the Crimean War
Aug 1856–May 1857	Works informally for the Royal Commission on the Health of the Army
March 1858	Appoints committee to oversee the Nightingale Fund
1858	*Notes on Matters Affecting the Health, Efficiency, and Hospital Administration of the British Army* *Notes on Hospitals*
24 June 1860	Nightingale School of Nursing opens
1860	*Notes on Nursing* *Suggestions for Thought* privately printed
1863	*How People May Live and not Die in India*
1864–68	Works with War Office on sanitary reform in India and with William Rathbone on workhouse nursing
1867	*Suggestions on the Subject of Providing, Training, and Organizing Nurses for the Sick Poor in Workhouse Infirmaries*
1870	Consultant for both sides about military nursing during the Franco-Prussian War
1871	*Introductory Notes on Lying-In Institutions*
1907	Receives Order of Merit
1908	Granted Freedom of the City of London
13 August 1910	Dies in her sleep

WORKS BY FLORENCE NIGHTINGALE

'Cassandra', in Strachey, Ray, *The Cause* (London, G. Bell & Sons, 1928), pp. 395–418.

A Contribution to the Sanitary History of the British Army During the Late War with Russia (London, John W. Parker, 1859).

Florence Nightingale's Indian Letters, ed. Priyaranjan Sen (Calcutta, Mihir Kumar Sen, 1937).

Florence Nightingale to her Nurses: A Selection of Miss Nightingale's Addresses to Probationers and Nurses of the Nightingale School at St. Thomas' Hospital (London, Macmillan, 1914).

How People May Live and Not Die in India (London, Emily Faithfull, 1863).

'I Have Done My Duty': Florence Nightingale in the Crimean War, 1854–56, ed. Sue M. Goldie (Manchester, Manchester University Press, 1987).

The Institution of Kaiserswerth on the Rhine for the Practical Training of Deaconesses (London, Ragged Colonial Training School, 1851).

Letters from Egypt: A Journey on the Nile, 1849–1850, selected and introduced by Anthony Sattin (London, Weidenfeld & Nicolson, 1987).

Notes on Hospitals (3rd edn. London, Longman, Green, Longman, Roberts & Green, 1863).

Notes on Matters Affecting the Health, Efficiency, and Hospital Administration of the British Army, founded Chiefly on Experience of the Last War (London, Harrison & Sons, 1858).

Notes on Nursing: What It Is and What It Is Not (London, Harrison, 1860).

Observations on the Evidence Contained in the Stational Reports Submitted to her by the Royal Commission on the Sanitary State of the Army in India (London, Edmund Stanford, 1863).

'The People of India', *Nineteenth Century* 4 (1878), 193–221.

Selected Writing of Florence Nightingale, ed. Lucy Ridgely Seymer (New York, Macmillan, 1954).

Suggestions for Thought to the Searchers after Truth among the Artizans of

England. 3 volumes (London, Eyre & Spottiswoode, 1860 [privately printed]).

Suggestions for a System of Nursing for Hospitals in India (London, Eyre & Spottiswoode, 1965).

SECONDARY WORKS

Baly, Monica, *Florence Nightingale and the Nursing Legacy* (London, Croom Helm, 1986).

Bishop, W. J. and Sue Goldie, comp., *A Bio-Bibliography of Florence Nightingale* (London, Dawsons, 1962).

Boyd, Nancy, *Josephine Butler, Octavia Hill, Florence Nightingale: Three Victorian Women Who Changed Their World* (London, Macmillan, 1982).

Cook, Sir Edward, *The Life of Florence Nightingale*, 2 volumes (London, Macmillan, 1913).

Cope, Zachery, *Florence Nightingale and the Doctors* (London, Museum, 1958).

Fink, L. G., 'Catholic Influences in the Life of Florence Nightingale', *Hospital Program*, 15 (December, 1934), 482–89.

Goldie, Sue, *A Calendar of the Letters of Florence Nightingale* (Oxford, Oxford Microform, 1983).

O'Malley, I. B., *Florence Nightingale, 1820–1856: A Study of Her Life Down to the End of the Crimean War* (London, Thornton Butterworth, 1931).

Poovey, Mary, *Uneven Developments: The Ideological Work of Gender in Mid-Victorian England* (Chicago, University of Chicago Press, 1989).

Quinn, Vincent and John Prest, *Dear Miss Nightingale: A Selection of Benjamin Jowett's Letters to Florence Nightingale, 1860–1893* (Oxford, Clarendon, 1987).

Rosenberg, Charles E., 'Florence Nightingale on Contagion: The Hospital as Moral Universe', in *Healing and History: Essays for George Rosen*, ed. Charles E. Rosenberg (New York, Science History Publications, 1979), pp. 116–36.

Showalter, Elaine, 'Florence Nightingale's Feminist Complaint: Women, Religion, and *Suggestions for Thought*', *Signs* 6, 31 (1981), 395–412.

Smith, F. B., *Florence Nightingale: Reputation and Power* (London, Croom Helm, 1982).

Strachey, Lytton, *Eminent Victorians* (London, Chatto & Windus, 1918).

Summers, Anne, *Angels and Citizens: British Women as Military Nurses, 1854–1914* (London, Routledge & Kegan Paul, 1988).

Tarrant, W. G., *Florence Nightingale as a Religious Thinker* (London, British and Foreign Unitarian Association, 1920).

Vicinus, Martha and Bea Nergaard, *Ever Yours, Florence Nightingale: Selected Letters* (Cambridge, Mass., Harvard University Press, 1990).

Woodham-Smith, Cecil, *Florence Nightingale* (Edinburgh, Constable, 1950).

Suggestions for Thought

to the Searchers after Truth

Among the Artizans of England

DEDICATION

To the Artizans of England

FELLOW-SEARCHERS,

I come to you not to declare the truth; I come to ask you (if subjects of moral truth have an interest with you) to join in seeking it with those capabilities which God has given to us. I offer the result of my own endeavours, and what I am able to gather from the endeavours of others.

But what are the many to do, who have no inclination to study such subjects? What are the 'poor and ignorant' to do for a religion?

Is the object of our desire in religion to be a religion suited to the 'poor and ignorant'? The object of our desire is to be Truth. All should have their faculties exercised and educated, for the purpose of forming a judgment of what is God's truth.

It is thought desirable for all to learn what is necessary to gain a livelihood. Arithmetic and other matters of instruction are taught for this purpose. But education is not pursued altogether with a right spirit and purpose. Man's education should be given for the purpose of *re*-generation; of putting him in possession of the capability of exercising his powers, so that those powers may reveal to him what, among the labours of mankind after truth, is really truth; may enable him to judge of the nature of God, the nature and destination of man, and how practically to pursue that destination.

But how forlorn, many say, thus to be left without an authority on the awful subject of religion!

We are not left without 'authority'. The Spirit of Truth will be our authority, if we will faithfully seek Him. Can there really have been an 'authority', when such different Gods have been believed in; such different modes of serving God pursued? Truth is, indeed, ONE; but the only way to 'unity of faith', is a true cultivation of the nature, and a true life in which to exercise it. If this can be discovered, *unity* of faith will exist.

Moses and Paul came forth from their desert, saying, 'this and this is miraculously revealed truth, which the world is to believe'. Should it not rather be said, '*this is truth*, viz., that man is to discover from the means within and without his nature, all the truth to find which that nature is competent'?

We offer you what we believe to be truth. We offer our reasons to your reason, our feelings to your feeling. *Judge ye if it is truth.*

Do we speak of what is important? Then consider it. *Is* it important? If not, hear us no further in this matter.

VOLUME ONE

PART I

Belief in God

1. You ask if we believe in God? If those who disregard
authority believe in a God at all, and why they believe Him
perfect?

The two questions have one and the same answer. I believe in
a perfect being, whom you call God.

But why do you believe in Him?

If you ask that question, we come immediately to the definition of the two words 'believe' and 'God'. What does 'I believe'
mean?

It means, in common language, sometimes doubt and sometimes affirmation. 'Is A. B. in London?' 'I believe so.' Here it
means, 'I do not know, but I think it probable'. 'Why do you
think he has been there?' 'I believe his word'. Here it means firm
persuasion. But even here the belief is qualified by the modest.
'I', which means, 'It is I who believe, I don't know whether
others do'. What is therefore to be understood by 'belief'?
Sometimes a sense of certainty, sometimes of uncertainty.

What will Johnson[1] tell us? The sense in which the word has
been used by certain writers, called classic. Johnson says that
'belief' is credit given on account of authority. But have we
really no other sources of belief than authority? There are means
of belief in the capabilities of human nature, and human nature
makes progress. At least in some things. Ideas make progress.

And the meanings attached to words which express ideas cannot, therefore, remain the same. A house may mean a house in all ages, though even in the case of words which express things, the house which we build now signifies a very different thing from the house built by the painted Briton. How much greater must be the difference in the sense of a word used to express a religious or a political idea! Either we must have new words or new meanings.

Johnson will define religion as 'virtue founded upon reverence of God and expectation of future rewards and punishments', and will quote Milton, South, Watts, and Law[2] for this sense of the word. Another theologian (belonging to an African tribe) thinks religion means jumping over a stick. If either of these be really religion, we want a new word to express so different an idea as the sense we have of our *tie* to God.

With what meaning, then, do we 'believe' in God?

Man advances to a consciousness and conviction that there does exist a perfect being (whom we may call God), exactly in proportion as his nature is well constituted, well-educated, well exercised. Human nature, when thus *well-born* and *well-bred*, will *admit* of his sense of this truth, and of others inferred from it, being as strong and complete as the sense of truth with which he asserts that the tree before his eyes is a tree, and not a house.

But we must be careful to know that the God whom we believe in *is* a perfect being. Men often think that they believe in a perfect God when, in fact, they do not, – when they are really wholly incapable of even conceiving of a perfect being. For instance, in the earlier nations, where revenge was considered a virtue in man, it would naturally be thought so in God. Many imperfections, as we now think them, were once deemed virtues, and consequently attributed to a God who was *called* perfect. The religious history of the Hebrews is especially curious on this account.

Again, the God 'of Abraham, of Isaac, and of Jacob', was certainly *not* the God 'of the whole earth'. It is true that the Hebrews *served* but Him alone; they *believed*, however, in the existence of many Gods. Their own God they reverenced, and

despised the other Gods. But it was not till long afterwards that
they rose with increasing knowledge to the belief that there was
but one supreme. Yet He cannot be perfect if there be more
than one. Is it, perhaps, that a knowledge of natural philosophy,
such as cannot be attained by an infant nation, is necessary for
the conception of one supreme being? The more we learn the
more cause we find to think that the whole system of the
universe is one scheme. Astronomy leaves no room, so to speak,
for more than one throne. The same legislation prevails everywhere. All becomes one whole, with one ruler.

Take those very Hebrews. Moses had learnt in Egypt, had
matured in the desert, his noble conception of a Divine Spirit.
But his savage Hebrew tribe was incapable of it; and he himself
was obliged to allow it to deteriorate to their level. Whenever
one man has endeavoured to impose the more perfect idea of a
supreme being, which has had its origin in his own more
advanced mind, upon a nation less developed than himself, we
see it degenerate.

If the stage of civilization be very low indeed, the race is
incapable of conceiving of a God at all. One of the French
'Sisters of Charity' (the only real 'women of the world') who see
all nations and all conditions, told me that the single race within
their knowledge, who did not possess the idea of *any* supernatural being, was a tribe in Australia, not far from Perth. They
were in the lowest conceivable state of animal existence. She
had with her one of their children, which she had bought for a
shilling, when about to be eaten by its tribe, and which appeared
little above an animal, except that it stood on two legs and had
no wings. It imitated like an ape, and stole like a magpie.*

I related this to an operative engineer, and he said slowly and
thoughtfully, 'That is just the condition in which most of my
fellow workmen are, and they do not know whether they
believe in a God or not. Sometimes they do and sometimes they
don't'.

*This child is now at a school in England, where it has advanced by the most rapid strides
from an animal into a human being. It now believes in a God.

I am trying to arrive at the meaning which we shall attach to the word 'belief', to prove that the highest state of belief, (viz., in the signification of the strongest conviction,) must be the result of the highest stage of development; that, therefore, we cannot be said to 'believe' in this sense, except when we have reached that state; and that at an earlier stage of development in man, 'belief' will mean a sense of uncertainty; at a later, a sense of certainty. Is it not possible that this sense of uncertainty it is which has led so many lately into the Roman Catholic Church, and some the most learned, the most earnest? Scepticism, not belief, has brought them there. They required their sense of a truth to be stronger and more complete than it was. The more they urged themselves to believe, the less real was their feeling of belief, till, at last, they took refuge in the belief of others to supply that which they had not in themselves.

In this age, however, by far the greater proportion of mankind, have gone the other way; in England, most of the educated among the operatives, especially in the northern manufacturing towns, have turned their faces to atheism or at least to theism[3] – not three in a hundred go to *any* place of worship; the moral and intellectual among them being, almost without an exception, 'infidels'.

These poor fellows, thinking so hard and so conscientiously, leave out the best element in the food which they so earnestly seek; the most divine element, that which makes confusion into order, that which makes the lowest into the highest; for the highest discoverable principle in existence, perhaps, is the feeling residing in the perfect One, which wills happiness; the thought of the perfect One, that happiness is, by its essence, worked out for the happy by exercise of their own natures and of other natures like theirs. *Time* is all that intervenes between man as he is, and man made one with God. Time intervenes only because that would not be the spirit of wisdom to which it was possible to will man to be one with God otherwise than through the exercise of man's faculties.

Whenever man rejects revelation, however, he is too apt to say immediately, 'God is incomprehensible, we will not seek for

Him, because we shall not find Him'. And he is left without a God, even where he does not deny the existence of one.

Such an one will think it fanciful to look upon the 'Holy Ghost' as a real existence. Hitherto we have rather looked for it, because it exists in the belief of so many, than felt it to be essential; but the love, the wisdom, the goodness, the righteousness, the power which *we* can, with our thought and feeling, recognize in law and its expression in the universe: these we may perhaps better call the 'Holy Ghost' than God, whom (as so much of the intellect of the present day says) we cannot understand. A distinction is necessary between what we can understand and feel, and what we cannot. Very much mischief has arisen from what has been said and written about the latter. That a Father of the universe exists, but incomprehensible to us, may be shown, not by mathematical proof, but by such strong presumptive evidence (by evidence, too, increasing with our knowledge and the improvements of our being) that man may live and feel in accordance with the fact, as with much else not mathematically proveable. But, with truth, it is said that we cannot comprehend Him, and, disgusted by the dogmatizing of theologians and churches, many are refusing to believe His existence. Instead of saying, 'I cannot understand the Holy Ghost', as we with many have said – instead of His appearing in the Trinity one knows not why – perhaps it is a Holy Ghost *only* that we *can* understand; perhaps we may find in these words the expression we want for that which each man can feel and comprehend of the Father.

Perhaps Paul unwisely said what we have beforetimes so often admired, 'Whom ye ignorantly worship, Him reveal I unto you'. He could only reveal that which he had himself felt and understood of God's truth,* and only to natures capable of receiving that revelation.

Let us distinguish God the Father as the spirit of perfection,

---

* This is the 'treasure which we have in earthly vessels', – 'that the excellency of the power may be' not 'of God', but of *man*.

incomprehensible to us; God the Holy Ghost, as what is comprehensible to each man of the perfect spirit.

To 'receive the Holy Ghost', what a remarkable expression that was! No wonder that those to whom it was addressed said they did not 'so much as know that there was a Holy Ghost'. This is just the state of those among the men called atheists in the present day, who are thinking and conscientious.

To 'receive the Holy Ghost' is to exercise the capabilities of man, in as far as each is able, in apprehending the spirit of perfection. Truly do these atheists say, 'We cannot understand God', so they leave the subject entirely as irrelevant. This true consciousness of not being able to understand, to feel God, has led, on the one hand, to being 'without' the Holy Ghost, the Comforter, 'in the world'; on the other, to the making Christ an anomalous being, called God, called not God. We cannot be too careful to admit our present ignorance, and any essential incapability in our nature. Neither can we be too careful to admit *no* incapability of attainment in human nature, while the individual human being, or successive generations of man, can advance towards attainment.

People have dogmatized about religion, building upon a few words in a book[4] (and a book the evidence of whose authenticity it is necessary to master) immense schemes.

Upon the words, 'Lo! I am with you alway', even unto the end of the world', (partly at least, if not entirely,) rests the fabric of the Church, with its high pretensions, its splendid temporalities. If we were to ask the bishops why they are there, will they not say, mainly because of those words?

If we ask the Roman Catholic church why *they* are there, they will say to hear confessions and absolve sinners. *They* have founded *their* scheme upon 'Whatsoever thou shalt loose on earth shall be loosed in heaven'.

We must admit that people have founded vast schemes upon a very few words.

Feeling the folly of this, others say that we are incapable of knowing anything about God. We cannot be too careful to draw a line of distinction between what we can know positively and what we can only conjecture empirically (*i.e.*, see reason to guess is true), and leave to be confirmed by the exercise of the faculties of ages to come; at the same time acknowledging our ignorance where it exists on those subjects on which it has been asserted that mankind has certain knowledge.

It is impossible to observe and reflect on what does exist and has existed, as cognizable by our various faculties, without tracing a vein of benevolent will, a wise will, and a powerful will.

Can it be denied that the signs, which make us assert that human will has been or is at work when we see machinery in action (even though no possessor of human will is manifest to the senses) – can it be denied that the same signs exist to manifest a will, differing from the human in possessing more wisdom and power to effect those same purposes which human will tries for?

But let us not go on to dogmatize, to *assert* that this will is perfect and eternal. Supposing the thought and purpose of God to be perfect, its perfect realization is the work of eternity. Therefore no perfect realization can have been recognized by man. Man can only recognize, in what he can learn of present, past, and future, *tendencies* from which he implies the perfect purpose.

Let us be most careful to keep accuracy in what we say we know, especially with reflective and conscientious men, who disbelieve what may be known, because required to believe what cannot be known.

Evidence may be brought of a will for long time past active, in which we trace *some* benevolence, wisdom, power. But we are seldom called upon to act and feel only by that of which we have certainty; we often have to act empirically.

The empirical must lead the way to the certain. Empirical laws are 'those uniformities which observation or experiment has shown to exist, but upon which we hesitate to rely, for want of seeing *why* such a law should exist. The periodical return of eclipses, as originally ascertained by the persevering observation of the early eastern astronomers, was an empirical law, until the general laws of the celestial motions had accounted for it. An empirical law, then, is an observed uniformity, presumed to be resolvable into ultimate laws, but not yet resolved into them'.

We find signs of benevolence, wisdom, and power, which appear to indicate that the will, in consequence of which that which exists does exist, desires the well-being of that existence at some time present or future. But there is and has been much suffering in every present with which we are acquainted, and we often cannot discern how it can be leading to a happy future *in detail*. Evidence may be brought to show, however, that it is leading, *in principle*, to a happy future – that, to the best happiness, the present is essential.

One and another cause of suffering disappears from time to time by the exercise of man's capabilities. We can see glimpses of how others might disappear, if he used these capabilities differently from what he has done. Great increase of enjoyment has been opened in certain directions by exercise of man's capabilities, and here too we have glimpses into immeasurable enjoyment attainable by man.

Do not such observations lead to the conjecture that the higher will intends man to work the way from suffering into happiness by exercise of capability?

The capability of each individual when born, the development and improvement of this capability, are obviously left in large measure to mankind. In no other race is there this dependence on the race itself. Do not these considerations point (shall we say empirically?) to the suggestion that man shall perfectionize man?

And since experience is evidence that exercise of capability is enjoyment, that without it there is none, does not this experience point to the belief that the Great Will made the happiness of mankind to depend on the exercise of the capability of mankind, thus calling forth the greatest degree of exercise, and with it the greatest happiness, in truth, possible?

I have tried to show that the highest state of 'belief' founded on conviction could not exist in some stages of national or individual development, but must belong to more advanced stages.

Undoubting belief, indeed, can easily exist in an early stage of development, which is ignorant of the sources of doubt presented by the advance of knowledge in the exact sciences. To this state of doubt, prevailing widely, as it does, in our present stage of progress, will succeed a more comprehensive, more impressive belief, as moral philosophy becomes fathomed by the understanding and raises the feelings.

I then tried to consider 'empirically' what a perfect being would do, if there be one; and to prove that he would appoint man to work out his own happiness. I now try to deduce from this the 'belief' that there *is* a perfect being, a God.

Here we come to consider the meaning or rather the meanings with which the word 'God' is used. It has been used to signify the most different ideas in different ages and nations. Can you attach any similarity of idea to the God whom his people whipped to make him do what they liked, and to the God who sate enthroned in the mystic phrase of Zoroaster[5]? Nothing is more common than to say, there never has been a race nor an age which did not believe in a God. *A* God certainly. But *what* God? What does the word mean? A cat? – a lamb? – a spirit? – a statue? These words are as synonymous as the different Gods in which different races and different ages of the same race have believed. When you ask, Why do you believe in God? I must ask, Which of the ideas of God do you mean? whether the God of the Old Testament, who commanded the extirpation of the Canaanites? or the God of the New Testament, who commanded submission to the yoke in many things in which, as we worship Him now, we believe that He commands the struggle for freedom?

We could not believe Him a perfect God, if He did not.

Authority does not teach belief in a perfect God. It is evident that very few have believed that their God was perfect. Some nations have not professed to do so; others have attributed to him qualities essentially imperfect, while giving him the title of perfect. For instance, the Greeks did not suppose their Zeus, Athene, etc. perfect. They attributed to them merely human qualities with superhuman power. In these earlier nations, *power* seems to have been the principal characteristic of a God. He or she was merely an engine to account for creation. Take all the thousand different meanings, which have been attached to the word 'God' by different nations and individuals in different ages, and some kind and degree of power above human seems to be all that is common to them.. In these days we profess that we believe our God to be perfect, but we attribute to him all kinds of qualities that are not – love of His own glory, anger, indecision, change of mind – and we try to believe, if we think at all, that a God with these qualities is perfect.

If you would, therefore, let me leave the question, why do you believe in God? – as not knowing which of these ideas of God you mean – I would say instead, I believe that there is a Perfect Being, of whose thought the universe in eternity is the incarnation.

It is evident that every nation, every age, *could* not believe in a Perfect Being – that it required cultivation, development to conceive the idea of perfection, and that the higher all the faculties of an individual, as also of a nation, have been, the higher has been his conception of God, the nearer perfection.

It is true, some of those called the most highly cultivated of the human race, Descartes, Laplace, Hume,[6] have not been able to conceive of a God at all.

But, have they been the most highly cultivated? Only intellectually so. And it seems evident that the *intellectual* idea of Him is *not* the highest. That is merely reducing Him to a master engineer, a mechanician-in-chief. Is not goodness for this purpose higher than intellect? Has not the innocent child probably an idea of God nearer the truth than that of Voltaire or Gibbon[7] 'Unless ye become as little children, ye shall not enter into the kingdom of Heaven'. We believe the carpenter's son, who humanly did not know that the earth moved round the sun, to have had a truer conception of deity than the philosopher, who had fathomed the laws of creation.

But he would have had a still truer, if he had known all that Laplace could have told him.

The more highly man's moral, intellectual, and spiritual

faculties are cultivated, the more nearly will he approach a true conception of God. But of reason, feeling, and conscience, feeling, truly cultivated, is that which gives us the truest conception of God; though, of course, a harmonious development of *all* these faculties would give us a truer still.

Thus the goodness of God is a higher attribute than His wisdom or power.

The question, Why we believe that there exists at all an Eternal Spirit of perfect goodness, wisdom, and power, I can only answer, By experience, and experience only. What mankind can learn of the past, the present, and the future is in harmony with the existence of such a spirit; without it, is unaccounted for. In earlier ages it was thought that what we see about us could not be accounted for, except by supposing imperfect qualities in the Eternal Spirit. But if, – as we make progress, we find a great many marks that He is perfect – if by degrees we should find that that very evil, which had made us *doubt* His perfection, is one of the truest proofs of it, shall we not come at last to think that He has done in the universe what we should have done, had we been perfect?

Thus increased knowledge, knowledge of the laws of God, is essential to our forming this idea of His perfection. Although a man in a dark room may often form a truer idea of Him than a philosopher observing the rotation of the sun, still, besides a man's *feeling* of what is *right*, his power of comprehending providence depends on his knowledge of the past, the present, and the future.

Instead, therefore, of directly answering the question, Why do you believe in a God? I would endeavour to set forth, –

I. Whatever exists, exists because there is one will and one power, which determines such existence to be.

II. The nature whence springs this will, in which resides this power, is eternal, is perfect, is goodness, wisdom, omnipotence, etc.

If it be said that this is reducing the wise and good God to the measure of my own understanding and heart, I answer, Not to mine, but to the accumulated and accumulating experience of all mankind. Sometimes the ancients may have been wiser than we are. Surely the ancient expressions of *wisdom, justice, truth*, are much truer than ours of a *wise*, a *just*, a *true* God. Athene was the goddess of wisdom, not the wise goddess. Themis was the goddess of justice, not the just goddess. So our Perfect Being *is* goodness, is wisdom, is power, not a good, wise, and powerful God.

It is often said that we cannot conceive of God as eternal, because, however remote the first creation may have been, there must have been beyond it, so far as we can see, an eternity of solitude and inaction. Unless we admit therefore that we receive the fact of His eternity from inspiration, we plunge into in-numerable difficulties. For instance, we may say that God may have been employed from all eternity creating; and that though the whole series of creations has been eternal, yet every particu-lar creation may have been at some definite point of time. But this makes some matter itself eternal.

In answer, we admit, first of all, that the idea of eternity is wholly inappreciable by the finite mind. A part cannot contain the whole. But the difficulty about creation is far-fetched. Matter is the incarnation or manifestation of God's thought – God's thought has been eternal, and therefore some manifesta-tion of it may, must, perhaps, also have been eternal. With regard to the question, whence the belief in eternity in those who wrote the sacred books, whether Egyptian, Hebrew, Per-sian, or Indian, that is indeed a difficulty. The idea has been so dinned into us from our earliest infancy that we can scarcely conceive of the stupendous effort requisite in the first human mind which imagined eternity – an eternity behind him, an eternity before him. It would be a curious inquiry to ascertain the first trace we can find of such a belief. The purely intel-lectual arguments, 'Something cannot come out of nothing', 'Nothing cannot come out of something', probably do not convince the *feeling* – do not make the belief present to us. Could we conceive the idea of eternity, of an Eternal Being arising in the minds of the first believers thus? – Look at the present state of things – whence came it? Whither is it tending?

Is it all confusion, springing from no will, tending to accomplish no will? In some aspects it does, indeed, appear so. In others, distinct, though imperfect, glimpses of *law* are discernible – of law, that is, of *will* determining the essential constituents of what is.

Determining them with what purpose? we next ask. Here again, in some respects, all appears confusion. Sometimes there is the appearance of benevolent purpose, sometimes the contrary, or the absence of it, or the absence of power to fulfil it.

Is there consistency, and is there unity of purpose? becomes the question. All historical religion shows the search of man for this consistency. The devil, the atonement, have been fruits of this search. It would appear that the idea of eternity has been its greatest result. There are many signs of benevolence in the creation, and yet, without the idea of eternity, they would be incomplete. Through eternity alone you come to consistency.

Where we recognize nothing but the finite and imperfect, we can discern infinity and perfection only through the idea of eternity. When the moral feelings predominate in ourselves, we begin to attribute to God the principles by which *we* should rule the universe, were it ours. We conceive of Him as like, not our actual, but our ideal selves. When the moral feelings of a people have advanced beyond their old mythology, scepticism follows, and no proof, no 'evidences', can make the old religion, the old divinity credible again. It is only by raising the moral condition of a people that we can raise their idea of God, but we cannot always by raising the moral condition of an individual persuade him to believe in a nobler God. The traditions of his childhood adhere to him, and he, perhaps, thinks it wrong even to examine them; or it may be that they are so repulsive to his improved feeling that he rejects the subject altogether. But with a nation this cannot long be the case. Mankind enlightens mankind. When the north of Africa was civilized, Christianity took root and flourished there. When civilization became extinct with the Moorish invasion, the burning of the libraries and the destruction of the schools, Christianity disappeared.

The questions, how has mankind arrived, first, at the idea of an Eternal Being with a past as well as a future eternity? secondly, at the idea of a future eternity for ourselves? can be only answered thus: 1st, That the more we learn of the laws of the universe the less we can imagine a time when goodness, power, and wisdom were *not*. 2nd, Perceiving as we do such proofs of wisdom, power, and goodness, and also such innumerable beings, to whom existence cannot be said to be worth having, we can only reconcile such suffering with our idea of perfect goodness, by supposing that there is an eternity for each, where the purposes of perfect goodness will be worked out.

It is said by one class of philosophers that we know nothing of any first cause, while religionists say we know everything. The more we advance from ignorance to knowledge, from imperfection towards perfection, the more we find that which exists referable to *one* cause, this cause being *a wise and benevolent will*.

II. *Questions relevant and irrelevant to this Inquiry, – what are they?*

II. How came this wise and benevolent will into existence? Was there ever a time when it did not exist, or is it eternal? are questions often asked.

We do not see why they are held of such importance, why it is feared that religion must fall if they are not answered, and why, therefore, religionists attempt absurd answers, or why some philosophers think that there can be no religion, *because* they hold these questions to be unanswerable. The capabilities of our nature truly exercised reveal to us a very wise, powerful, and benevolent will, *in many instances*. In looking through existence we are led to question the existence of such a will *in other instances*. But the *tendency* of improvement in the knowledge and the being of man is to increase the number of the former, to decrease the number of the latter instances. Moreover, this most important observation opens upon us from actual experience, that much evil which looked like *absence* of a good, wise, and powerful superintending will, is remedied by man. This leads to the question, may not all evil to man be remedied by man? And to the farther question, if this *is* so, may not all evil point to a wise and good superintending will, to a will that man shall have the means and be the means of rising from the ignorance and imperfection whence (alone) evil comes, to the knowledge and excellence whence well-being comes? If such a will exists, is it not a wise and benevolent will?

One man places a child in circumstances where he will have means to exercise his faculties aright; another does the child's work for him; which man's is the wiser will? Would you be of the bird's kind, which builds its nest unerringly with a smaller range of faculties, or of man's kind, wanting and suffering, as he has been, before his habitation was skilfully built? Would you be as the bird with its small range of duties and affections, or as man, with his aching heart, his wounded conscience, wringing other hearts while his own is wrung, all in ignorance? But is not the ignorance blessed which points to the possibility, in removing it, of rising to the divine and perfect? Oh, man! bless your sufferings, even your agonies, while gallantly you strive to work out, through them, peace and bliss to mankind. Rather we would hope that the bird, in another mode of existence, may rise to learn through suffering, than that man may find peace in being instinctively taught his path.

Does not a perfectly wise will include omnipotence, that is to say, *all power to fulfil the will*? Christ dwells constantly upon 'faith'. He seems to have had the idea that you could do whatever you *believed* you could do. 'If a man believes, he shall remove mountains'. How singular seems this idea! If a man is wise, he will wish only what is wise; he will purpose to fulfil only the wise wish; he will not believe that he can fulfil the wish unless he really can do so.

Perhaps in no book is so much spiritual truth to be found as in the Bible. 'In Him is no variableness, neither shadow of turning'. What an insight do these words show! Is not law the 'invariable' wisdom, modifying and modified by the succession of events? The sun rises every day: wisdom wills no change in that. One day is fine, another rainy: wisdom wills changes in this. The changing and the unchanging alike come from the wisdom which never changes. The placid sunshine and the raging storm both spring from His will, yet in that will is no variableness. Time, or the *succession* of events (it matters not which we call it), makes the only difference in the nature of events. That is wise in this phase of succession, which would not have been so in a former.

In proportion as we stretch our natures to comprehend His, many questions which puzzle us now will appear unimportant. Such as, could there be existence without beginning? Is time what can be called an existence, or merely a succession of events? Is matter an existence? If we can make out to the satisfaction of our natures that the cause of whatever has been, is, or shall be, is a wise and benevolent will, what matters it whether that will has been eternal? Probably we shall not be able to help believing that it has been so, but what matters it to us? Knowledge of all being, and improvement of our own, will bring into view eternity before us.

The important question to us is, have we a righteous Ruler? The evidence that we have such an one stands or falls with the evidence that human existence is a portion of that progress which befits our nature, or of preparation for such progress. Such is the constitution of human nature, that thus only can existence be of real value to man. These are creatures to which the amusement of the hour, without connexion with past or future, is all that they are fitted for; such is not man's proper nature. But many live through their human existence in a state quite at variance with their nature. Many, if this life were all, had better not have been born, supposing it true that righteousness is the soul's health.

Yet God's laws determine the constitution which befits human nature. God's laws determine what each man has actually been. Such laws existing, there can be no righteous Ruler, *unless* human life is a road to righteousness, even though it may be a circuitous one. Many descend in this world to the hell of sin and ignorance; it may be that they have also to endure it in other worlds; but all will attain to be as it is befitting their nature to be; otherwise, there would be no righteous Ruler.

We believe in a righteous Ruler, not because it is our desire. We *seek* Him because we desire Him above all desires. We have none that do not include His existence. We *find* Him in the tendency, the operation of His laws, which alone come home to us, as what could tell us that He exists.

It is said that the desire, the tendency of mankind to believe in a future existence is alone sufficient evidence for it.

But this is no reliable evidence.

We can have no desire to believe it or to preach it, if it is not true. We cannot believe it so as to do us any good, unless from such examination that we should believe it because it is true, not because we wish it. We have a greater fear of believing what is untrue than readiness to believe what we should feel glad to believe.

There is little use in *speculations* concerning the existence of a God, or concerning His nature, unless He may be discovered to be the object for trust, love, reverence. Unless the question be thus made practically helpful, we would rather say with the conscientious unbelievers of this day, 'It is better to try to remedy the evils of man's life than to confuse one's self in metaphysical speculations concerning God's life'. Let us, there-fore, rather inquire whether there is *such* a God than whether there is a God, and what He is.

But with what faculties are we to inquire? The Germans on the continent, and Mr Newman at home[8], say that there is a special faculty which they call the *soul*, or 'intuition' (*anschauung*), which apprehends God, which knows Him, as the senses know the external world. There is a school (Unitarianism as it was) which says that this faculty is *intellect*, and that man apprehends religious truth by a process similar to that pursued in any other scientific investigation. Mr Martineau[9] has looked to the moral nature of man, and shown that man cannot appeal to his *conscience* without coming to religion.

Why should Mr Martineau, or Mr Newman, or the intellec-tual school, expect to find religion revealed by *one* faculty, independent of others? If we wish to estimate a man rightly, to hold right intercourse with him, all our faculties are wanted.

We shall not rightly estimate mankind, or live well among mankind, unless every faculty we have is in exercise. Should it not be so as to religion? A man will be really religious in feeling and act, will apprehend religion rightly, in proportion as *all* his capabilities are rightly exercised, and in proportion as the society in which he lives is organized so as to afford full and free exercise for his nature.

But the conscientious unbelievers of the present day say, that, when all is said and done, and the whole of the faculties exercised, etc., all that we can discern with these faculties is the law of nature.

Is there not an absurdity in saying that all we can discern is that whatever *is*, *is* according to law? For is it not our experience of law that it *always* springs from a will, from a purpose?

If we went to some new country and found a law in operation, but could have no information, no trace of the person who willed, who purposed in that law, we should nevertheless feel an entire certainty, a consciousness that will and purpose had existed in regard to that law.

When we discern a law of nature, we can generally at the same time trace *purpose* in it; is it, then, philosophical or reasonable to say, 'We can know nothing as to whether there is or has been a will, a purposer;' we having so much experience that where there is a law and purpose, there is will and a purposer? In the laws of nature we can trace will and purpose of the same kind as exists in man; for instance, love of order, love of beauty, benevolence which wills convenience, ease, comfort.

Mankind has been jarred by circumstances unsuited to right constitution, right development, right exercise of the nature. The thinking part of mankind has been irritated and disgusted by dogmatic assertion of superstitious notions. A revulsion takes place. Many thinkers say in consequence, 'I will do my work and believe nothing but phenomena recognized by my senses'. Reason and philosophy are now in arms against superstition and dogmatism rather than in peaceful search after truth.

But does it not seem that reason and experience suggest, when we trace law, a will and a purpose?

It is very evident that this will and purpose concerns mankind, for the whole of our existence (our existing at all as man and our mode of existing) is in accordance with these laws – springs, in fact, from these laws. All the power which we have to influence our own mode of existence, or that of any of our kind, or, indeed, to influence any mode of existence, material or other, is by working in accordance with some law or other, whether we know what it is or not.

Can it then be uninteresting, can it be practically unimportant, to inquire into the nature of the *willer*, the purposer of these laws?

We find in some cases marked unmistakeable purpose to secure human well-being, as, for instance, in the laws of astronomy and anatomy, which concern human habitation and the human frame.

In these instances, power, wisdom, above human in degree, though like human in kind, are evident in the will and purpose.

In other instances, the effect of these laws on human habitation and the human frame is suffering.

But can it ever be said that malevolence, or a wish for suffering, becomes evident? If it were so, would not the evil be irremediable and permanent? Can we point out any evil and say, 'There is strong reason to believe that the united efforts of mankind never would be able to prevent its recurrence?'

Prejudice is now setting in a contrary direction to credulity, and prompting to disbelieve what reason and philosophy would prompt us to believe, viz., that laws of nature *are* discernible; that reason and experience say that law implies a legislator with a purpose; that this purpose in the laws of nature is discernible to be a wise and benevolent one – benevolent where it causes well-being, – benevolent where it causes suffering, which it does, *unless* man's faculties are exercised aright.

Now suppose we discern –

1. Law.

2. A legislator, implied by law.

3. A benevolent and wise purpose in the legislator, – what then?

If the whole of man's nature were penetrated with this, as truth, there would be practical benefit to life, *i.e.*, if he thought and felt and acted congenially, consistently, in accordance with this belief.

In theory, the admitting thus much would lead not to *proof*, but to assurance, (not differing in its practical effect from proof) of an eternity to come, in which each individual would attain to the perfection of goodness and happiness through the exercise of his own nature and that of mankind. If not only the reason were convinced, but the feeling were imbued with this belief, man would, even in suffering and privation, feel himself sharing the omnipotence of God. He would feel, 'I wish no *law* altered'.

As to the present effect of law in causing suffering and privation, he would consider all this to arise from that part of God's law, in consequence of which mankind are to make their own way out of ignorance to truth, out of imperfection towards perfection, by the exercise of their faculties – God in His various laws supplying means and inducement.

Would not the practical effect of such a belief be to inspire vigorous effort, where effort can be made, – calm patience where it cannot be made, not doubting but that the time will come when effort can be made?

Would not love be inspired by One whose law was love – veneration by One whose law was wisdom?

There seems a difficulty in imagining the nature of God, when we try to think of Him as an Eternal Will, manifesting itself in law. We suppose all existence to depend on this will in order to *be* at all, to be what it is entirely by and through this will. But when we have said this, in relation to the nature of God's existence, we have a dissatisfied feeling, as if we supposed something after the imagination of the Hebrews, who thought that victory in the battle depended upon Moses holding up his arms. One cannot hear this without an uneasy feeling at the barreness of Moses' task of holding up his arms. Our arms ache, and our spirits are weary under the imagination. And we feel something of the same sort in reference to the nature of God's existence, when we have read the words about law here used.

Go to the Sistine chapel, however, and imagine the nature which painted that roof. There was a will without which that roof would not have been; that will determined each stroke of the pencil – but the first stroke had regard to the last and to every intermediate one. Was it a weary existence thus to will? Perhaps you will say, 'No, because the artist varied as he advanced, and was occupied in thought'. But, in proportion as a man is a great artist (whatever be his work), he does *not* vary as he advances. Is he making a speech, organizing a society, arranging a battle, building a hospital, painting a set of pictures for a church, writing a book of history, poetry, or metaphysics – in proportion as he does well, will his first *will* determine the whole, his first word or stroke of the pen or pencil concern the whole. It is not because he varies in thought that he will not be weary of *willing*; on the contrary, the more oneness of purpose, the greater his interest and satisfaction. The great mind, through its work, is developing one will throughout, and that mind has most interest and satisfaction.

May we not conceive that God's present will is one with every stroke of the past and the future, which is and will be ever developing itself? The artist who begins upon twelve pictures to fulfil one purpose, has one will throughout, by which will they are developed into being. He *is* not those pictures, but they are the manifestation of his will when done, its development while being done. Is it not so with all external existence, with regard to God? the God whom Œrsted[10] fancied 'developing Himself into planetary geologies and polarized light.' Why developing *himself*? No more than Michael Angelo was developing himself when St Peter's dome arose at his will; no more than a painter is his picture when his picture developes at his will, does it appear that God is developing *himself*.*

* For Pantheism we can see no *evidence*.

The acorn developes into the oak – such is its nature. We have no reason to believe that there is any thought or purpose in the acorn, in consequence of which it so developes.

If we had seen Michael Angelo at work, we should have been quite sure that there was a conception in his mind of what was to appear on his canvas, a purpose that he meant to fulfil. We should have seen that he did not make stroke after stroke, like a child, pencil in hand, but no purpose in his mind; we should have seen *purpose in process of realization*.

How it comes to be that the painter's hands mediate between the will and the canvass, we understand no more than how the Highest, without hands, developes His pictures before us. 'The whole universe a single intellectual aim', we might add a *single aim* of the spirit of love, of beauty, of order, of righteousness, of benevolence, of every attribute which man can appreciate as right, and good, and true; of others, it may be, which he cannot appreciate.

The reason of our suffering the grievousness of inefficiency is the want in us of this consistency and comprehensiveness of will. If I knew how, I too would have a *single aim* of righteousness, and love, and benevolence, and beauty, and order; but I have a different aim every half-hour, without comprehensiveness, connexion, consistency. In *this* only can I be comprehensive and consistent. I can say, 'thy will be done;' I accord with that will; I acquiesce in waiting till we find out how to be comprehensive and consistent, till we attain that blessed oneness.

There is an oneness of seeking external amusement, of doing what it is conventionally agreed is to be done; this saves present suffering, but does not help on mankind.

Better than such an oneness there is a blessedness, even in the suffering of ignorance and inefficiency, in trusting that we shall work our way to light at last. Then when we remember these days of darkness, may it be with the wish to deliver others from suffering and privations which we have known by experience!

Is it an insuperable difficulty for us to believe that love, goodness, wisdom, which we can now trace as the spring of law, have *always* existed? Is the constitution of our nature such that

---

We may discern conception of something to come, purpose determining what shall come, in the history of the oak as it developes from the acorn, and lives through its centuries. Yet such conception, such purpose, does not reside in the oak. Therefore to talk of God developing Himself in the oak is an imagination, standing on no evidence, not consistent with what we see going on.

To say that thought, purpose, *manifests* itself in the history of an oak *is* consistent with what is going on before us. In the oak itself indeed the conception, the directing purpose, can be only imperfectly read, but in the connexion of *each with all* in the universe, in successive time, it is to be looked for, and even from our limited point of view we may obtain a glimpse.

we cannot help believing that whatever is must have begun to be?

To us it appears more difficult to suppose that wisdom and goodness began to be from not being, than to suppose that the nature, which we discern to possess these attributes, is eternal, and that all other beginnings are merely changes of one present state to another (though all manifestations of one unvarying purpose), these changes arising from the existence of this eternal nature.

With regard to matter, it is probably impossible for natures like ours ever to prove that it exists at all. We see no means of approximating, of advancing one step towards proof.

Nor does it make the slightest practical difference to man whether it really exists or not otherwise than as the thought of God. Grant a nature eternally possessing perfect goodness and wisdom, and you account for all that is. One existence consists with, is harmonious with, another. All spring from the same will, tend to the same purpose. The more we penetrate into the characteristics of various natures, into the effect which they are calculated to have upon each other, the more traces we find of such a nature. The geologist, the antiquarian, as he opens the closed leaves of the history of existence, invariably shows us the will at work consistently, harmoniously with this one thought, viz., mankind, or preparation for mankind, *i.e.*, for a race of beings whose nature it is to *attain* the divine nature, God providing in eternity means and inducement for each and all. The true prophet will see vistas in the eternity before us, as the eye, which penetrates into the past, sees them in the past eternity, all disclosing the same will.

What are to be our witnesses if not miraculous revelation, is often asked.

Experience and consciousness – are they not that to which we have to refer for truth, as to our feeling of the existence, the presence of a God?

Many say, 'our experience and consciousness tell us nothing of a God'.

We are not to conclude from this that there is no God. It is man well-born, well-developed and whose present nature is in right exercise (when he tells you his experience and his consciousness) to whom you are to refer. And he cannot be well-born and well-bred and in present right exercise of his nature, unless many besides himself are and have been well-born and well-bred.

If each individual were to refer to his own experience and consciousness, and question whether there is a God, what would the answer be, supposing him to refer to no authority of book or word, merely to the spirit as interpreting itself, manifesting itself to his spirit, if it does so manifest itself?

A man is not to set himself down satisfied that there is no God, if *his* experience and consciousness tell him nothing of one. That the blind man is not conscious of trees and flowers does not prove their non-existence. That the farmer, who has looked at trees and fields, in reference only to value of crops, is conscious of no spirit of love and wisdom speaking in them, does not prove such a spirit a fable. Even the conscientious aspirant after truth, who says, 'O God, if thou dost exist and dost intend that I should know thee, tell me of thy presence', may not conclude that, if he receives no answer, therefore there is no God. For to ask that question *thus* may not be the way in which the spirit of truth and righteousness sees that it is to be answered.

Let each mind ask itself, is there not, if I look through as much of existence as I can take cognizance of, some degree of wisdom, and goodness, and power above man's, as the spring of *some part* of that existence? If so, is it not important to try to make out something concerning this power, and wisdom, and goodness? If it is important, let us be ready to wait, still inquiring, while man is so imperfectly constituted and cultivated that we cannot trust his answer on a subject which requires the right exercise of all the faculties of all mankind to answer it. My own consciousness is that there is appreciable to my nature a spirit, a will of righteousness, goodness, and wisdom in the universe – a spirit of the same nature as that of which I, at times, am conscious in others of mankind, and in myself. Thus much we can say without any straining after mysticism. When we seek truth, if we are not seeking it from man, it is from this spirit that we seek it.

Whether we seek truth as to a (comparatively speaking) great or a small thing, – 'is there a God?' or 'what shall be my food', or as to some scientific fact, or in order to arrange the intervals of music so as to produce a scientific and harmonizing effect, we are seeking truth of the source of truth.

Will it not be asked, are you not seeking it of yourself?

Have I any consciousness that I am the source of truth? I have a consciousness that I am a means of finding truth by the exercise of my faculties.

How much there is wanted a Baconian way[11] of treating these subjects! Man studying physics says now, 'My assertions and my conjectures shall be founded on phenomena recognized by man's senses'.

May we say of subjects *not* recognized by the senses, 'My assertions and my conjectures shall be founded on experience and consciousness?' To trust to the senses, they must be in a healthy state; to trust to the consciousness of a being, the being must be in a healthy state.

But man does not say this, he does not go to his experience for facts, when studying these subjects, he goes to a book for authority.

That sort of exercise of the mind called speculation is indeed not suited to the nature of the case. But most of those who 'speculate' have not a full consciousness that the time is coming, and now is, when on the exercise of man's nature is to depend whether mankind have a religion or not. Scarcely any of us, who have been brought up under a supernatural religion, *can* feel ourselves absolutely dependent on the exercise of mankind's nature for our conviction. On more or less impression of a supernatural revelation of religion, most of us, who *have* any religion, depend. By degrees the astronomy, the geology of the Old Testament have been *generally* rejected as not true[12]. *Some* now see that the political economy, the moral philosophy of the New Testament, is not always true.

It will remain that Christ will speak to all eternity the truth
that is in him – but *what* is truth (of that which he is reported to
have said) will be sifted by man – and it will be discovered to
have sprung from the exercise of *his* nature, as in other cases in
which man attains truth. Let us bring ourselves clearly to see the
state of the case; then we shall see that our consideration of
these subjects is not mere speculation for the amusement or
gratification of the intellect, but that the question is
approaching. Have we, or have we not, a religion? Many specu-
lators, probably, are not conscious that this is their question.
Vague feelings, which the having taken for granted a supernatural religion has implanted in them, prevent this consciousness. Let us then awaken to a sense that our question is, Does
religion exist? – That Christ's words, or the words of the
followers of Christ, contain much of mistake as to God's nature
and laws, as to man's duty and destination, – is proved by
discoveries, since the time of Christ, as certainly as such discoveries prove that there are mistakes in the astronomy, etc., of
the 1st chapter of Genesis. The discovery of such mistakes will
in no wise prevent our appreciating that which was true and
right and loveable in him; but the discovery of such mistakes *will*
prevent our feeling that we may believe in God and a future
state, because Christ speaks of God as existing, and of a future
life for man as to exist. Let not what we say be supposed to
mean that a mode of being, called man, is, by exercising its
faculties, to discover a mode of being of different nature, called
God. The exercise of the attributes of God, as existing limited
by physical law, will reveal those attributes existing unlimited by
physical law. God, working truth into the concrete, – God,
manifesting truth in life and work, thus reveals the thought, the
sentiment, the purpose, the law, in accordance with which the
imperfect *lives* truth progressively, till it rises to the perfect
comprehension of the whole.

Before belief in the supernatural is quite exhausted, let us
strive to work out belief from the workings of our own
nature. It is *right life* which must prepare true belief to be
general.

Are not almost all mankind children in religion and moral philosophy?

If we knew how, we would endeavour to organize life for children, so that it would exercise all their nature. We would then endeavour to have ready, at each step, assistance for them to *express* the feelings which such exercise would naturally call out. The life would awaken the heart to ask,* and the heart would awaken the intellect to answer its questions. We would have matins and vespers, such as the heart and the intellect, thus awakened, would want, as soon as the child was developed enough to accept assistance gladly, in order to express feelings beginning to want expression. The true feeling of the importance of the day begun upon, the true feeling of union in their common work, of the general purport of their common work, we would endeavour to awaken; as also a true *appreciation* of God – the all-comprehensive nature; and, when awakened, we would endeavour to help it to the enjoyment of feelings of love, trust, sympathy towards this nature. The peace of the early morn, suitable music and singing, appropriate expression from architecture and painting, all the sources to give to children enjoyment of the religious feelings, which are natural to them, we would seek, with which to begin each day. Each should be a *holy-day*, a holy day for work pursued with zest, not the misnamed 'holiday', so often wearisome.†

---

* Comte's[13] idea.

† Children are naturally early disposed to religion, and if they had some help, would accept it gladly.

What *is* the help offered to them? Doctrines, sermons, prayers, alike for the old and young, springing from the thought and feeling of ages ago. Children, at eight or nine years old, will sometimes find satisfaction in certain modes of their own, certain prayers, and the reading of certain books, but seldom show the least *interest* in any of the prayers or sermons prepared for them, though they do not object to them, but take for granted that it is right. A child of six said to his governess *quite* simply, 'You don't think about God; I'm always thinking about God'. – The husband of Lord Byron's first nurse says of him that, when 'a mere child', he was 'particularly inquisitive and puzzling about religion'. – How was this tendency developed? 'I was sent at five years old to school. There I learnt little, except to repeat by rote the first lesson of monosyllables (God made man, let us love Him), by hearing it repeated without learning a letter. Whenever proof was made of my progress at home, I repeated these words with the most rapid fluency, but on turning over a new leaf, I continued to repeat them, so that the narrow boundaries of my first year's accomplishments were detected, and my ears boxed (which they did not deserve, seeing it was by ear that I had acquired what I had)'.

The time is coming when, more and more, others as well as ourselves, will discern the little dependence to be placed on supernatural revelation; consequently, let us search to the utmost the *real* grounds man will have for a religion when the unreal grounds crumble away beneath him. The divinities of Greece and Rome, how powerful they were! But they are laid low. Hardly a trace of belief in them remains. The belief in all supernatural foundation for religion will give way in like manner. Many ideas in the present theology are more opposed to natural feeling than those which prompted the worship of some of the pagan deities. *E.g.*, law is *traceable* in all existence, in history of every kind, history of successive generations, of their opinions, their characters, their actions. In vain, then, should we expect the doctrines of particular providence and of forgiveness of sins, to retain their hold on our belief. Yet these doctrines are the staples of religion, as now believed, or as taken for granted. Law is *traceable*, *i.e.*, glimpses of it have been *traced*. When law was traced in astronomy and geology, Genesis ceased to be authority in those sciences. When law is traced in the history of events, and in moral philosophy, Christ will no longer be considered as supernatural authority, speaking, as He does, of providential interference and forgiveness of sins. And when this day comes, where will be our religion? Religion *might* be more

---

Children generally have the feeling that grown-up people do not care about religion as they do.

Comte thinks that there is an inevitable resemblance between personal and social progression, and that the 'individual' will pursue his 'proper evolution' in rising from simple fetichism at the beginning to real polytheism, as did the *race* before him.

Is there any confirmation of this in any of our experience of children? Such an opinion goes against that which we find to be the case, viz., that it is a part of law that the nature is *influenceable*.

'Social progression' is according to law. So is 'personal progress'. But it is a part of law that the *wise regenerate* may develope truly the *ignorant unregenerate*. There is no law compelling the unregenerate to go through a definite course of error, as would be the case if each individual must be a fetichist and a poltheist. Till the influence of the regenerate can arrive at the unregenerate, he does so; he sees objects inverted and double, etc., but the purpose of education is to lead from ignorance to truth, not through falsehood. To present that which is truth to the regenerate, but incomprehensible to the unregenerate, would not indeed be leading from ignorance to truth. A true education will gradually develope, following the lead of the questions which seek answer, the feelings which seek gratification. Such an education will not drag each individual through fetichism and polytheism to truth.

felt, more comprehended, infinitely more influential on life than
it ever has been. But we must work that it may be so. Nothing
comes without work. If your work helps another, it is by
helping him to work. If circumstances of any kind help a man, it
is by helping him to work. Let us not suppose that our highest
and best knowledge, and feeling, and life can come but by work.
All must work to reveal our common Father. All must work that
the Father, in the Son, may live His thought – that the life of the
Son may raise him to partake in the all-comprehending thought
of the Father.

Is then human nature so working as to make progress? We
should indeed concern ourselves with this question far more than
we do. How few ask for it, how few care for the answer? But
might not human nature make continual progress if mankind
would but have it so? What is meant by progress? Advance in
becoming what our nature is fitted to become. '*L'éternel devenir*'[14]
is always going on. Mankind is always on the *way* to progress
through God's will. But there will be no actual progress until it is
man's will to find and pursue the road upon which he should be.

Look at the aims of men in general. To earn a livelihood *must*
be the object which mainly directs life in a large proportion of
mankind. But how is it with those who are free to employ life as
they please? What directs their course? Generally speaking, to
live as others live in their line of life. To live thus passes for
right; although one part of duty is to meet at church in order to
say that all we do is utterly and entirely wrong.

But what would we have men do?

Could not 'two or three be gathered together', not to say
they do wrong, but to try to find out how to do right, to try to
find out from God's laws what a MAN should not be, how
mankind should live?

Let us not be satisfied with what we are told by men,
although believing themselves inspired to teach us, when we
may learn from God Himself through His laws.

Men have joined in the attempt to spread what they accepted
as true belief, to live according to it. Such were the Moravians,
the Quakers, the Roman Catholic religious orders.

We hold a different belief as true. We tell it in the hope that
what there is of truth in it may sometime reach the minds of
men, so that in like manner they may try to live and to gain
others to live according to what they accept as truth concerning
the nature of the Ruler, and concerning 'the whole duty of
man'.

What is called *speculation* on religious subjects is now not
uncommon. Such a word is entirely unsuited to the subject,*
which should engage our deepest thoughts, and should lie at the
foundation of the whole of our practical life. On such 'speculation' we have no desire to enter. Our object is real practical
progress for mankind through true religious belief. We hear of
the 'rise and fall' of empires. Now one country, now another, is
in the ascendant. We hardly know why or wherefore. Real
continuous progress for mankind at large will only be through
men uniting to learn from God's laws what man ought to be,
how men ought to live – through their uniting to bring about
that so men shall be, so men shall live.

In our times there is also much critical observation on
religious subjects, showing doubt or disbelief of creeds, of which
the foundation is *miraculous* revelation; but there is no strong or
united purpose to find out what *is* true on religious subjects.

There are reasons now increasing in force why the time is
coming, and now is, when those who doubt or disbelieve are
called upon to look for what they *can* believe, what they *ought* to
believe if they can.

The belief of universal and invariable law has necessarily

* Scarcely a day passes but books, by the orthodox and the unorthodox, by men and by
women, are advertised, with titles as follow (I take these at random): '*Passing* Thoughts on
Religion', 'Musings on Manifestations of God to the Soul of Man'. As for the 'Impressions', the
'Aspirations', their name is legion. Now, can we call this anything but *impertinence* to God? What
should we say if we saw advertised, 'Passing thoughts' on hydrostatics, 'Musings' on clinical
surgery, 'Impressions' on life assurances? Everybody would laugh, and nobody would read the
book. Is religion, confessedly the most important of all subjects, to be the only one on which
anybody's *passing* thoughts are good enough? Is the nature of God the only science not worth
study? I am not aware that any book called '*Fancies* on Religion' has yet appeared, but the title
would be by no means a misnomer, for much that is written consists of nothing but fancies. A
life of the Virgin Mary, which I have read, in eight volumes, called '*La Cité Mystique de Dieu*', by a
Spanish nun, who believed it to be the work of inspiration in her, is not more the work of fancy
than are some of these Protestant effusions.

gained ground gradually, because its foundation is observation and experience. To those who in past ages had not the possibility of recognizing law, it was natural to see superhuman power chiefly in the more interesting and startling events of life, and to seek help through prayer or other means, which human experience represented as likely to please or propitiate. Men *could* not then believe what now stands on evidence. They naturally imagined a revelation which satisfied their (then) moral and physical wants.

But more light has been gained, more truth on morals, on physics; and now if we would look, we might find a revelation founded on evidence to all, not on hearsay to a few.

People who inquire on religious matters generally take separate subjects, or whatever may have happened to attract their attention. – 'What is the evidence for the existence of a God?'

We have endeavoured to show how vague is this question, since no one word has been used to express such different conceptions as have been included in the word 'God'.

'Is there a future state?' means often (perhaps generally) is the future state to be, which is alluded to rather than described in the Bible? Are we all to be called to account for our actions, and rewarded or condemned accordingly, to live above the clouds 'in the bosom of Christ', 'to be called to glory', or to suffer 'everlasting damnation'?

The intellect of the day rebels against such belief, but constructs no other.

Or 'have there been miracles?' or 'how shall this or that passage in the "sacred writings" be understood?' Or questions arise in the various existing churches or religious associations as to particular doctrines or modes of government.

All these questions, pertinent in their day, and to be respected while they were suitable to that phase of human nature, to *that* state of human knowledge, are left behind, if God's universal, invariable law is recognized. And the questions which God's laws reveal to us, as those which we *ought* to ask, which include all others, become those with which we set out.

The answers to them refer to every human being; those with

whose sufferings before we were born we have sympathized; those whom in our day we love or yearn to help; those whom we are to leave behind in the struggle of this life when our own is over.

Will some answer, 'I do not feel these struggles: life is joyous and pleasant?' Such have not known *human* life: their feeling is more that of butterflies than of men.

The answers to these questions would be one truth for all, one principle in life for all, one truth lived, worked out in all human life, though in ever-varying ways.

'Unity of belief' has been fought for, struggled for by fire and sword. The most grievous torments which man has inflicted on man have been, sometimes conscientiously, sometimes from selfish motives, inflicted to bring about *unity of belief*.

From a spirit of truth and duty men have borne, and sometimes inflicted, these terrible sufferings.

Now some satisfy themselves with excluding persons supposed to hold 'dangerous opinions' from their society, and from certain employments; while others, called 'liberal', say 'all men cannot think alike'.

Rather say, all cannot believe certain doctrines which (they are told on human authority) stand on divine authority. There is truth referrible to divine authority, for which there is *evidence*, which all may examine and understand, – evidence which not only all men can believe, but which none can help believing (that is, none that have healthy well-developed minds), if it were only well explained.

It is not the case now in astronomy, that some believe that the earth goes round the sun, others that the sun goes round the earth.

If religion rested on evidence addressed to those powers and feelings in our nature which are capable of receiving it, as little would some believe in the 'atonement', others not; some in 'eternal punishment', others not, etc.

For the following propositions this section is intended to lay the way: –

1. Evidence of the universal and invariable law on which our creed is founded.

2. How, if universal and invariable law be admitted, the questions hereafter proposed will arise.

3. How, if universal and invariable law be admitted, it will give answers to these questions.

Our Creed — what is it?

We have spoken of law as revelation, which stands on evidence to all mankind, who cannot *all* accept any of those revelations, each of which is by some believed in. Why do we expect so much from this 'law'? In the succession of phenomena, physical and mental – in the change throughout all that is susceptible of change, which the present exhibits from the past, what *is* now shows *this* relation to the past; viz., that it is *conditional* on the past; it is not merely that there is a change from the past. Even this is not at once obvious.

We learn partly from what may be now observed, partly from inference from such observation, that since this world existed as a solid ball, it has had a past of ages, exceeding in number *such* number as our minds can form any conception of. We learn of changes taking place in what seems least to change, in the ocean's bed, in what we call the 'everlasting hills'; we go on to learn that such great and remarkable changes come to pass by small and imperceptible changes, not to be conceived, only to be expressed by saying, that all that *is*, all that has existence, (except the unchanging ONE, whose will is the source of all other being,) is always changed in time present from what it was in time past. That present time, so quickly passing, that before we can say, before we can think that it *is*, it is gone; yet has changed all existence but the ONE who directs ALL.

It is not merely to be observed that there *is* change. The *very* change may be observed to arise out of *some definite conditions in the past, and in what co-exists with each change*. What is, would not have been, if those definite past and co-existing conditions had not existed. Herein is exemplified what we mean by *law*.

Preceding, simultaneous with each individual physical phenomenon, each state of mind, there have been and are conditions without which that particular phenomenon or state of mind would not have been. It would be again – the same conditions existing. But they never will exist again *precisely*. Mark the eternal road, without beginning, without end, in which all that is marches, ever the same in *principle*, *tending* all the same way. In all that is now there is repetition of what has been, but also variety; never exactly the same; never quite different. For the conditions which regulate the present are never *quite* different nor *quite* the same, but enough the same, differing enough to reveal that the resemblance and the difference mark a relation, a connexion, which is what we intend to express when we say that all change manifests law, as the *constitution* of each individuality manifests law. The history of each individuality, the *tendency* of that history, manifests law. If *this* has been, *that* is invariably. If *this* is, *that* will be certainly.

This is maintained on no man's *ipse dixit*[15], or opinion, or belief, that it has been revealed by Omnipotence to men long ago departed from this world. It is open to all men to examine whether it is or is not so. Observe, examine, vast nature is before you. Your own thoughts, what you wish, what you will, the consciousness ever present to you (which *is* yourself), all is there to answer the question whether this is true or not of law.

PART VI

Law

'*Predestination*' infers one of two things, – either that whatever we may will, and whatever we may do, certain consequences, such as our state in the next world, will inevitably take place, by the *decree* of God.

Or it means that God, at his appointed time, calls a certain number into that state of grace, which will have for its consequences hereafter salvation, and leaves the rest in the state in which they are by nature, of sin and death.

In one sense indeed we *are* predestinate. We see a ragged creature, brought up in Field Lane or Saffron Hill[16], at the 'thieves' kitchen and seminary for the teaching of that art to children', and we truly say that he is 'predestinate to sin and death'. We see the child of Lois and Eunice brought up amid great objects 'unspotted from the world', and we can truly say he is predestinate to grace and salvation.

All children, however, brought up in St Giles's[17] do not grow up thieves; all who are carefully and piously educated, as we but too well know, do not grow up good men. Is there something besides the inevitable action of circumstances, as it is called?

These exceptions are also the subjects of law; the effects are also traceable to some circumstances, unknown to us, but which could have no other effects.

Then, it is said, this is implying an unbroken chain, held in the hands of God, from the first beginning of things, upon which is strung every event, act, feeling, thought, will of a man's life; effect following cause, as link follows link, immutable,

pre-ordinate. None of the insulated phenomena of predestination. None of the recalcitrant exercise of free agency.

But there is no cause but God; all the rest is the effect of His
laws or thoughts. A certain circumstance brought into contact
with a certain nature, must always have a certain, the same, and a
definite effect. It will not have sometimes one effect and sometimes another. Nature and circumstances remaining the same, to
say that any other effect will occur is contrary to experience.

The nature, however, it is said, remains under the free will of
a responsible agent.

This is to say, in fact, that God interferes with some things
and not with others, that He, by an act of arbitrary will, lays
down certain landmarks, and leaves man to live as he likes
during the meantime. How do you explain 'insulated phenomena'? Can such be? Phenomena are only the manifestation of
God's thoughts. Insulated phenomena are as much as to say that
God thinks at one time and not at another.

This, it is said, is a far more dangerous predestinarianism than
that of Calvin[18].

It is true, we are predestinarians, each in his own sense. The
difference between this predestination and that of Calvin is, that
we believe all are predestinate ultimately to the happiness of the
Creator himself: any idea of punishment, not intended to
improve the creature, being inconsistent with a Being of perfect
goodness. We believe cordially that the laws of God are so
arranged as to flagellate us with our sins, and to attract us with
their opposites, so as, at an appointed time, (appointed, not by
decree, which is an express volition of God, but by *law*,) to bring
us, *i.e.*, all, into a state of grace, as it is called.

Then it is said, we have nothing to do but to lie still and wait
till '*the laws*' whip us into goodness. Free will, adieu!

But what is meant by free will? A power to will whatever I
please? Certainly, you may will whatever you please; but the
very question is, what you will please? What you will please is
decided by your nature. Do you wish to include in the word a
power to will contrary to your nature? No, it is said, a power to
choose whether I will will a thing or no.

That is to say, that you can have two wills at the same time. Two wills? rather three. For you must have a third to decide between the two.

Is this to say that I am not free to will to go into that room or not as I please?

But you will not please, – that very *as you please* is the bar. There are strangers in that room; your nature is not to please to go among strangers. In half an hour you have an appointment, and your nature is to be punctual, and therefore in half a minute you will get up and set out, in order to keep it. You can certainly do as you please about going into that room – that is, there is no external force to prevent you – but you will not please. You will not will; the force is internal. No mysterious force, but the force of two qualities – punctuality and shyness, formed in you without your consent, and prior to any volition on your part.

Supposing that you were to go into that room at once to show me that you can will it, still you will only be willing as your nature prompts you. Your nature is to be piqued, and you may be piqued into going into that room; but what does that prove?

But you say, I can bring my will into such a state as that it will choose to go into that room. *There* will be an exercise of free will. I can overcome my shyness and lay my punctuality aside for once.

We do not know each other always enough to predicate whether you can or cannot; that is, whether you will or will not. But if you do, it will only be because some other motive is strong enough to overcome your shyness or punctuality.

Then where is our responsibility? is the final counter argument.

The word responsibility expresses but a low conception of the relation between man and his Creator.

God himself may be said to have the 'responsibility' of ruling the universe, to be accountable for us; but what does responsibility mean? *answering to* – has God no higher motive in administering the universe than that he has to answer for it? Answer to whom?

To himself.

But does a mother take care of her child only because she will have to answer for it? Of such a mother, nay, even of a hired nurse, we should say that all love for the child must have ceased.

The word 'responsibility' is applicable where you take a housekeeper, and say, 'there are so many towels in that closet, will you take the charge of them? here is the inventory'. Where there is an express or even a tacit agreement, by which one party offers, the other undertakes a charge, there is responsibility incurred. The housekeeper expressly agrees to *answer for* that linen. In many human transactions a similar compact may be traced. Where men live together in states and societies, there is a tacit agreement that each shall not live by marauding on the rest; in return for which he claims the protection of the rest, and submits to certain penalties if he infringes this agreement. There is a farther agreement, not that each shall protect the rest, which would take up too much of his time, but that each shall pay something, so that one be appointed to protect all. By becoming a subject, you claim the support of your country, and you subscribe to its stipulations. Such compacts we can understand. You become responsible to your country, and your country to you. If you do not like the terms, you can leave the country.

But between God and man there is no such agreement. Man did not ask to be born. God never asked man whether he would undertake the charge of himself or not. Many an one, if so asked, would certainly say, No, I cannot undertake this anxious existence, not even in view of the ultimate happiness secured to me. But He is too good a Father to put it into His children's power to refuse it. If He were to do this, timid spirits would all resign at once. According to the theory of responsibility, suicide would be justified. For a man may put an end to his service, if dissatisfied with it.

But you must account for your talents, it is said.

How can I account for what I do not know is there? The housekeeper might justly say to me, You never told me you committed any table cloths to me, if there were none upon the list. God does not tell man what talents he has given him. He furnishes him with no list of his powers. A man often finds out all at once at forty years of age that he has a talent for something which he had no idea of.

It is degrading, it is debasing the whole relation between God and man, to put it upon the footing of responsibility.

Then what is our relation? our tie to our Creator?

It is a training, by which we are to be gradually raised to share in all our Father's powers, in all His happiness, in all His truth.

Even in the relation between master and servant, so often insisted upon, if the interest of the servant becomes the same as the master's, if an affection springs up, such as is seen between an old nurse and the children she has reared, and she espouses their cause as if it were her own, does not a higher relation take place? And when we come to have one cause and purpose with God, during the short moments even now in which we can feel, 'I and my Father are one', is that responsibility?

The Calvinists tacitly admit that free grace implies irresponsibility. If we miserable worms are to be scaling heaven when and how we please, where would be our sense of reverence and awe when we look up to God, of humiliation and utter helplessness when we look down upon ourselves? they ask. God alone can call us, of His free grace and election, according to His purpose before the foundation of the world.

This predestinarianism reduces us to the level of animals. A man is no better than a dog to which its master all at once begins to teach tricks, and which has neither art nor part in them.

If this be so in partial pre-ordination, often called election, observe that, on the contrary, universal (not partial) pre-ordination is the only system of things by which any power at all can be given us from above. Without the laws of God, which pre-ordain the minutest connexion (we will not say, consequence) of things, how could man have any power at all for carrying his will into effect?

But it is said his will is, according to this doctrine, the

offspring of his nature, which is the offspring of previous circumstances; therefore his will itself is not free.

The word 'freedom', however, is improperly used in this case. For 'freedom' should we not rather substitute the word 'power'? And this power to put his will into effect must be wholly dependent upon law. If circumstances were to have sometimes one consequence and sometimes another, how could we calculate so as to produce any effect which we desire?

Often we do calculate, and are deceived! Not, however, because the law has failed, but because some other laws, unknown to us, are concerned, which, when we know them, will ensure our calculation, based upon absolute fore-knowledge that effects can never vary nor be uncertain or indefinite. When we know all God's laws we shall be omnipotent like Him, for we shall desire nothing but what He wills.

This is a quibble upon the word omnipotence, it will be said. Killing every wish that cannot be satisfied is not omnipotence. Supposing we know and can employ all God's laws, it does not follow that we shall not desire something which those laws will not give us. It is an old story: the child who cried for the moon.

But what is God's omnipotence? To satisfy our idea of omnipotence, must it be able to do everything which tongue can speak – to effect a contradiction – to effect that a thing should be and not be at the same time – that a thing should have been and yet not have been – to make the past not be – to make injustice justice, cruelty mercy, wrong right? Is all this necessary to satisfy the condition that 'all things are possible with God?'

If God repented, or wished to make the past not to be, He would not be God. He would have made a mistake. A Being who could wish to effect a contradiction or an absurdity would not be God; and that Being who could wish to make wrong right, we are quite sure, would not be God, but devil. Is it necessary to make God able to do that which he does not wish, to satisfy our idea of omnipotence? If not, the same definition, which answers our conception of God's omnipotence, will also satisfy it in man's case.

When man knows all God's laws he will perceive the full

beauty of them; it will be impossible for him to wish one to be altered, for he will see that if one were other than it is, man could not attain the full happiness prepared for him; it will be impossible for him to wish other than what God wishes, because he will see the perfection of it. Is not this the meaning of what St John says, 'We shall be like Him, for we shall see Him as He is'. Then shall we no longer say, 'Father, not my will, but Thine be done', but 'Father, Thy will is mine;' and therefore all that we desire will be done. Do we wish for a greater extension of omnipotence than this? Faith truly makes men omnipotent.

This dreary rationalism, it is said, strips the universe of the presence of God, and causes it to be inhabited only by His laws.

But what is the difference between God and His laws? His laws are, after all, only the expression of His thoughts. If thought is invariable in Him, so must His laws be also invariable. But we have got into our heads that law is some mysterious chain, which God creates and then leaves – a machinery like the watch, which the maker manufactures, and then sends to a distance out of his own hands. If, however, it is correct to define law as but the unvarying thought of God, law is the continuous manifestation of God's presence – not a reason for believing him absent.

Great confusion arises from our using the same word law in two totally distinct senses, viz., as the cause and the effect. It is said that to '*explain away*' everything by law is to enable us to do without a God.

But law is no explanation of anything; law is simply a generalization, a category of facts; law is neither a cause, nor a reason, nor a power, nor a coercive force; it is nothing but a general formula, a statistical table. Law brings us continually back to God instead of carrying us away from him. To say that a stone must fall *because* of the law of attraction, is but saying that one stone must fall *because* another does, or because the earth tends to fall towards the sun. The *law* of gravitation is merely a general formula, embracing all these facts.

So Quetelet[19] makes his computations that so many people will commit suicide, that so many widowers will marry three times; and we call it, and justly (supposing the computation correct), a law, and then, with our vague ideas that a law is a coercive force, we cry, 'Oh! how horrid – then there is a law which compels so many people to commit suicide in a twelve-month.' But the law, which is merely a *statistical table*, has no *power* to make people commit suicide. So you might as well say that Newton's law has the power to make the stone fall as Quetelet's table to make the people commit suicide. Newton's law is nothing but the statistics of gravitation, it has no power whatever.

Let us get rid of the idea of power from law altogether. Call law tabulation of facts, expression of facts, or what you will; anything rather than suppose that it either explains or compels.

But there is another meaning to law besides this. The Divine Legislator makes a law, 'Thou shalt do no murder;' the human that Jews shall not sit in the House of Commons.

Law, indeed, in the first meaning which we have been discussing, carries us back to another kind of law, a first cause, a conscious intelligent will. If law is in itself no cause, it must bring us back to the cause of law. If law has no power in itself, it must be the expression of a will or power, mental, not physical; and thus laws are only the expressions of the thoughts of God.

The thought, however, 'Thou shalt do no murder', is quite a different kind of thought from 'Attraction is proportionate to or diminishes as the square of the distance', for murders *are* committed, but stones do *not* remain hanging in mid air.

'Thou shalt do no murder' means, if thou doest murder such and such consequences shall follow. The law of attraction means, if the stone is not lodged in the fork of a tree it will fall to the ground. Where is the difference? We cannot break a law of God; we see that we do not; such education and such temptations acting upon such natures, we see by Quetelet's tables that such a number of murders takes place. Is there any breaking of a law here? Such a body being brought within such a distance of such another body, such an attraction takes place.

Law is, 1st, a general formula, expressing, not explaining facts which co-exist invariably with definite circumstances; 2nd, an intention, or will, in a conscious intelligent being, divine or human, for some uniform co-existence or succession.

All calculation, all foresight, becomes impossible, if we admit NO law or pre-ordination, no inevitable and unalterable con-nexion of facts. If 'the Father of lights, with whom is no variableness nor shadow of turning', governs the world, how can phenomena, which are but the manifestations of His thought, be variable and indefinite?

It is urged that the whole doctrine of reward and punishment is by this theory swept away, for how can the human being, whose will is formed for him, be, in any way, with justice, a subject of reward or punishment? he only does what he is made to do. The Creator has made his creatures what they are. How can He punish or reward them for it?

Let us give up altogether the ideas and the words implying reward and punishment. In sermons and pious books, 'sinful pleasures' are generally treated as the natural desire of the human heart. 'The heart is desperately wicked and deceitful above all things'. These words are quoted as reason for the belief. By the *nature* of man, the constitution of man, we mean the state which *befits*, which is appropriate to man according to the laws of his being – and thus understood, the proper, the healthy nature of man is averse to sin. It 'thirsts after righteous-ness'. In sickness, a man loses what is called his natural appetite. So it is with a corrupt mind, or a mind not constituted, or not developed so as to feel the *natural* wants of the human mind. Wrong is invariably suffering or privation of man's proper *well-being*. Right is invariably well-being, or the road to it.

This eternal immutable (we will not say connexion, but) *identity* of right and happiness, of wrong and misery, is very commonly lost sight of, and it is thought that our nature tempts us to sin; that sin would be pleasant, if only God, by His arbitrary will, had not decreed that we should be burnt for it.

How can there be any right and wrong if there is no 'free will?' it is asked.

It is a law of God that a certain wind acting upon a tooth in a certain state, tooth-ache shall be the consequence. Because you

could not help it, does that tooth-ache cease to pain? Do you
say, it was not my fault; I will not care about it? On the
contrary, the very pain is the motive which compels you to get
rid of it and to avoid it in future. Right and wrong are as
immutable as pain and ease, the one to produce happiness, the
other misery. And we talk of 'God making allowances for the
frailty of His creatures', 'not being prone to mark what they do
amiss', 'having mercy on his erring children'. This mercy would
be the height of cruelty. As long as His laws have not inflicted
evil consequences on our sin and ignorance till no vestige of
either is left in us, mercy means to leave us in sin and consequently in misery.

Mercy for *past* sin would mean a change of mind in God.
What does it change in us? or in that which is past?

It is said to mean that God, knowing our weakness, makes
allowances for it, and does not require from us more than we
are able to do.

Allowances for what? Allowance to do wrong? – allowance to
be miserable?

It is said to mean a remitting of the punishment for what we
have done that is wrong.

Punishment, in the sense of suffering consequent on wrong-
doing, and designed by the eternal laws to drive the criminal to
another course, we can understand, and such punishment we
cannot wish to have remitted. But punishment, when there is no
further power of amendment, there is hardly a human being
who would wish to inflict.

It is said that removing the feeling of self-blame does away
with all bar to every licence. There is no danger. Could Bonaparte go on being Bonaparte to the end of time? Could a selfish
tyrant go on being a selfish tyrant for ever? No, the laws are
such by their essence that selfishness and tyranny bring their
own fruits, their own inducements to goodness and benevolence. A man cannot go on being a Bonaparte if he would. Can a
doctrine be immoral where goodness *is* happiness, not connected with or the cause of it, but identical with it? – where
wickedness is misery? The other doctrine says that there is

always a hope that God will forgive, – that we may sin and yet escape the punishment. But the only happiness worth having is God's happiness; and the divine happiness, that happiness which we are *all* to share, is not the consequence of goodness; it is goodness. But where happiness is made to depend upon some change of mind in God, and not in man, – where, as in the case of the dying but repentant sinner, God is supposed to forgive, that is, to change His mind towards him, and bestow happiness as an arbitrary gift, – can there exist than this any more immoral doctrine? God *gives* us nothing. We are to work out a happiness, like His, in ourselves, in accordance with His laws.

The story of the penitent thief, so often quoted, is not relevant. It is very evident that the man was very far from being all evil. The very high state of spiritual perception necessary to believe in Christ's kingdom at a moment when his nearest friends considered their hopes blasted and his kingdom destroyed; to pray not for life, not for being saved from the cross, but only for moral salvation, shows that he was already very far on the road to happiness. As far then as he was right he will enjoy happiness, identical with the right. *In* his wrong, not *for* his wrong, he will suffer till his evil becomes all good. But to obtain happiness complete, eternal, while there are any of God's laws unknown, or unobserved by us, is an impossibility.

This conclusion is, it is said, contradicted by our every day experience. We see the selfish man enjoying, the good man suffering, the criminal infinitely happier than the philanthropist.

Happier do we call him? Insensibility to privation is not happiness.

As in a medical case any pain is better than paralysis, inflammation more hopeful than mortification; so the murderer, who is conscious of no suffering, is in a worse state than the man who, knowing and observing some laws, suffers for his ignorance of others. Therefore we say, not that misery is the inevitable consequence of evil, but that evil *is* misery, identical with it.

Man is 'predoomed to misery' only on his way to something else, and in order to give him something else. What is the

Creator's own character? He cannot choose between good and evil. *Cannot* is indeed a wrong word, as implying that He would if He could. But to suppose the Creator willing evil, is a contradiction. In this sense God himself has no free will. The nature of the Spirit of Goodness is turned unvaryingly to good. What may we suppose is His object with His creatures? Not that they should attain a free will to choose between good and evil, but such a nature as that nothing but good will attract, no evil will tempt it. Surely if you were bringing up a child, you would not wish to educate it to make a free choice whether it will be a murderer or not, but to be one to whom murder is impossible. When, therefore, our natures, by the Creator's laws, have been brought into that state that we not only know that right is happiness, but feel it, – know how 'to incline our hearts to keep this law', we shall not will to commit evil, – not because we shall have acquired what is called 'free will' to make a choice between good and evil, but because we shall no longer be capable of willing evil.

As a means of attaining this state, the pre-ordination of inevitable consequences is essential. Without this, right would produce sometimes happiness, sometimes misery, calculation would be at fault, motive would be wanting. There would be nothing to incline the will more to good than to evil, without the pre-ordained connexion between good and happiness, evil and misery.

VOLUME TWO

PART II

In order to see where our doctrines will lead us practically, we must push them to the extreme and ultimate limit which they will admit of. This is the only test. Now, our whole real relation with God, with each other, with ourselves, is practically over-thrown by what is commonly called the 'free will' doctrine. These relations cannot be based upon any other idea than that of (not necessity but) law.

Take, first, our relation towards ourselves.

Our belief amounts to this: that I may look back on any particular moment of the past, and truly feel, it was impossible at that moment (God's laws being what they are, and having operated on all preceding that moment as they did,) that I should have willed otherwise than as I did.

We believe this to be just as true as that it was impossible at any particular moment that the earth should not have pursued the course she did: God's laws being at that moment and having been till that moment what they were.

It is, therefore, untrue and useless for me to cry out, Oh! how worthy of blame, how deserving of punishment I was! My good friend, I should rather say to myself, don't be afraid, you will have suffering enough in what you have done. You exhaust the powers which you have in you for finding out the laws to alter nature or circumstances, by these exclamations. 'Come back', I would say kindly to myself, 'I know you could not help it. Let us have patience with ourself, and see what we can do'. But it is the custom in our religion to appeal almost exclusively to the conscience. A wretched drunkard tries to awaken himself by tormenting this faculty. He says, I am very wicked; I hate myself; I am a dreadful sinner. He exhausts himself till he too often flies to that very drink again to escape these terrors of his conscience which he has roused to save himself. A butler once denounced himself to his master, in great agony of mind, and before 12 o'clock the next morning when he was to meet his master, to be dismissed, as he had himself entreated, in order to escape a temptation too strong for him, he was drunk again.

That we would not have him go on in his course without troubling himself about it, we need hardly say.

But take the common course of a drunkard. He may abstain once, by force of conscience or even feeling, or some other motive, but his physical state, which has been accustomed to stimulus, will want it more at the end of 24 hours than of 12. We must consider the whole of the nature on which we wish to work, whether it be our own or any one else's. It is not enough to address yourself to the conscience, while, perhaps, the nerves, the spirits, which have also their laws, may be in a state of severe suffering, from want of the stimulus to which they have been accustomed. But what do we do? Twice a week, we say, we have done nothing we ought to have done, and we have done everything we ought not to have done (in order to make sure of leaving nothing out). And we mean to lead an entirely new life from this moment, to do something entirely different. But it is very certain that we do not, because we intend to say the same thing again in the afternoon. The science of moral recovery is at least as intricate as that of physical recovery. Imagine if a man with a broken leg, or an inflammation of the lungs, were to say, there is not a fibre in my body that does not give me pain – every function I have is going wrong; but I mean, as soon as it is half-past twelve, to walk about as if nothing had happened. I propose that nothing more shall be the matter with me (intending to repeat the same thing at a quarter before three). You would say, he may well say the same thing again, because there *will* be no difference. His intellects are affected, as well as his frame.

Of all the fatal mistakes that have been made to impede the progress of the human race, this perhaps has been the most fatal, viz., the superstition that we have nothing to do but to exert the will, as it is called, and all former error will be rectified, all future good secured. If this mistake had been made with regard to the physical health, mankind would probably have come to an end. If we believed that a man with one diseased lung has nothing to do but to will, in order to have two good ones; if we believed that a man when he is hungry has nothing to do but to will in order to eat, the human race would soon perish. Are not the laws of the spiritual world at least as numerous, important, and worthy of study as those of the physical?

But we don't *only* say 'will'! There are 'means appointed' for our 'growth in grace'.

The means usually enumerated are, self-examination, observance of the Sabbath, public worship, including the communion of the Lord's supper, reading the Scriptures, and prayer.

Self-examination, – we undertake the practice, over and over again, of examining ourselves once or twice a day, and insensibly leave it off from dislike to the operation. Which of us who have ever tried it cannot tell the same tale? Suppose you were to say to a man afflicted with tic-douloureux[20], now twice a day examine yourself diligently for one quarter of an hour (that is not much) to see where the pain lies, whether it is better or worse. And be very sorry for it, remember to be very sorry for yourself while you are doing it, and reproach yourself bitterly that you are no better. Then make a resolution that you will be quite well for the rest of the day, and observe yourself carefully from time to time to see whether you are keeping your resolution. Why, it would be better to try and forget your pain or your sins altogether than to do this. But no, it would not, anything is better than to be altogether careless, because the pain you feel may drive you at last to take some means for cure.

With regard to the Sabbath, one day in seven set apart by common consent of all the world for finding out the spiritual laws of God is indeed an inestimable advantage. We should like

to have two. Even in discovering the material laws which
everybody acknowledges to be very important, how many hind-
rances people find, in consequence of the consent of mankind
not being with them. Some are hindered by hunger, others by
the 'laws of conventional society', unfortunately not the same as
those of God. Those who are prevented by the fear of starvation,
and those who are frightened by that of being 'thought odd', are
therefore equally out of the pale of true discoverers. Now, a
Sunday which is granted by universal consent both to the very
poor and the very rich is inestimable. Only let us use it as such.

As to a 'common worship' as it is called, instead of having it
once a week, we would have it every day, twice a day. The word
'worship', however, seems hardly to express what God wants of
us. He does not want to be praised, to be adored, to have his
glory sung. We can scarcely conceive a good man, a very limited
edition of God's perfections, wishing it. How inappropriate,
then, to Him all this praise! And many only give it, because they
are afraid of Him, for how can He be really thought good, with
such qualities as are ascribed to Him, vanity, anger, revenge.

What He desires seems to be accordance with Him, that we
should be one with Him, not prostrate before Him.

It is said that the parallel between a good man listening to the
singing of his own praises, and God doing the same, is no
parallel, because humility is one of the essentials of a good man.

What is meant by humility we do not well know. Great harm
is done by striving after what is called 'humility', by checking
what is called 'pride'. It is a cry of nature to wish to be
something – to do something. To check it is to check the
appetite for activity which God has placed in our nature.

Humility is thinking meanly of ourselves, placing ourselves
below others, and being willing that others should do so too.

Is not this rather absurdity and untruth? What I want is a
true estimate of myself, not a false one. I want to see myself as
God sees me. If a man with great physical strength were to say
to one who has none, you are stronger than I, you can cut down
that tree better than I: we should say 'how wrong!' If
Macaulay[21] were to persuade himself (for the sake of being

humble) that he could not write history so well as any of the people at that moment walking down the Strand, would that be true or desirable? The maxim, let a man know what he can do, and do it, is not compatible with that of humility. Humility, if logically carried into our conduct, would lead to our giving up everything we do into the hands of those whom we are to strive to think can do it better than ourselves.

Pride and conceit are not qualities either which will contribute to our oneness with God. But pride and conceit become impossible when we have a knowledge of the laws of God. If his laws have made me what I am, if without them I could not be what I am, and with them cannot be than what I am, how can I possibly be proud of what I am? They do away equally with pride and humiliation. The laws of God have brought me where I am. His laws will carry me through.

You wish to believe that God has done everything. We wish to prove it. You say, how horrible for man to think that he has merit – that his virtues are self-derived. We say, too, it is untrue, for God does everything (by means and inducements).

What is morality to be referred to? Is it not to our sense of right? But we have referred it to a book, which book makes many contradictory assertions. Discoveries are being made every day in physical science; but in the most important science of all no discoveries are made or can be made. Why? because the book is final. Supposing Moses had written a book about mechanics, and this book was regarded as the ultimatum, we should have made no progress in mechanics. Aristotle was supposed to have written such a book, and for 1,800 years people disbelieved their own actual experience before their eyes, because they could quote chapter and verse of Aristotle to a contrary effect. Yes, with the sound of two weights falling simultaneously in their ears, they maintained that the weight which was ten times heavier than the other fell in one-tenth of the time of the other, because *Aristotle had said so*. Is not this an exactly parallel case?

Religion under this view, it will be said, will consist partly of assertions considered to be proved, partly of subjects for further consideration among mankind. Much is to be learnt from the

Bible, and probably from all books which have been accepted by large portions of mankind as inspired; but man's capabilities of observation, thought, and feeling exercised on the universe, past, present, and to come, are the source of religious knowledge.

But how may we ever hope to accomplish such improvement of our capabilities? Let us look at our foundations for hope. We have principles to go upon:

I. Religion is discoverable to man through the exercise of his nature.

II. Life ought to be the manifestation of the religion so discovered.

III. It is possible to man to make life the manifestation of religion.

In the doctrine of prayer unbelief and inconsistency reign triumphant in England. Did we really believe in the efficacy of prayer (in the sense of *asking*), there are things which we wish for so much that we should be all day and night upon our knees till we obtained them. But how many do we ever see on their knees in England? except twice a day, when they say what is called a 'form of prayer'. That is a good word – a *form* of prayer. The Evangelical Germans are different, they really kneel down in the middle of what they are saying, and go on, in the same voice, 'Now, dear Lord, give me' so and so. They believe in prayer, and they act upon their belief. But we say we believe, and we do not. We care so little about it that we don't even note what the effect is which follows our prayers. We don't look to see whether it comes or not. The Prussian mystics believe that prayer has a distinct objective effect, that it influences an external will to do something for them which is beyond their control, and they act accordingly. We are not quite sure whether it does or not; but we think it as well to try and take the chance.

A clergyman once asked to be told a certain fact, on the plea that without such information he would not know which of two things to pray for. Here was a distinct practical belief. He believed that if he gave God certain information, and asked for one set of things, a certain definite effect would follow, different from what would follow, if he informed God of something else. This is real belief, logically pursued to its practical consequences. But this we rarely find in England.*

At least it will be allowed that belief in the objective effects of prayer, in its changing something in the will of God, is less often found than it was. But belief in its subjective influence, in its changing something in our own wills, this, it will be said, still exists.

A religious mind in prayer *is* already observing the laws of God; is already *one with* Him. But to send a drunkard or a profligate to prayer, would probably be to send him back to vice. He would be disgusted with an employment, for which he was so little in tune, which had no relish for him.

I gave up praying, in the sense of *asking*, from experience, and not from theory. When I was young, I could not understand what people meant by 'their thoughts wandering in prayer'. I asked for what I really wished, and really wished for what I asked. And my thoughts wandered no more than those of a mother would wander, who was supplicating her Sovereign for her son's reprieve from execution. The Litany was not long enough for me. I wished for all those things, and many more; and tried to cram in as many requests as I could, before the *spell* at the end came in the form of St Chrysostom's prayer. I liked the morning service much better than the afternoon, because we asked for more things. In private prayer I wrote down what I asked for, specified the time by which I prayed that it might come, continued in prayer for it, and looked to see whether it came. It never did. I have papers upon papers, 'by the 7th of July I pray that I may be' so and so. When the 7th of July came, I looked, and I was not.

Sometimes, indeed, I was, but then I knew very well how it was, and that it would have been just the same if I had not

---

* Mademoiselle du Vigean requested S. Vincent de Paul[22] *not* to pray for her conversion, because, he having '*credit* with God,' she might be converted against her will. But S. Vincent continuing to pray without her consent, she became a nun (according to her own account). This is real practical belief.

asked; I could not bamboozle my own consciousness and say, as in the case of a sick man, 'if I had not prayed, this laudanum would not have given me sleep, or my doctor would not have thought of it;' or else, 'this sleep is the effect of my prayer, and would have been, whether I had taken the laudanum or not'.

I always prayed for something definite, specifying the how, the when, and the where of my want. People generally take refuge in the indefiniteness of their prayers (so that they cannot say whether they have been answered or not), from the disappointment of finding out that God has not heard them.

I was always miserable if I was not at church when the Litany was said. How ill-natured it is, if you believe in prayer, not to ask for everybody what they want. If the burning of the 'Amazon'[23] had taken place, and I had not prayed at the Litany the Sunday before, with all my heart, for 'all that travel by land or by water', I should have felt bitter remorse, and believed that their blood was upon my head, in proportion to my share among the prayer-sayers in England. I well remember when an uncle died, the care I took, on behalf of my aunt and cousins, to be always present in spirit at the petition for 'the fatherless children and widows'; and when Confalonieri[24] was in the Austrian prison of Spielberg, at that for 'prisoners and captives'. My conscience pricked me a little whether this should extend to those who were in prison for murder and debt, but I supposed that I might pray for them spiritually. I could not pray for George IV. I thought the people very good who prayed for him, and wondered whether he could have been much worse if he had not been prayed for. William IV. I prayed for a little. But when Victoria came to the throne, I prayed for her in a rapture of feeling, and my thoughts never wandered.

In short, I believed what I believed about prayer, and I should have thought it as disrespectful to God not to wait for the answer as if I had been a servant, which I truly believed myself, sent on a message.

I thought it rather absurd to pray every night, 'Give us this *day* our daily bread', but I supposed that people were not attending to what they said, and that they meant, give us *to-morrow* our daily bread.

Once a friend of mine who died of scarlet fever, showed an intense anxiety to live through the Sunday, in order to be prayed for in church. She died immediately after the service.

It did strike me as odd, sometimes, that we should pray to be delivered 'from plague, pestilence, and famine', when all the common sewers ran into the Thames, and fevers haunted undrained land, and the districts which cholera would visit could be pointed out. I thought that cholera came that we might remove these causes, not pray that God would remove the cholera.

At last, not from thinking what was likely to be, but from observing whether prayer was answered, and finding it was not, it occurred to me that this was not God's plan, that His scheme for us was not that He should give us what we asked for, but that mankind should obtain it for mankind; that we were not paupers asking at a Poor Law Board for relief, but men working for themselves and their fellow-creatures.

It always comes as a surprise when a prayer *is* answered. We record it in little books. We print 'Encouragement to Prayer;' 'Extraordinary Answers to Prayer'. A man prays for 'three and sixpence' over night, and it comes by post the next morning; straightway it makes its appearance as being *extraordinary* in 'Illustrations of Faith', or some such like book. But is it not rather extraordinary, if there are so many millions praying twice a day all through their lives, and if that *is* the way in which God imparts His gifts, that there should be so few of these instances, instead of so many?

It will be said, if we are to have no prayer, we lose our chief support and comfort in this painful world.

Never, never let us be understood to mean that there is *no* communion with the One Perfect. Is there nothing but asking? Can it be that man has nothing to say to the Perfect Spirit of Love, in whose presence he is always dwelling; to the Spirit of Power, of Wisdom, in whom is his trust, in the struggles which convulse his life; to whom he refers the bliss of existence to

which he feels himself destined? Man is capable of love, reverence, sympathy with right, and truth, and goodness: shall he not
feel these towards the only Being who can give them full
exercise?

How are we to speak to Him, if we are not to pray? it will be
asked.

We cannot dogmatise on this highest intercourse. There can
be no 'form of prayer' which will be the voice from all hearts.
Yet, (to man in his true state,) to have intercourse with God, to
be at one with Him, to feel devoted to His purpose, is the
highest happiness that man can enjoy, is essential to give reality
to every other interest. Unless we know what we are working
for, and whom we are working with, we shall work with no zest
or zeal. To be without God in the world leaves every joy
without brightness, to be with Him makes every sorrow in some
sense bliss.

But what is the intercourse we now have with God? Prayer,
in its present sense, is to give utterance, at stated times, to a
form of flattery and to selfish or unwise requests. It is, as in the
Litany, to say to God, 'Don't go this way, don't go that way', till
we have marked out the whole line which He ought to go, and
interdicted to Him the fulfilling of almost every law which He
has made.

What ought to be our intercourse with God? It is not well
with any man who does not desire such intercourse. What it is
to be in private, each enlightened man's nature must tell him.
What it is to be in public, let us try to learn each other's hearts
and discover – in order that when that solemn period of an
eternal existence called a day, begins, we may meet with our
fellow-creatures, and be sent forth to it with all that is within us
of divine roused to activity by words of truth addressed to the
reason, by music from the human voice, expressing the wish to
go forth with right purpose, with love and gladness to God's
appointed work, by sympathy with our brothers and sisters in
this preparation for it, by true emotion resolved into true work;
in order that, when evening comes, we may again meet to thank
God and hail our fellow-workers before we sleep.

We want, it is said, the direct personal communication with God and Christ, that we may ask and hear them answer. Do not take from us, is the cry, our Saviour, the Christ who died upon the cross for us.

And does not God do much more than die upon the cross for us? Is He not in every one of us, going through sin and suffering, 'descending into hell' with us? Does he not suffer, not once for us, but every day in us? And can we want anything more than communion with the perfect and eternal Father?

I want, it is said, communion with Christ, my divine brother, who feels for me.

And you will have it with the Son, the divine in man, with many Christs, who suffer for all mankind.

But we want a Son 'to make intercession for us'.

Do you suppose that Christ is ever 'making intercession' for us? It is true He 'ever liveth', to work for us, but – to 'intercede' for us? He had better not exist at all, God had better not exist at all, than be employed in this way; the one in persuading, the other in being persuaded.

But we want an answer. It is no comfort to say that God may hear me, but He does not speak to me. Man wants an answer.

Can he receive it from the Eternal when he cannot comprehend what eternity is, – from the Infinite and Perfect, when infinity and perfection are beyond his understanding? Were God to speak to him, could he hear? Were God to tell him His plans, could he comprehend them?

But God does not refuse to answer the longing, devoted spirit, which says, Speak, Lord, for thy loving child heareth. He hears as the Father; He answers as the Son, and as the Holy Spirit. I could not understand God, if He were to speak to me. But the Holy Spirit, the Divine in me, tells me what I am to do. I am conscious of a voice that I can hear, telling me more truth and good than I *am*. As I rise to *be* more truly and more rightly, this voice is ever beyond and above me, calling to more and more good.

But you have to invent what it says.

We believe that each man has his Holy Ghost; that is, the

best part of himself inspired by God. But whether it is I who speak, or whether it is God speaking to me, I do not know. We call upon our fellow-creatures to study this subject. That prayer, as *asking*, will entirely cease, we are certain. If we give up *asking*, *confessing* our sins and formal *praising*, will it be said, what remains to be expressed to God? Surely, infinite are the sympathies, infinite the thoughts and feelings, of man towards the Perfect Spirit, with whom he desires to be one.

The Perfect exists in three relations to other existence.

1. As the Creator of all other existence, of its purpose, and of the means of fulfilling its purpose. This is the Father.

2. As partaken in these other modes of existence. This is the Son.

3. As manifested to these other modes of existence. This is the Holy Ghost.

What reason, it will be asked, is there for a belief so fanciful? We revert to what we have formerly said.

Grant a perfect being, as inferred from what is what has been, and what may thence be deduced is to come, and it follows that, if the two former of these relations be denied, the perfection we have asserted is denied.

The Being would not be perfectly benevolent, who, being omnipotent, did not will other modes of existence, with the purpose of producing happiness. The Being would not be perfectly wise, who did not will the means to exist for fulfilling his purpose.

Neither would the Being be perfect, who did not cause others to partake in that which constitutes well-being.

We find that that which constitutes well-being of the highest kind is the exercise of goodness, wisdom, power, those attributes which we have ascribed to God as existing in perfection in Him. These being the essentials of the highest mode of well-being, God would not be perfect unless He caused other beings to partake in them.

To say, then, that God is perfect is to say that He exists in those two relations, which relations have perhaps been felt when He has been spoken of as the Father and the Son.

The third relation seems to consist in our consciousness of the existence of these attributes, in the communication which, if we seek it, these attributes hold with us. Ask of perfect wisdom, you will have an answer above and beyond yourself. Speak, articulately or inarticulately, to perfect goodness and love, such existence hears you, answers you, through the exercise of your own nature, it is true, but it is not your own nature which answers you, but a higher. It is not the mere fact of using words which brings this answer. Many, many are the words spoken to this Holy Spirit which receive no response. Time has already disclosed conditions which, if kept, allow a communication between the holy spirit of God and the holy spirit in man. It used to be thought that God spoke occasionally to individuals, with no other condition than that it was His arbitrary will so occasionally to speak – that He called man out of his sleep with no reference to any particular state in man, the consequence of which would be always communication of the divine in man with God.

But experience shows that there are times when man may ask this communication, but cannot have it, because the conditions for having it have not been kept. He has strayed after false gods. But let him have patience to find out and to keep these conditions, and wisdom, and love, and goodness, which he will feel above his own, will dwell with him; he may interpret their words.

Evidence for this may be found in experience. We believe, from experience, that man is capable of living always, as it were, in a state of reference to that higher Being – that, as the world's ways improve, far as we are from it now, man's intercourse with man will be regulated so as to help this higher intercourse, to keep it unbroken, whereas now it is almost impossible not to break it as soon as man is with his kind.

Deep souls who wanted it fled to wildernesses, to monasteries, and as always happens, others who did not comprehend them, imitated them, and fleeing from the world became a fashion; although it is hard to understand what it means, since the world is what we have to mould, not to fly from.

Everything which is only a part is dull or false. It is only as
part of a whole that anything can be interesting. As part of a
whole, even the most trifling events of every day are interesting.

It is said that mysticism is mistaken in urging man to isolate
himself with God, and devote himself exclusively to his Creator;
whereas man's natural inclination, implanted in him by God,
urges him to devote himself to his fellow-man, urges all mankind mutually to unite in benevolent ties. But those who say this
do not see that the first motive for mankind to unite is devotion
to God; that devotion to God is the spring of love to man, makes
it neccessary, is the same thing. One with God, one with man.

The novel – what a false idea it is – brings two people
through 'no end' of troubles, to make them at last – what?
exclusive for one another – caring alone for one another –
'wrapped up', as it is called, in each other – an abyss of binary
selfishness.

The Methodists,[25] again, have tried for intercourse with God,
by exciting discourse, by imparting their 'experiences', and have
sometimes mistaken the workings of over-excited nerves for the
still small voice of God.

Would that our intercourse with each other could be such as
that to be together *were* a means of being more, not less, in the
presence of God! Would that we felt that awful, though loving
presence, so as not (while we profess to be especially seeking it)
to be repeating words without feeling, to be telling lies with
such indifference that we are not conscious of them. We passed
the church yesterday morning, which was Sunday, on our way
to visit a sick person. The people were all in church, saying that
they had done everything that was wrong, and nothing that was
right, and that they meant to do quite differently in future. As
we came back, they were just going into church again to say the
same thing. It was to be hoped for the sake of their sincerity
that they had done something wrong between this and then,
otherwise they would be telling a lie. But how dare we say this?
We said it last Sunday; have we led an entirely different life
since then? And what expectation have we that we shall do so

next week? What prospect have we? Have we taken any means?
Have we any hopes?

We say that we wish to conform ourselves to the pattern of
Christ. The Roman Catholics, some of them, do act somewhat
after his pattern. They go about doing good, they beg about
without shoes – but what do we do? The most we do is to
confess every Sunday that we are not like it. There have been
holy souls who, in silence, like the Quaker, in excitement, like
the Wesleyan, in form, like the Anglican, have sought and found
this presence, but the imitators of such often find it not, yet are
not aware that it is not there. They go to church or to chapel
because it is a 'duty', and feel no want in not having seen God
there. They did not expect His presence – they are not disappointed at not finding Him, because they did not expect He
would be there.

PART III

SECTION VIII

What a choice it is before a woman! It is notorious how few are
her acquaintances among men; a few out of the few are likely to
give her the opportunity of marriage, and how slight is the
acquaintance which she has with *them*! If, then, among these
few, to those who like *her*, she says, 'I know you so little that I
cannot make up my mind to marry you', she will but express a
very common situation. The anxiety of mothers to marry their
daughters is a current joke. When daughters are grown up,
mothers do not know what to do with them; they are aware
that the daughters have not what is called a 'sphere' at home,
are not satisfied, and the mothers think therefore, naturally

enough, a great deal about the marriage of their daughters, perhaps hardly consciously to themselves. Therefore, the usual talk about children staying at home to take care of their parents means nothing.

Now, if the daughter does not marry, what is her alternative? She is penniless, unless in exceptional cases where she may have had something left her; she must remain at home, it is said, to take care of her parents. It is the hardest slavery, either to take the chance of a man whom she knows *so little*, or to vegetate at home, her life consumed by *ennui* as by a cancer.

What does she take to? In the absence of other spheres of action she very often takes to *governessing* her parents. Where she is fond of her home, this is generally the case; an active spirit doing nothing must find something to do, and this is the nearest thing at hand. People who have nothing to do generally take to playing the policeman over their relations; if too gentle or too indolent for this kind of action, *ennui* consumes their lives. We do the best we can to train our women to an idle superficial life; we teach them music and drawing, languages, and *poor peopling* – 'resources', as they are called, and we hope that if they don't marry, they will at least be quiet.

SECTION IX

It will be said that this doctrine sets the father against the son, and the mother against the daughter, and there will be five in one house divided, three against two and two against three.

Granted, if we were to lock them all up together in the same room. But this is just what we want not to do. We want to send them forth.

But the children often don't want to be sent forth, they have nothing which they want to do; they are like canary-birds which you let go, and they come back again.

We don't want to *force* them out. But, if they are *not* canary-birds and want to go, we would let them out. If they are quite satisfied, let them stay, by all means. But, in general, they are not satisfied at home, and yet have nothing they want to do abroad.

But do children owe their parents no duty, no love or gratitude for all that they have done for them?

Certainly they do; but what is duty? Not to sacrifice but to improve life. Love and gratitude? Certainly. But they can't be grateful to people for making slaves of them. They acknowledge the kind intentions of parents with all their hearts. They are grateful in two ways – for what parents have done which is kind, and for what they intended to do which was kind. But gratitude is a sense of kindness, and they can't love and be grateful to people for enslaving and injuring them.

But there is to be no forbearance, no respect, no mutual self-denial? Is every member of a family to think only of improving, or developing himself, without any regard to the duty of yielding to one another's desires, or even caprices?

There should always be a *whole* in our dealings with everybody, that is, we should always see the whole of our intercourse, or a type of it, before us. If, for instance, I were to see before me the whole of my intercourse with my child, or friend, not merely what I should like to give her to-day, I should not let her go on interrupting me every half hour; there would be no *type* in that; but I should settle with myself what amount of time and forbearance I ought to give her. I should not sit to-day two hours after dinner listening to her, thinking, 'To-day it would not be kind to go away;' but I should consider *her* whole life and *my* whole life, and the type of each, and how much we ought to give one another. And I should not allow these things to be determined by accident, by momentary impulse, – vibrating like a pendulum, between resentment and remorse, – resentment at having so much exacted from one, remorse at not giving so much as is expected of one. A woman who accomplished one of the greatest works which has ever been accomplished, either by man or woman, mentions that she had had the plan of it three years in her head, before she did anything. Why? because she had no type of what her intercourse should be with her own family, nor had they, and she allowed them to monopolize all her time, – the time for doing the thing to which God had called her, – and thought it was ill-natured to go away after breakfast or after dinner. Some say such a family will say to her, 'How could you? You saw, and we did not see, and you let us. How could you suffer us to do it?' A friend of mine had a crooked finger, because when she was a child, she would not let her nurse take off the rag, when it was hurt, to dress it, and the nurse allowed it. Might she not say, 'I was a child, and did not know; how could the nurse let me?' How could she indeed? And what is a deformed or crippled finger compared with a deformed or crippled *life*? Is it well to go on without a type, leaving it to the accident of the moment to decide? Thus is frittered away our life. When we think of the lives around us, squandered by the fancies of children who know not what they do, we cannot but see strongly the danger of having no type. For, if you were to ask people seriously, 'Do you intend your life to be spent in this way?' they would say, 'Oh! no, it is only for to-day; it would be thought unkind not to give way to-day'.

The audacity of people in forming an opinion, and not only forming, but urging one, merely 'because it is my opinion', is curious.

It is because they have no *type* before them. When they give unhesitatingly their opinion that such and such should be done, – that A should go to college, for instance, B study the law, it is because they are thinking, 'What will people say? They will say what a bad thing that he should not go!' not because they have any clear type in their minds of what A will be when he leaves college, or how the study of the law will suit B.

SECTION X

'God makes the family'. So it is often said. Perhaps it is just the contrary. God makes attractions, and the principle of the family is *not* to go by attractions. There may be one tyrant in the family, and the tyrant may go by attraction, but the others do not. In an amiable family, the common course of things is for every one to give up just enough to prevent such collision as would make it intolerable.

But is it not good for the character to give up its own way? Does not God intend all our peculiarities to be softened, our selfishness subdued in this way? is often asked.

The question is a very simple one. Are we intended to go by attraction or by repulsion? Are we to put on a strait waistcoat? Good people make themselves resigned to a family. They do not kick nor struggle, and unquestionably this is much better than mere impatience of it. But it is as if we were to say, There are plenty of things in that room for one to do, plenty of people whom I could help and whom I could work with, but it is good for me to deny myself; I will put on a strait waistcoat, and I will be resigned to it, I will sit quiet and not complain nor resist.

Then, is there no truth at all in the universal opinion of good and earnest Christians, that it is right for us to practise self-denial and forbearance, to give up our own way, and have our sharp corners rubbed off by a little contradiction? will be said.

It is good for us to walk about and exercise all the muscles which are in our body. But to graze our elbows, and our shins, rub the skin off our knuckles, how can that ever be anything but an evil? God means us to do what we like, first learning to like *the right*.

'For joy that a *man* is born into the world', Christ says. And that *is* a subject of joy. But a woman must be born into the *family*. If she were born into the *world*, it would be joy too. But what joy is there in her being born into the smallest of all possible spheres, which will exercise perhaps no single one of her faculties?

Every one will say this is preaching doctrine subversive of all morality. But what right have a man and woman to absorb all the powers of four or five daughters? The right is all the other way. If I have brought them into the world, *they* have the right to expect that their powers shall be exercised, their lives made worth having, opportunity given them for developing all their faculties. I brought them into the world without consulting them; they had no choice in it, and I ought to have thought of this, whether I was able to give them all this, before I did so. 'The mother that bore you' is often mentioned as such a subject of gratitude; as if life were such a boon that the mere circumstance of *my* having given *you* life entails slavery upon you. But whether it is a boon or not depends upon whether parents can make it so for children. 'Bore you' to what? To take care of me? By the beautiful arrangement of Providence that the good of one shall tend to the good of all, and *vice versa*, that one cannot be injured without injuring the whole, the parents are injured as well as the children by this absorbing of their services.

And how often is there unsuitableness in the characters of the members of the same family. Look round the families you know, and see how many you know in which they do not think there is something very peculiar in them. 'We do not go on well, but', etc.; 'I should not like it to be mentioned, but', etc.; 'there is something *"very peculiar"* about that child', 'such an unusual reserve', or, 'I know there is a *"peculiar"* deficiency in myself'. Do you know one family where the mother has what may truly be called a beautiful relation with the daughter? One which you would call a very happy family, except the 'happy family' in the cage which travels about? 'If I had but children like so and so', we hear constantly said in private, 'but mine are so *"very peculiar"*'.

'Robbed and murdered' we read in the newspapers. The crime is horrible. But there are people being robbed and murdered continually before our eyes, and no man sees it. 'Robbed' of all their time, if robbing means taking away that which you do not wish to part with, slowly 'murdered' by their families. There is scarcely any one who cannot, in his own experience, remember some instance where some amiable person has been slowly put to death at home, aye, and at an estimable and virtuous home.

With regard to time, however, it is often said that if people made the most of their odd moments, they would have not much to complain of, – but they waste their spare quarters of an hour so grievously.

The maxim of doing things at 'odd moments' is a most dangerous one. Would not a painter spoil his picture by working at it 'at odd moments'? If it be a picture worth painting at all, and if he be a man of genius, he must have the whole of his picture in his head every time he touches it, and this requires great concentration, and this concentration cannot be obtained at 'odd moments', and if he works without it he will spoil his work. Can we fancy Michael Angelo running up and putting on a touch to his Sistine ceiling at 'odd moments'? If he did he would have to take it out again. But the value of fresco is that this cannot be done, and that is one reason probably why great masters preferred fresco, and said that oils were only fit 'for children and dogs'. The very gist of fresco painting is that it should be all painted in at once from one master idea, not niggled and dawdled at.

The Chancellor Oxenstiern[26] is recorded to have written a folio volume during the ten minutes his wife kept him waiting for dinner every day.

It was not worth his writing, then, nor our reading. Everything that has ever been done at 'odd moments' had better never have been done; even a letter, written in a 'spare quarter of an hour' had better not have been written. Can *any* work requiring thought be done at 'odd times'? Perhaps the mere writing what has been carefully thought out in the watches of the night, – yet hardly even that, to do any good.

Then are we to do nothing with our odd times? Are we to waste the spare moments which make up the greater portion of a woman's life? If you are to do *any* thing, you must do it then, is again said.

When people give this advice, it sounds as if they said, 'Don't take any regular meals. But be very careful of your spare moments for eating. Be always ready to run into the kitchen and snatch a slice of bread and butter at odd times. But never sit down to your dinner, you can't, you know'. We know what *can* be done at odd times, a little worsted work, acquiring a language, copying something, putting the room to rights, mending a hole in your glove. What else is there? I don't know. Nothing requiring original thought: nothing, it is evident, which requires a form, a completeness, a beginning and an end, a whole, which cannot be left off 'at any time' without injury to it, which is not 'mere copying', in short.

When Beethoven wrote a bar, he must have had the phrase, the movement, the quick time which was to succeed, the slow movement which came before – the whole piece, in short, in his thought. And could he write a bar now, a bar then, at an 'odd moment'? This is what we call being a 'dilettante', when a man does work in that way, and most of the works of Dilettanti had better not have been. Women are almost always dilettanti, and have women ever produced any original work, any, with a *very* few exceptions, which the world would not be as well without?

Many, indeed, are the stories told of great men mastering a whole science in their spare moments.

There are, no doubt, some minds which can work, and some employments which can be taken up at odd times – where it is *acquiring* which is to be done. But if there is no digesting done, or if there is no time for digesting afterwards, the acquiring perhaps is not of much benefit. Or a mind may become so possessed with a subject that it can work at it at *all* moments, but then the moments cease to be 'odd'. The greatest genius which cannot and ought not to work without seeing the whole of its subject before its eyes, the most important subjects of thought which require this, these cannot be referred to 'odd moments'. People get out of the difficulty by not having *any* subjects of thought, which require to be pursued at other than 'odd times'.

How, in a family, where the one has to wait for the other – where, if they have any amiability, the employments of every one are constantly called upon to give way – how can the members, excepting those who have professions, ever have anything but 'spare moments'?

How, indeed? We constantly hear it said, 'So and so has given up all her music since she married, or her drawing, – what a pity,

such a first-rate artist as she was!' A married woman cannot
follow up anything which requires exercise, and if, even for such
second-rate things as these, people cannot command the time
necessary, how will they do for subjects of *thought*? And we are
slower still to apprehend that we must not rob you of the state
of mind *with* which to think, than of the time *in* which to think.
If visitors come in, the lady of the house often complains that
she will not have time to do this or that, she does not complain
that she will not be in a state of mind when they go, to do it, if it
is something important and requiring thought. She settles *that*
by not having anything important to think about.

Half the people in the world have, indeed, no power of
thinking. 'What does it matter to give me time for that which I
cannot do?' is often said.

But 'half the world cannot think', *because* they have never
tried. How is it possible? People get up in the morning and
come down to breakfast, can they think then? After that, they
read the newspapers or write letters, or sit in a room reading a
book, where everybody is reading bits out of their own book
aloud, or talking, till luncheon. Then they ride or drive, then
they read a book or write letters till dinner. Then they spend the
evening together till bed-time. This is interspersed, for women,
with housekeeping, and visiting the poor people; for men, with
House of Commons, managing their estates, the bench, and the
board. Now, how are you to think? When are you to think? Not
sitting with your feet on the fender, that is only dreaming. Few,
except Descartes, ever thought without a pen in their hands.

A mother will say to her daughter, 'Now, my dear, all the
people are gone, you have all the afternoon to yourself, you can
go up and employ yourself in your own room'. But is she in a
state to think? Is not her power of attention all frittered away? If
she has breakfasted in a crowd, if she has been standing about
for two or three hours afterwards, not knowing whether she
might go away or not, how is her mind in any condition to think
after that time? Sir Walter Scott[27] even did not write his novels
in that way.

But we are not all Sir Walter Scotts, nor Michael Angelos,

nor Beethovens. On the contrary, such geniuses only come once in a thousand years.

How do we know that? We are often struck by the richness of organizations at 17 or 18, and how they go off afterwards. We are oftener surprised by the power than by the poverty of young characters. In many families there is one with a great dramatic talent, another with a genius for music, and a third with one equally remarkable for the pencil; a fourth writes like Coleridge. Yet we know perfectly well that these will be neither Michael Angelos, nor Beethovens, nor Mrs Siddonses,[28] nor Miltons. Why? A lady friend of mine and Michael Angelo both had a turn for architecture. Michael Angelo studied it. My friend never did. All she did was pure genius. To compare her with Michael Angelo, of course, does not come into our head for a moment. How could she be compared, indeed? The one had no possibility given her, the other had. But people never think of this. They think nothing of being in a *state of mind* to think a great thought, to do a great work. They will fritter away all their power, and then think they have enough to do anything *they* want to do with it. They will let others play with them all the morning, and then think, 'I shall have the afternoon to myself'. You may do your accounts, or you may play with the children, or you may read an idle book, but do anything important which requires thought you cannot. And therefore the best way is to give up all subjects of thought, and that is what people do.

Many say there is not the absolute want of steady application in a family here mentioned, because there is 'reading aloud' almost always going on. But don't you feel, when you are being read to, as if a pailful of water were being poured down your throat, which, but that it comes up again just as it goes down, would suffocate you? Very few swallow it at all; fewer still digest it. Many people like to read aloud; but how many can bear being read to without going to sleep? Yet *everybody* can't be reading aloud.

Women like something to tickle their ears and save them the trouble of thinking, while they have needlework in their hands. They like to be spared the *ennui* of doing nothing, without the labour of doing something.

Those who have a great power of receiving impressions, a ready perception, thus like to be read to, but a reflective person does not, because there is no time nor opportunity given for reflection, and therefore he ceases to attend. I remember hearing Lord Jeffrey[29] say, only the year before his death, that he hated being read to. He always read to himself, at eighty years of age. In a family the common practice is for one to read aloud and for the others, of course, to listen, or – not to listen. What does it signify in the latter case whether I am there or not? Generally, *I* am not there, though my body is, for the others would be very much vexed, of course, and think it *very* unsocial if *my body* were not, even though it be asleep.

One person can do nothing after eight P.M., but goes to sleep. Another can do nothing before ten A.M. But both unfortunates are obliged to be present in the body at whatever is going on, although *they* are not *there*. We shall think it curious, looking back, in a future state, to see that we have condemned people to do nothing, and called it a duty, a self-denial, a social virtue.

This, perhaps, may be one reason why grown-up people seldom improve. We ought to improve, of course, every year, as long as we are capable of gaining *any* experience, and the more experience the more improvement. Young people, during the time of their education, do improve. But it is set down for granted that old people are not to improve. Does any one ever say, 'Do you think Mrs —— is improved since last year?' Nobody ever thinks of such a thing, unless, indeed, there is exercise of some faculty. For instance, it is said, 'Pauline Viardot[30] is much improved since last season; she shows marks of careful study;' and this after she has arrived at mature age. Or, 'George Sand's[31] style and ideas have undergone a complete regeneration since she began writing'. Or, 'Sir Robert Peel's[32] powers as an orator are sensibly greater than last session'. Raphael, it is well known, changed his manner, and most, or all but the pre-Raphaelites, would say for the better. Schiller[33] made the most tangible progress, so that Goëthe[34] said of him, 'If you met him after the lapse of a week you did not know him again'. Is it not evident, then, if exercise goes on in mature age, as it does in childhood, that progress will be made in the same way? Nay, probably even faster, as the vantage ground of experience becomes greater. But people have no *type* before them, neither nations nor individuals. We say vaguely that 'times improve', whereas sometimes it is evident that they do *not* improve, as in the Roman empire, as in Spain, where they degenerated. In England it is always taken for granted that we are making progress. Then comes some statist,[35] and says there is more crime, more disease, more madness than formerly. Macaulay says the contrary, and shows that food is cheaper, that the 'condition of the working classes' is more comfortable, education and literature more diffused, etc. No one seems to know which is the case. Both these statements may be true, and are not inconsistent. How can nations improve, however, if they have no type before them?

It is perhaps incorrect to say that they have no type. England has the type of making money. In commerce, in trade, in many manufactures, in railroads, in mercantile speculations, she is far beyond all the rest of the world, – and, (which is having a type), she seems to make money for making money's sake. A cabinet minister, of the highest moral worth, subscribes to Hudson's[36] testimonial. When Hudson lost his character without losing all his money, he was still 'received'. A man left nine or ten thousand a year to a boy of nine years old whom he knew nothing of, to his only sister with whom he had lived in the most affectionate intercourse all his life, a small annuity, (and this was prompted by his attorney), to his niece nothing; and all for the sake of keeping a large fortune together after his death, which he had spent his life in amassing. Lately a most distinguished and respectable man left his whole enormous fortune to a young nobleman, known to him and to all the world as a profligate, and deeply in debt, so that the fortune was tied up till these debts were paid, while he left to some of his best friends nothing. Such things as these could perhaps happen only in England, where money, for its own sake and not for that which money procures, seems to be valuable.

Perhaps the type of France is a type of art in everything that concerns the eye and the ear. Some women furnish their apartments to suit their complexions. The barricades were a study for the painter. No Frenchwoman is ill-dressed, no Frenchman or woman does not know how to talk. You have only to enter their gay capital, smiling and beautiful, like a gem, to see the difference of its type from that of ours. You had only to go into the Great Exhibition of 1851, and see their counters, arranged with an artist's eye, even to the *papeterie*,[37] so as to be perfect studies; and then look at the beautiful English silks, set up upon a thing like the ornamental paper of an inn fire-place, in order to see the difference of the two nations. Then the cleverness of their talk, by which their wits become sharper every hour – the point of everything they say and write. You see at once that their type is to elaborate ideas into conversation;* but no one would say that this is an English aim, and therefore the sooner, perhaps, they give up a mere attempt to imitate their neighbours over the water, the better. The French elaborate their thoughts into words, the English into work. The word is good, and so is the act; but can the two nations ever interchange? A copy is seldom worth having.

Perhaps no nation or individual has a tangible type before them now. All they do is to imitate. When the Greeks believed in their gods, there came forth an Apollo Belvidere, a Ludovisi

---

* In a review by one who knows both French and English society thoroughly, it is said, speaking of Paris; – 'The sociability, the love of conversing, is an absolute necessity. We know men who had rather live in extreme poverty in Paris than go away for a comfortable income: not from any love of its localities, but they are afraid of being *ennuyéd*[38] for want of the conversation they find in every *salon*. Why does a man in London prefer his club to a drawing-room, where a lady presides? And why do men in Germany never go to one but by special invitation, with a supper to make it bearable? They are as fond of their homes as the French, but they have less need of companionship in their wives. But whatever is the cause, the effect is certain; and in consequence of this preference for their society, the middle-aged and the old ladies have the same relative value, according to their intellectual merit, that men have. We never heard anybody in France call a man an "old woman" because he was a fool of a particularly twaddling kind. Old women are thought quite as capable of wisdom as old men, and in fact they have more influence. * * In England a woman's beauty and her virtues are what every man thinks of as the charm of his house. He talks with rapture of the woman who will nurse him and pour out his tea. In France you do not hear much about a woman's coffee. "Est-elle aimable?" (*aimable* does not mean a virtue, but an *agrément*[39]) "A-t-elle de l'esprit?" is the second question, if not the first, that every man asks. It does not mean anything wonderful: it means, Has she the quick perception that seizes what is said, and returns change for your thoughts?'

Juno. Now we no longer believe in them, but we still imitate
them. And there come forth Titian's Venuses and Canova's
Perseus. When the Italians believed in the Virgin Mary, see what
holy families Raphael and Guercino and Guido[40] produced; and
the same Titian, whose Venus is an earthly profligate, paints a
virgin fit for the skies. *We* still go on painting the holy family,
though we have ceased to believe in it. And what holy families!
Could we not advance to paint a new whole family, the holy
family of mankind? If we were inspired by that, as the Greeks
and Italians were by their gods and goddesses, a new era of art
would come in. But go into Mr Vernon's gallery, and see horses,
and cows, and game, and cottages, and dogs, and little boys
grinning, and ladies on horseback, all very beautiful in their way;
but no holy families, nothing of what in the future *might be* – of
the ideal – of the type which God intends mankind to reach, and
poets and artists, who are our prophets, to set forth.

PART IV

SECTION V

It is a radical mistake fatal to all progress to say that we are to
remain in the position 'in which God has placed us'. The very
object of all the teaching which we have from God is that we
may *find out* the 'calling' to which we are called.

He leaves *us* to find it out. If He were to rub out the wrong
figure in the sum and put in the right one Himself, would that
be exercising our faculties at all as it does to make us do it
ourselves?

There is no idea now of organizing a life to act out our
religion. We are to get on as well as we can *in our life* with our

religion. What can we expect, then, other than what we do? It would be truer to say at once, 'I know that I shall do so all my life, but if you like I will come once a week, and say that I will not'.

We think so much more about having done wrong than about doing right. We talk so much more about what we have done, and our 'desperate wickedness' than about doing otherwise. To ask God's pardon is the main part of our religion; perhaps all the religion we have.

Now, if we think that the very kernel of God's plan is that we *should* make mistakes, asking pardon for them, instead of learning our lesson (His lesson) from them, does indeed seem counteracting His plan, and mistaking goodness for badness. What a difference it would make in our feelings towards each other if we could but get into our heads that this is God's purpose.

God's plan is that we should make mistakes, that the consequences should be definite and invariable; then comes some Saviour, Christ or another, not one Saviour but many an one, who learns for all the world *by* the consequences of those errors, and 'saves' us from them.

Instead of saying to ourselves, as we have so often done, 'we will begin next Sunday, and never do wrong any more', we ought to say, 'I know that I shall do wrong; there will be (not one 'fall' visited upon all mankind, but) many falls. I know that I must make mistakes. It is part of God's plan. I will (not ask pardon for them, but) take them in conformity with God's purpose, and strive to learn His purpose. The consequence of my falls, indeed, will be upon the human race till a Saviour comes'. May we all be Saviours in some way to humanity!

I yearn to be and to do right; but, before I knew what I was about in existence, the time was passed when I might have cultivated, have exercised capabilities which I now no longer possess. Inefficiencies, ignorance of the way I should pursue, habit, all render powerless the wish I have to will aright. What shall I do? I live on, strengthening much that I know to be wrong; though I desire above all the right; though the only times

on which I look back with any pleasure are those when circumstances *did* help me to true and right feeling. I care for nothing
that is called amusement. Ambition, as it is called, the externals
of the world, have not a charm left for me. But incapacity
blights me. Not a day passes, not an hour, in which I do not feel
myself mistaken, in the wrong, either in thought, in feeling, or
in doing. How shall I find help?

At all events I am convinced that to beat down my already
depressed spirits, to thicken the cloud of darkness by self-
reproach for that which arises from the laws of God, would be
untrue. I can point out to myself many helps and consolations. I
can assure myself that all *shall* be well; but I do not ask to live
upon such assurance. No; existence is made up of *presents*, and
each present is to be cared for. To live on the future (or on
contemplation of any kind) is obviously not intended to be
sufficient to man. In an imperfect state of things, in a life
modified by no comprehensive view of what they are, and what
they might be, who are to live it, it is difficult to exercise the
nature aright. But from day to day I can see, helped by my own
experience, means by which I may improve my course. And let
me not think that there can be anything selfish or wrong in
striving for the healthy nature of a human being, because that
being is myself. The only question is, *will* my thought and care
improve that being really? If it will, so I may help, or prepare to
help, mankind. If I can really help myself or any human being to
be better, *so* I undoubtedly am working with God and for man.

I *wish* to avoid any course of thought, any talk which is
deteriorating, but I have not the capability to lead, to elevate
myself or others; life takes its poor course; with a sorrowful
heart I follow, unable to lead.

I never will offer to myself the false doctrine that I may be
good and happy in any circumstances, *if I will*. Since God intends
man to modify life into one righteous course, dissatisfaction
with any other course is His admonition, teaching me that *this is
not it*. Let me be thankful, at all events, that I am not dead or
paralysed, so that this voice does not reach me. But helps I can
have. I can look into the detail of my life, I can try for wisdom

to steer through it aright, *when I can*. I will not flatter myself that
I can enter upon an unbroken course of life, that I can say, 'I
have been always wrong, pardon me, O Lord, because I am
conscious of it, and confess it. *Now* I will try never to be wrong
again'. I accept God's will that mankind, and I, as one of
mankind, am to learn – to *work* my way. Let me awaken to see
the nobility of such an existence, to see it in my own feebleness
and ignorance, and in that from which I suffer, in others. Let me
look how not to deteriorate, look even to the less rather than to
the greater deterioration. If I cannot avoid what I feel
deteriorating, there is a feeling with which this may be borne,
which is elevating. The general run of moral books and of
sermons are full of precepts which come home to nobody. How
few can say practically that they have been better in consequence of them. To hear or read them is thought right in itself;
but who says that they have helped him to be, to live better? Yet
how *one* may help *another*, when a true life shall become the
object of mankind. I heard yesterday a concert of instrumental
music; how perfectly one fell in with another, what harmony!
Such harmony will therefore be in life when man strives to find
out what it ought to be, to make it such, to help man by means
of man, each to take his part so as to harmonize with each other,
engaged in the performance of the same piece.

When I feel low, and poor and miserable in a drawing-room
life, where I can do nothing, is not that His word to me, saying
'Now you see that in this life human nature is not exercised to
anything like the degree which it is capable of. You feel very
uncomfortable, therefore change it as soon as you can, pick up
everything you can from it while you are in it; but find out the
life, as soon as you can, which does call out all the goodness and
wisdom of which human nature is capable?' Can He speak
plainer than He does? Could it, if He spoke in words, be more
clearly His voice to me?

But there is nothing about God in the lives we lead; we are to
do what is *usual*. The visits we have to make, the people we are
to ask to dinner, that which is 'usual' determines all these
things. We never ask, What is the nature of God? and what is

His purpose for man? What is the nature of man, and what his destination? or, if we do, we have only a Sunday answer. It is surprising that *what God is* is a question which interests no one. They take, without inquiry, what is set down in a book.

Dr Arnold[41] was right in taking a country curacy, and letting inquiry alone when his mind was disturbed. Those who take the miraculous view and think that God has given a revelation to the world, must think that, if He has given one, He has adapted it to the normal state of that world; therefore, if any one doubts it, it must be owing to some defect in his own nature. What *he* has to do, then, is (not to inquire, but) to improve his own nature that he may be able to accept God's revelation.

We have long since done with the miraculous view. We think God has entrusted it to the exercise of our own faculties to make the revelation. But, for those who hold such a view, Dr Arnold's course was the only wise one, viz., to lay aside inquiry, adopt an active life, and try to improve his being.

SECTION VI

People constantly say, would God have left us without a revelation of Himself? Would He have left such an important question as religion to the unassisted reason of His creatures? All that we can say is, He *has* done it. But it is said people might believe Christianity if they liked it. Could those who lived *before* Christianity, could those now living, who have never heard of Christianity, believe in it, if they liked it? It is said, this is a mystery. Then He *has* done it. People allow that there are 'doctrines upon which eternal life depends, and yet of these not a whisper was heard on earth until there came a revelation' 4,000 years after the world began. They do not see what a God they have made when they say this; they do not see how they have been insulting Him. We, who say that revelation has to be worked out by the exercise of man's faculties, can readily believe (and

thank God for it) that 4,000 years and much more might pass
before the revelation came. We can reverence and esteem God
for it. We can even be in a 'rapture', like St Teresa,[42] in
contemplating the perfection of the scheme. But if the revelation was to be given by God, as these men say, why not give it
sooner? What reason could He have?

There have been three parties – those who have said that
there was a revelation through the book; those who have said
that there was a revelation through the Church, or through the
book and the Church; and those who have said that there was
no revelation at all. Now we say that there is a revelation to
every one, through the exercise of his own nature – that God is
always revealing Himself.

Then how come men to believe in so many other revelations?

The Church is necessary to maintain those beliefs, in the
atonement, the incarnation, the sacraments, etc., which were
the natural growth of minds, in the times in which they sprung
up; but which, in these times, in which they are not the
'intuitive effluence' of our natures, could not be maintained
without a Church. The Anglican Church has not authority
enough to do this; and therefore she maintains them but very
imperfectly. The Roman Catholic Church alone can do it. As she
says herself, she is the only Church who can.

Is there any consistency in this age in any Church but the
Catholic?

There can be no religion in arguing that you should stay in
the Church into which you were born. The struggle now going
on between the Roman Catholic and Protestant appears to be
not at all a matter of religion. We hear the argument daily used
by the Arnold school (the names of which we reverence beyond
most, the principles of which we are hardly able to understand),
that men ought to stay in the Church into which they are born.
There is no religion in this; there is something else, there is
conscientiousness, there is reverence; but there is no religion, if
religion be our tie to God. Surely the God who orders the
Roman Catholic Church must be a very different God from the
God who orders the Protestant Church, still more different

from Him who orders the Church of the *future*. If you believe
that He does the things which the Roman Catholics say that he
does, how can you stay worshipping Him in another Church
which says He does not? There can be no religion, at least, in
doing so, though plenty of something else, love of kindred,
regard to duty, etc. And, indeed, can you go into an Anglican
church, and think there is any devotion? You see no prostration
of spirit, no intensity of feeling, as among the Roman Catholics;
you see people very nicely dressed, you see great care to come in
good time, you see a feeling of having accomplished a duty when
it is over.

No one can call the Church of England the Church of the
Apostles. The Catholics may say that their Church is the Church
of the Apostles; but we do not call our Church the Church of
the Apostles, except in the creed. We know that it is the
Church of Henry VIII, not of the Apostles. And what a Church
it is! The best thing that we can say of a clergyman in these days,
is that he does not *interfere* – 'a very good man, he never
interferes' – that is, he may interfere with the poor people, he
may go and say, 'I did not see you at church last Sunday, how
was that? I think you might have managed to walk so far'. But
he must not say such a thing to the 'upper classes'. That *would* be
'interference'.

The Church of England is expected to be an over-idle
mother, who lets her children entirely alone, because those
made her who had found the Church of Rome an over-busy
mother. *She* imprisoned us; she read our letters; she penetrated
our thoughts; she regulated what we were to do every hour; she
asked us what we had been doing and thinking; she burnt us if
we had been thinking wrong. We found her an over active
mother, and we made the Church of England, which does not
'interfere' with her children at all.

But, if mankind can find out God by the exercise of their own
faculties, how does it happen that we have not long since found
Him out, that we have not long since a Church dedicated to that
search?

Hitherto all the efforts which have been made in religion,

since Christ's time, have been either to cut off error, or to believe what you *say* you believe. The Catholics say, 'Christ says, be poor like me, leave your family for my sake, *we are going to do it*'. And the religious orders are the consequence. The Evangelical party[43] says, 'You tell us that Christ died on the cross for us; this really makes a great impression upon us; we cannot go and laugh and dance as if He were not dead'. These are the efforts which have been made to act out what *was believed*. Luther[44] and the Reformers were the men who cut off some monstrous errors. *Protestants* they rightly called themselves; for *to protest* was all their business; and there is nothing very high or noble in protesting. To search for truth has yet to be brought forward as an object.

Everything that we have now in religion we should then have more of. You want to believe that Christ 'died' *once* for you. We believe that God is always dying for us. You want to believe that we 'do nothing of ourselves'. We believe that God is in all of us; that we are, in fact, His activity. You want to believe in 'Free Will'. We believe that God's whole purpose is that man should learn (of himself) to be God. You want to believe in a future state; we would teach really to believe in one, – not a future state which is to be given us, but a future state which we are to *create*. The mistake of all religions seems to have been, 'Let us renounce this world and all its vanities, and look forward to a better'. We say, too, 'Let us renounce this world', but 'let us *create* a better, let us show an example of a better'. There is no fault to be found with this *earth*; we have no reason to suppose that there is a better earth anywhere else; we have no reason to suppose that there *is* a 'better world', unless we have created it; it will not be given us; let us then begin without delay to *make* one. Again, you think Christ was 'inspired', we don't well know how; we believe all men to be inspired, to have God dwelling in them. All, excepting the Atonement, we shall have. Suffering *instead* of a person seems to be without meaning.

Without the belief in miracles, in prayer, in a man-God, it is said, we can never have that fervent conviction which Saint Teresa had.

Remember these words, 'Lo, it is I, be not afraid'. Some
great artist should paint a series of pictures, where man is
passing through sorrow, and God says, 'It is I, be not afraid;'
where he is passing through sin, even through sin, – yes, *most*
through sin, and God says, 'It is I, be not afraid'. God is so
much more there than 'walking on the sea', which is, after all,
very paltry. Raphael paints Him performing the miracle of the
fish, and makes him so divine that we lose sight of the absurd
nature of the miracle. But, if he had painted him saying to man
in a state of sin and degradation, 'It is I, be not afraid', how
much more divine!

Saint Teresa was in a 'rapture', but we might be in a much
greater rapture than hers. We have so much more to give us
'rapture'. For what made her in a 'rapture'? Because Christ had
appeared to her with a crown upon His head, and had told her
that He would keep one door of her monastery and His Mother
the other. And what was her monastery for, and the life she
intended to live? To live at other people's expense and pray all
day. If she could be in a 'rapture' about such things, it shows the
power of loving in her nature. And we who have so much more
to love, shall *we* not be in a much higher 'rapture'? We, who see
our God always, not with a crown upon His head occasionally,
but *always*, acting out the perfect law of love and wisdom in
everything? Saint Teresa did not know whether her 'raptures'
were from God or the devil. It was a misery to her all through
her life that she never could be quite certain of this. But *we* shall
be quite certain that our 'raptures' come from God. Because
what we have to do *is* the searching out and finding what is
consistent with perfect love and goodness. And this consistency
will be the cause of our raptures. And therefore we shall have no
doubt that they are not 'the devil'. Saint Teresa was never sure.
Did we really believe in God, *i.e.*, in a *perfect* Being, whose
scheme was that of perfection for *all* His creatures, should we
not be in a continual 'rapture'?

What evidence we have for miracles! is often said.

But no evidence could convince us of them. You wish to
believe in them, because you think you find your God there. We

should lose our God, if we were to find Him performing miracles. That is the difference.

But the Roman Catholics have not lost their God. They are, perhaps, the only people who have found Him, who are one with Him.

The Roman Catholics, it is true, believe in such a God that we should find it impossible to love Him if we did believe in Him. But, then, they have an organization ready for their truly religious people to step into – to act out the irreligion. They have a *life*. Like them, it would become impossible and disgusting for us to do anything which was not *one with* Him, if we organized a life, of which unity with Him was the purpose and end.

When all mankind shall have *one* purpose, then will there be real unity. And what a world that will be! all pursuing the same purpose, though with different means.

People make such a point of having the evidence of eye-witnesses to a miracle. But here we have the evidence of St Teresa that she saw two little devils round a priest's neck. We have the evidence of St Paul that he saw a light in the sky, and heard a voice. We are as certain of their honesty, we are as certain that they believed it, when they said they saw the devils and the light, as I am that believe it when I say I see an inkstand on the table. There is no more ground for suspecting imposture in the case of St Paul than in that of St Teresa; but that the devils were not there, and that the voice was not there, we are equally certain. Therefore, what is the 'evidence' of an 'eye-witness'? Wherever miracles have been believed, they have been seen. We feel as sure that St Teresa believed she saw the miracle as that she did not see it. There is no difference in our certainty.

NOTE. – Baden Powell[45] truly says, Testimony is but 'as a second-hand assurance; a blind guide that can avail nothing against reason'.

We agree also with Pattison,[46] that '*evidences* do not constitute theology'. We cannot, however, agree with him as to what *is* 'theology'.

PART V

The Church of England has for men bishoprics, archbishoprics, and a little work (good men make a great deal for themselves). She has for women – what? Most have no taste for theological discoveries. They would give her their heads, their hearts, their hands. She will not have them. She does not know what to do with them. 'You may go to the Sunday School, if you like it', she says. But she gives no training even for that. She gives neither work to do for her, nor education to do it, if she had it to give. Many women would willingly give her their life's work. Luther gave us 'faith', justification by faith, as he calls it; and the Church of Rome gives us 'works'. But the Church of England gives us neither faith nor works. She tells us neither what to believe nor what to do.

No, it is said, she has wisely refrained from telling us what to believe. She does not wish to make slaves of our intellects, but to let each man judge for himself. We do not wish to believe all the dogmatic absurdities of Christian churches, to have an Inquisition forcing us to believe.

Does any educated man, now, really believe in the incarnation? There *has* been, perhaps, more of feeling excited by the incarnation than by anything else. People were tired of hearing about the beauties of nature, and God's skill in contrivance, and about their 'creation, preservation', etc. But the idea of a God dying for their sins awakened much of feeling for religion.

People must *make* a God till they can *find* one. It has always happened that some have made such a God as could be imagined by them, and others have taken Him from them. Few have looked about to find the true God. Indeed, it is hardly likely that they should. If we are to make a God for savages, or for men living in a false state of refinement, this is not finding God as He is.

'What is religion without prayer?' says Gerbet.

Rather, what *is* prayer? Mrs S, when she lost her daughter, said, 'I prayed that she might die without pain, and my prayer was heard'. Think of a sweet gentle innocent creature whom you would not hurt for the world, – and that God should have given her pain! and for no reason!! Because He desisted when the mother asked Him. It can only be (on this view) because the mothers do not ask Him to desist that He gives the children pain. And this is the God made by our theory of prayer. Well may it be said that we are idolaters, and have not found the true God.

It is said that the Protestant religion gives no discipline to the character, no feeling of duty.

There are these three phases of character, – selfish indulgence, necessity of duty, and accordance with right. We have got out of the second phase (duty), and we have not got into the third phase (right). Therefore we have fallen back into selfish indulgence. Formerly, there was much more of conscientiousness. It was all laid down what we were to do, and we did it. People did not think of what they liked, but of what they ought to do. Now duty is so difficult, it is so little known what it is, that we only think of what we like. We have not come to 'accordance with right'.

'Right', is the voice of God. It is natural that people should say, 'I can't hear what He says; I can't hear distinctly. I want a man to speak to me, and tell me plainly what He says, and what I am to do; a man or a Church'. In the Catholic orders, it is the Superior who speaks with the voice of God. But the Protestants are *between* heaven and earth. They have neither an earthly superior nor a heavenly one. They doubt whether God speaks, unless indeed they open the Bible and find some text which tells them. But then they find contradictory things. They will not allow a man to speak as from God, which they call interference with religious liberty. But we *might* have the same certainty about God's purpose which the Roman Catholics have. Only we must have it through the exercise of our own nature.

Sometimes indeed His voice whispers, and sometimes it does not speak plain.

But can we *wish* to hear it, except through the exercise of our own and others' nature? If God did tell us things, a little detail here and a little detail there, what a confusion it would be! Supposing we were to ask Him how to make the steam engine, and He were thus to tell us!

Two inquiring spirits among the operative class (a man and a woman) have at different times told me, that they had asked Him to tell them *if He was*, and when He did not, they concluded that either He was not, or that He did not care to have it known to us. This is as if Galileo were to ask Him to tell us if the sun stood still in the centre, and to conclude, if He did not, that either it was not so, or that He did not care to have it known. These earnest spirits were exactly in the position of Lord Herbert of Cherbury,[47] expecting a voice from heaven.

It is indeed said, what is religion without prayer? But is it not impiety to ask anything from Him who is always giving, who regulates everything by wisdom, righteousness, goodness – who *is* goodness?

When we can hear His voice plain, we shall hear Him saying, 'Do not regret anything that is past. It is all right. *I did it*. Do not be anxious about anything to come. It is all under my laws, in accordance with my nature'. We should have perfect trust.

But we should doubt that He exists, it is said, if we did not recognize Him in revelation, in answers to prayer.

Can we ever doubt that He exists? It seems ingratitude to do so (as if we were to doubt the goodness of the kindest friend), after such proofs as we have had of His goodness.

- - - - - - - - - - - - - - - - - - -

SECTION VII

Not 'turning away from evil', but pursuing good is the means for good; 'cleansing the soul from iniquity' does not answer, but rather taking every means to feel and think and do what is good. If we are thinking of 'self-mortification', we are thinking of ourselves, whom we had better forget; it is in itself a kind of self-seeking, and the end is much better attained by going out of ourselves than by trampling upon ourselves.

Luxury, indeed, enslaves the soul, and renders it unfit for charity. All history is an example to us how nations decline when seated in their easy chairs. Soft chairs and luxuries are an impediment to love and charity; but if we were to put such nations upon hard chairs, would they do anything for the world?

There is so little of the 'spirit of understanding' now. 'One great duty which we owe to God is faith in his providence, which is made known to us by external circumstances, well considered by the light of reason and divine grace', say the Roman Catholics.

We do not owe it as a *duty* to God to have faith in His providence; but if we rightly understood His providence as it is 'made known to us by external circumstances, considered by the light of reason' and of feeling, we *must* have, we cannot but have faith in it. 'I know in whom I have believed' are pregnant words; but how few *do* 'know'! To 'do things *considerately*;' how few ever do anything with consideration! And yet the least thing would be better done if done with consideration.

'Doing all things with consideration and disregarding all human feelings and inclinations' is the Catholic precept.

It is not disregarding our natural feelings and inclinations, but endeavouring that our *nature* shall be such that our *natural* feelings will be those which we *can* follow, that is the wise course. The Roman Catholic says, that I am 'not to seek my own interest, but to be intent solely upon the work of God and upon the benefit of my neighbour'. It should *be my own* interest, the greatest interest I have, to do the work of God and the world; 'to benefit my brethren' would then be to 'seek my own interest'.

The law of love and that of our own feelings and inclinations may be the same. How many laws have now become the strongest impulse of our own feelings which were formerly not even acknowledged to be laws. Take a glaring instance. In some of the most civilized nations of antiquity, the marriage of a brother and sister was not only tolerated, but was almost enjoined, as in the case of the Ptolemies.[48] Experience proved such marriages to be fatal to a race; they are now illegal; and what is more, the strongest feelings which exist in our nature are enlisted against them; they are become not illegitimate, but simply impossible, a crime we may not even think of.

All moral laws should be thus unmistakeably supported by our warmest impulses, as this physical law is by our (instinct, we should say, were it not that we see, by history, it is not instinct but) experience; here we say, it is not duty, it is *nature*, such a crime is *unnatural*; we do not say 'disregard your *natural* feelings and inclinations'. So it should be our object to create in ourselves such a nature that the seeking our selfish interest would be *unnatural*, and that the *not* doing God's work would be 'disregarding our *natural* feelings and inclinations'.

The mistake is in considering man a selfish animal. If we mean by 'selfish', one constituted by God to follow His highest satisfaction, man *is* a selfish animal; but well constituted and well developed, man is a generous, a devoted animal, devoted to God and mankind; and devotion to God and mankind *is* his highest satisfaction, his greatest selfishness.

The Roman Catholics talk about 'abnegation of will'. Abnegation of will is the exercise of the highest will, the will, that is, of the highest part of us. 'Mortification' is not the highest pursuit of the soul; to 'mortify ourselves' is to think of ourselves. To do the work of God and mankind is the highest work; and we could trust ourselves more if we could do this work, enjoying the feast which God has carefully prepared for us, yet able to leave it instantly *for His work*, than if we make ourselves uncomfortable for fear we should not be able to leave our comforts.

It is the rule of the Catholic orders 'to *seek* zealously greater denial of self in all things, and as much as possible continual mortification', and it gives them far greater liberty of spirit and much more freedom to serve God. It sets them free from all those little '*recherches*' which perplex and enslave us.

But it is not a very high pursuit to make oneself uncomfortable, though it is a higher pursuit, certainly, than making oneself comfortable. But we may embrace and welcome what *comes* in the way of making us uncomfortable, instead of shrinking from it – as wishing to be one with God, and this without putting ourselves in the way of it. Oneness with God, benevolence towards man, and interest in the exercise of one's faculties, ought to be the 'end of society', and if they were so, we should take with thankfulness the comfort, and with thankfulness the discomfort, as being one with God.

The Roman Catholics always take the bull by the horns; they say, for fear I should not be able to leave my comforts, I will make myself always uncomfortable; for fear I should prefer *anything* to God's work, I will prefer to have *nothing*. But we are in a higher state if we leave, for instance, our warm bed or our good dinner at God's call for something which would be a higher gratification, something for God or for man, than if we make our bed cold or no bed at all, and our dinner distasteful or no dinner at all, for *fear* we should not be able to leave them at such a call.

It will not be found necessary to 'bury' the 'old man'. A new man would spring up directly in a life organized to call out the religious feeling, instead of being organized to depress it – amidst intercourse, which called out our good, instead of our bad.

But what discourse 'tends to good' now? If *we* 'gave ear' to such only, to what discourse should we give ear? To 'live apart' from men is now perhaps wise, because there is so little to be gained from men; but, if we were all in progress towards perfection, we should gain by living together. In order to make this possible, the Catholic orders lay down certain rules. They are 'to keep nothing hidden from their Superior', and to be glad when their defects are told by others to the Superior. They are to feel an 'equal love for all men', to give up their own opinion and judgment for that of another, to wish to be accounted fools, to esteem every man superior to themselves. They are to strive that 'holy obedience' may be perfect in all its parts, in the outward action, in the will and in the understanding. They are 'to hate the things which the world loves and cherishes, to cultivate the spirit of mortification, to choose always the poorest and worst things of the house'. If we did not look upon fault as blame, if we really wished to do the work of God, and to improve *in order* to do it, if our master, or leader, or superior were really our spiritual physician, we too should wish our fault to be told to him; (just as we are, when ill, grateful to any one who will explain our symptoms to our doctor), not for the sake of 'mortifying' ourself, but for the sake of true improvement.

There is a necessity for perfect 'obedience' in great works, and in learning individual things. But the whole being is not to be given up. For there is no one who has the power to conduct the whole being.

God the 'Superior-General'. For each great work and department, a human 'Superior', under whose guidance we place ourselves, and in whom we really recognize the voice of God, because, if we were to listen to His voice in *everything* that He says, we could not hear. He is speaking in everything all day long. We cannot, each of us, listen to all. Each had better listen in his or her peculiar department, and communicate to the others. Then we should be truly said to be listening to the voice of God, when listening to these. This is not rendering up the *whole being* to any one. It is each man hearing the voice of God as well as he can in one thing for the rest. Each is the Superior in one thing. We cannot be supposed to listen to the voice of God in astronomy, in chemistry, in theology, in natural history. In all these things there must be leaders for each.

Obedience forces the mind (which is a great help), from

'Shall I do this little thing or that?' And for the Superior to be freed from the consideration, 'Shall I be obeyed or not?' is necessary. Without these things no great work can be done.

'Let us do instantly whatever we have to do, without even staying to finish the letter we are making', the Roman Catholics say, 'For it is the voice of God that calls'.

It is the spirit of order, or punctuality, or duty, and that *is* the spirit of God. But it *is not* the thought of God that we should be like a 'dead body', surrendering up the whole being to the Superior.

We cannot 'feel an equal love for all men'. Our interest for them *must* be in proportion to how much we know them.

How can you 'give up your own opinion for that of another?' It *is* yours. It is like saying that *you* can *become* another person – that you can see that blue is green.

To 'esteem every one superior to ourselves', would, if pushed to its ultimate practical consequences, become folly and untruth. Then would a Galileo be seen giving up his opinion to any ignoramus.

To 'wish to be accounted a fool' when you are not a fool, is to wish that some one should make a mistake, an error in judgment.

There may be a pride even in humility, a self-seeking in suffering 'abjection' (all pride is the effect of a narrowness of view), and therefore it is far safer not to be thinking about ourselves than to be seeking for 'mortification'. Besides, it is ungrateful to God, when He is seeking to give you pleasure, always to take the worst – *not that some one else may have the best*, but only for the sake of mortifying your*self*, and especially, if you do this for the sake of having the best in another world.

To 'renounce worldly enjoyment' implies a mistake. It should *be* our enjoyment to do the world's work.

It does not improve us to 'hate' anything. One might easily excite oneself to hate all these luxuries. But it does us no good.

The Catholics say that 'through love of Christ's poverty the religious man should be glad when he has the poorest and worst things'.

Surely it is a mistake to recommend poverty. Surely it is a higher pursuit to have property, in order that we may devote it to Him and do His work with it.

Christ was the most spiritual being who has ever lived. But surely he made mistakes. He is generally considered *either* as God or as an impostor. Now, much progress cannot be made unless we admit that he made mistakes, and we, Protestants, who profess to be the upholders of the Bible, do admit it practically, though we assert theoretically, that He was plenarily inspired, a man-God. What do boards of guardians make, for instance, of this his counsel of 'poverty'? Those who do not admit His wonderful spirituality cannot make much progress either. He was not a reasoner, certainly. For sometimes he speaks of leaving father and mother and lands as a sacrifice, and offers compensation elsewhere; and sometimes he tells us to hate them, and then it cannot be a sacrifice. He certainly was so indignant with the lukewarm spirit of the times, which was always making excuses, that he spoke in very strong words, 'Let the dead bury their dead', 'Hate your father and your mother', 'Who is my mother and my brethren?'

The truth of the matter is probably that the attraction between husband and wife, and between all other friends should be this, that those two can do the work of God better together than apart, and then there would be no occasion to 'leave them for His name's sake', but the contrary. When you have taken a wife, and undertaken the responsibility of children, *without* any such attraction, certainly there is no right in leaving them. With regard to leaving brothers and sisters, and father and mother, you have undertaken no charge with regard to them, and these should be left anyhow for God's work.

Christ spoke 'with authority', it is said. 'Thou shalt love the Lord thy God'. 'Thou shalt love thy neighbour as thyself'.

But the command does not elicit the feeling. We do not say, Thou shalt love thy husband, or thy dearest friend. The thing is to show God to be such a Being as one can love, as one *must* love. Christ's God was *not* such. What a gospel there is to proclaim; the 'good news' of a *perfect* Being. This *is* a gospel, and one which has never yet been preached.

It is said that we make God, make Him after our own image. But surely we can trace the existence of a spirit of benevolence, of wisdom and goodness, *not ourselves*. We can go further and show that *all would be as it is*, if there were a spirit of perfect goodness and wisdom, and would not this be evidence that such a spirit *is*?

There are depths of intense bliss, yet unknown, in the perfect trust and reverence, the untold happiness which to live consciously in the presence of such a Being must be. St Paul felt it. He says that 'eye hath not seen, nor ear heard, neither hath it entered into the heart of man to conceive the things which God hath prepared for them that love Him'. And yet *his* God was far inferior to our God.

Luther left *his* God just as he found Him. He only swept away some absurdities. All he did was negative. But think what, if we did realize what He is, (not *all* that He is, for truly is it said that He is incomprehensible,) but if we did realize Him, not through *special* providences, but through *all* His providences – think what it would be to live in His presence, devoted to Him!

Think what the gratitude would be! Now we have such strange gratitude. We are grateful to Him for having broken one arm and not two, but if we could be grateful to Him for His laws, those essences of perfect goodness and wisdom, what gratitude that would be!

There are three phases of theology; the miraculous, the supernatural, and the 'positive' theology. At first it is quite natural (in an infant state) that infants should think God works by miracles, and should see Him in miracles and not in law; then that they should see Him in special providences, which is really almost the same as the first; that is the supernatural theology; – lastly, we see Him in law. But law is still a theology, and the finest.

We love that which is loveable, and surely we must love the God of the perfect laws.

But how silent God is! Through all this difficulty and suffering, when just to hear His voice would inspirit us to do anything, He remains silent.

That silence is so speaking. *We* could not resist the temptation which, humanly speaking, to so loving a Father it must be to speak. But *He* does. Because, if He speaks at all, He must speak always, and then we should be machines. We must be either interfered with occasionally, or passive recipients of perfection, which, if we could see it, we should feel to be a contradiction.

This belief will make no martyrs, it is said. There are none now. And this belief in the God of 'law' will make none.

In former days, the Christians thought that they had nothing to do but to testify to God. It did not matter whether their truth were received or not. If it were not, they would still be martyrs, and would go straight to God. It did not matter that their persecutors would be then in the farthest possible state from receiving the truth, in the very opposite of the state in which they *wished* them to be, when proclaiming that truth.

But we have now no truth which we are sure of, which we wish to proclaim, which we feel anything at all about. It is therefore no wonder that we have not the zeal of the martyrs.

But, having a truth, we may have a wisdom in choosing how and when to speak, which they had not, because they were thinking of a crown for themselves. Let us, with more wisdom, have the same or a higher zeal.

Their way was easy compared to our's. For Christ had to prepare men for death, not life; and his followers had to bear their testimony, and if they were made martyrs, so much the better..

'What zeal does he experience for the attainment of perfection?' is one of the questions the Catholic orders ask.

And were that question asked of anybody here, could it be said that they feel any?

The Catholics say that 'everything is to be preserved for the honour of our Lord alone, and therefore held sacred, that nothing be wasted; thus all actions, even the most common and trifling, will be sanctified'.

We cannot say to our servants, 'This is God's, you must not waste it', but, 'this is mine, you must not waste it', and that makes the difference.

"'Not to be curious about trifles" is another rule'.

But, in 'society', what else is there but trifles?

The religious orders insist upon the *intention*, that every action may be done to God, through the best and purest motive.

We ought always to know the moment our intention is wrong. It is possible to know directly whether one's intention is with God or not, just as one is conscious that one is cold, even though one should not be able to alter it directly.

SECTION VIII

Wesley[49] was the first man who brought about the renewal of Roman Catholicism in England, for he first shook the Church of England. People had never thought of inquiring before. The Church of England said, 'don't use your own judgment', and she remained unquestioned; but *then* people began to see that in the Church some maintained the doctrine of baptismal regeneration, and some did not. Among the Wesleyans, some held Calvinism, and some did not; and they began to look about for what they were to believe. Only one Church could offer them 'one Lord, one faith, one baptism, one God'. The Church of England now said, 'use your own judgment, but only so far as to see that the Church of Rome is wrong'. She said 'look to the Bible'; people looked to the Bible; and this once admitted, authority once admitted, the Church of Rome must follow. Again, the Church of England says, '*Don't* use your own judgment, or at least you will be damned if you do' (*vide* Athanasian creed).

Dr Arnold led the way to Puseyism;[50] he urged an earnest religion, – an earnest religion on authority, – and Puseyism naturally followed. So Wesley strengthened the hands of the Church; he diminished their numbers, but moralized their lives, and thus the Church was really strengthened. So Luther moralized the Church of Rome. We often do what we don't intend, while at the same time doing what we do intend. Dr Arnold urged earnestness in religion, without saying, 'think for yourselves'; and by his influence he produced a great feeling in religion; but then his pupils began to want authority. If 'to believe' was of great importance to them, they wanted to know what they should believe. The Church of England did not tell them, or, at least, it told them different and contradictory things, and they had recourse to a stricter authority. In the same way, the moralization of the Church of England led to the Church of Rome.

It is said that the persecution of the Catholics led to their increase. There is no *law* which makes persecution favourable to development. A persecution which weakens or paralyses the organization or a slow system of disabilities, as the privation of education and privileges – such persecution tends to destroy. The Emancipation Act[51] gave an immense impulse to Roman Catholicism in England, just as its worst enemies said it would. But any persecution which tends to make a thing conspicuous, to attract attention of any kind to bring it forward, and which does not tend to enfeeble – such as the persecution of the early Christians, – the murders, tortures, blood, which made their faith notable, which made people ask, What is this which enables them to bear so much? – such persecution gives to the persecuted power, it is true.

Roman Catholics say, the Church shall think for me. 'I can't understand, but I will believe, because the Church tells me so'. Protestants *protest* – that is the meaning of the word – they protest against any one thinking for them, but they don't think for themselves. They say, 'I am far too busy to think out these things for myself, but you shall not think for me'. They like to be told what to think; in fact, they pay many thousands a year to fifteen thousand people to do this. They say, 'Our *teachers* shall all think so and so. They shall tell us so and so; whether we believe it or not is our affair. We "protest" against being *made* to believe it'.

They don't read the 39 Articles, not, at least, unless there is something to be got by them.

Some read them because they don't believe them; but are they read by those who call themselves Church of England? They say, '*our teachers* shall believe the 39 Articles', but *they* don't believe them themselves.

The heap of reviews on an English table is exactly the Protestant spirit. Reading a review is being told what we are to think; we are not bound to think it. This is just what we do with our religion. We go to church, the clergyman is to tell us what we are to think; we go armed to criticize what he says, what he thinks, what the service is like. We must be told what the Church thinks, but we will not be obliged to think it. It is all a contradiction and a mystification, whereas the Roman Catholic never thinks of criticizing; he says, 'I can't understand, but I can believe, *credo, quia impossibile est!*'[52]

As long as the Church of England enforced herself by penalties and laws, by hanging people who did not belong to her, and punishing those who did not come to church, she did very well; but when she became moral, when she said, No; I don't think it right to compel and to punish – when she rested her claim, not on her authority, but on her morality; then she lost ground. Wesley's secession made people think she was not infallible; and then they looked about them, and found that there were contradictions in her teaching.

Look at the doctrines which she teaches, – forgiveness of sins, for instance.

What is meant when you say the word 'forgiveness'? People forgive, but how do they do it? Probably they think of something else. If a man knocks me down, and if I feel that he is the greatest sufferer, because he is further from the way of right or happiness by the act of knocking down than I by the fact of being knocked down, and if I feel that by the laws of the universe he could not have done otherwise than he did, I can – not forgive, but – feel no resentment, for he could not have done otherwise. But if I am told that I am to forgive another because God forgives me, what have I to do? I must think that that man has been very wrong; but then I have been very wrong, too, against God, and He has forgiven me; and if I don't forgive this man, perhaps another time God will not forgive me. What does that mean? It means that I think of something else, of God's wrath and my sins against Him, and so I forget what has been done against me. Can any other meaning be attached to the theory of forgiveness?

Forgiveness is certainly a *step* beyond revenge. In the first state of society, it was considered right to revenge our injuries; in the next state, it was considered right to forgive them; though how this is done we do not know. Still, this is a step in advance. This is already a 'future state' to the first. In the next 'future state' it will be considered that there is nothing to forgive; and that will be a doctrine as much higher and truer than this of forgiveness, as this of forgiveness is higher than that of revenge; but the philosophy of the will must be first understood.

With regard to forgiveness in the Creator, the theory is no more intelligible. 'God cannot forgive' is true, and it is curious how people lay hold of a little bit of a truth. *God cannot forgive*; His laws have assigned consequents entirely definite to every antecedent. Do we pray that he will prevent oxygen from uniting with hydrogen in the proportion of eight to one to form water? Neither can we pray that he will alter the laws of perfect goodness and wisdom with regard to spiritual things. *He* would not be perfect goodness and wisdom if He did. But the theory of forgiveness, as the Anglican Church holds it, is, besides, a confused one. What sign have we that we are forgiven? How do we know when we are forgiven? The Roman Catholic is more sensible, who takes his beads and says so many paternosters for every sin, as his confessor orders. 'We don't know how to pray', he says, 'therefore we take our Saviour's form of prayer, which is much better than anything we can say, and we take each sin in succession, and say, "Forgive us our trespasses, etc.;" and then say, "that sin is forgiven", now on to the next'. Is not this the theory of the rosary when used 'in union with' our Saviour's sufferings? The Roman Catholic does think of his sins enough to tell them each and individually to a priest, who is the intermediary, and who tells him whether he is sorry enough, and, if he is,

gives him absolution, though what takes place when we are
absolved we do not know. But Protestants have such a 'slovenly
unhandsome' way of doing the business. We will not even take
the trouble of enumerating our sins, but we say, in order to save
ourselves that trouble, 'We have done those things which we
ought not to have done', in order to include everything, and
then '*bang* comes the absolution', without more ado. But what
takes place when we are forgiven? Is it a change in God or in
man? What is it? We know no more than if you were speaking
Chinese.

'Taking a clergyman's duty', the very words are significant, it
is a *duty* to pray to God; and when the clergyman wants to do
something else, he gets somebody to 'take his duty'. We do it in
the most lazy way we can. We get one man to say it all for us
(while we sit by), – to say that we have done everything wrong.

The doctrine of forgiveness, though an advance upon that of
revenge, is still, therefore, the great mistake with regard to
God's character, the character of the Perfect, of perfect wisdom
and goodness.

The parable of the two debtors says, to him 'who sins against
me most I shall have to forgive most, and he will love me most'.
This is the substance of it. 'Can this man have power to forgive
sins?' the Jews once asked. Here they were right. But they did
not go farther and ask, can *God* have the power to forgive sins?
What does forgiveness mean? and if it means anything, is it not a
contradiction? In the case of the blind man, they asked, 'Who
did sin, this man or his parents?' and Christ did not say,
blindness is not the consequence of sin at all, but of some
physical law. He said, 'That the works of God should be made
manifest'. He was so filled with the idea of impressing the
people with the power of God, that he really seemed to imply
that the man had been made blind on purpose. Or, rather, he
did not turn his attention to these subjects at all; his feeling was
perfect, and he came to save from ill-feeling, not from bad
moral philosophy; and when a man feels very intensely on one
subject, it is not rare that he should overlook another. Christ
certainly did believe that sin was visited with ill-health, and that,

if the sin were forgiven, the ill-health would be removed. In the case of the man with the palsy, he implied, 'If I say, thy sins be forgiven thee, or say, arise and walk, what does it matter?' in either case the man would be cured.

But what a character his was! When he talks about the baptism and the fire he has to go through, how expressive those words are! A baptism of fire he might well have called it. Every person must be baptized with fire who would do anything which is not usually done in the conventional walk of his life, which is not provided for in the ordinary course of things. Every person must have a baptism of fire who is not satisfied with the world as it is, and who would fain help it out of its rut. 'And how am I straitened till it be accomplished!'

But there are many things he said, which are very beautiful, and yet are not true. When they brought the woman taken in adultery before him, and he turned aside and wrote in an absent mood on the ground, and then said, 'he that is without sin among you, let him first cast a stone at her' – that beautiful tender spirit felt truly. But still there is a right and a wrong about adultery. This would be putting an end to all law and justice. If no one is to execute the law unless he be perfectly pure himself, the Lord Chief Justice and the Chief Baron must vacate their seats on the bench, and the police be disbanded, and the criminal jurisprudence of a country come to an end.

And when he implied that we should take no more thought than the lilies of the field, is that absolute truth?

And what he tells the Samaritan woman of the 'living water' is very beautiful, but when she does not understand, he seems to make no effort to explain to her. He was so filled and absorbed with his own thought that he seems to have spoken absently, and hardly to have cared whether she understood or not. He even sometimes says, 'That seeing they may see, and not perceive, and hearing they may hear and not understand'. Might not the people have said, if you are to teach us, would it not be better to speak so that we can understand?

What a point he seems to have made about faith, believing that we can do a thing! 'Faith can remove mountains'. Now, it is very true that very often we do not believe we can do a thing, which, if we did believe it, we could do. But we may believe we can do a thing which we can't. A great many, from ignorance of the laws of God, have done so. Believing does not make us able to do it; does not make the law of God by which to do it. He seems to have known the first fact, and to have confused the second with it.

But what have we made of Christ in these vulgar times? We have daubed him all over with bright colours, so that we can hardly see through to the original beautiful form underneath. The churches have made him a God, and said, What! do you think you are like Christ? while they are preaching to you to imitate him. The Unitarians have made him a perfect man, preaching that of which you see a great deal is not true. If we could but show him in his original form! The idea of a divine being dying to save you from another being does excite some feeling; but to tell you to listen to preaching which is perfect, and which you see is imperfect, and the whole of which you *cannot* believe, excites no feeling at all. If he is to be merely a teacher or merely a God, he is nothing.

We have such a strange idea of our God. 'If we don't forgive, perhaps He will punish us more'. A mother who lost her little boy, said 'she must be resigned, or a worse thing might be sent'. If we believe that God puts in His hand now and then, we may believe that He says, 'Another lesson must be yours, if you don't learn the first'. But it is worse, it is like a great boy who says to a little one, 'I will hit you harder if you cry'. No wonder we love Christ for having come to save us from Him.

But have moral and physical laws no connexion with each other?

It is all planned from the beginning to bring imperfection to perfection. Unless the perfect one wished to make the imperfect perfect, there would be a contradiction; and, therefore, it may be asserted with certainty, that, if there is a spirit of perfection, this is His plan.

But how do we know that there is a spirit of perfection?

We see signs that there is. We do not assert it. It is evident that, in some stages of our development, it is impossible for man to *conceive* even of a spirit of perfection. The more he advances, the more he finds reason to believe that there is. But we assert that, if there is a spirit of perfection, it is a contradiction to say that such was not his plan.

There is some rough truth in the superstition, A died for the good of B, A was drowned in order to teach B sympathy. For, it is all a vast scheme for bringing the imperfect to perfection.

But it is implied, if B had had more sympathy, the water would not have risen and drowned A.

Now we *cannot* say, *if* B had had more sympathy – for nothing could have been otherwise than it is. If B had been different, all the laws of God would have been different, and the imperfect would not have been progressing to perfection. God knew perfectly well that B would not sympathize any more for A's death. He did not require to be told of this. He was not trying experiments. It was all in his scheme. To write history with 'if's' is unmeaning nonsense.*

Then why do we not sit still and do nothing?

The laws of God visit us with consequences till we do something. We may try the experiment; we may sit still, if we like; but, while we do so, God's laws will never cease molesting us. His laws have provided that it shall be impossible to us – that our nature is such, our desires, energies, inclinations such, that we can't continue to do nothing.

To say, if 'A had been different, if B had had more judgment, and C had had more feeling, how easy it would have been!' – to wish that it had been otherwise is to wish that the imperfect should not be on its way to perfection, – is, in fact, pure nonsense. In many cases we can *see* that it has all been 'for the best'; but, even when we cannot, to say, 'if it had but been otherwise', is using words without meaning.

With regard to 'special providences', if there were any, there would be no universal general providence.

---

* A historical writer in French actually sets forth a different course which *God might* have taken in history, '*if*' the Elector of Saxony had but been different.

Each particular thing is, indeed, brought about by Providence, in accordance with His law, as a part of the whole.

If, when I come to London and go into Oxford Street, I find Mrs C at home, God had it before His thought that I should carry out some purpose through her means. God took me there. God always has before Him in His thought what the whole plan is, and the purposed results.

Now, nobody reasons; there is good feeling and good conscience, but it is reasoning power which is most wanting in the world. The Church does not reason; society reasons still less. How worse than useless it is talking to any one about religion! Can we expect anything else with the existing code of society – when people go on paying morning visits to each other, although they *know* that *both* sides will be glad if they are not at home? The B's said they left London that nobody might say any more, 'There now, we have *done* the B's', when they had been invited to a dinner, – to a dinner, too, to which they did not wish to go.

Much is said now about the tolerance of society.

We may have, it is true, any opinions we like about Gothic architecture and Italian pictures, because that is only amusing; it involves no change. We are not likely to be pulling down York Minster in consequence. But if we have any opinions which require a change in society or in anything else, even if seen to be true, 'it won't do'. You must only have fancy opinions – not working opinions.

- - - - - - - - - - - - - - - -

PART VI

No science has been so unfairly treated as religion. From the awe which it has inspired, it has never been allowed to be on the same footing as any other part of our knowledge. Emotion, imagination, and self-interest have been its main sources. Up to a certain period in the development of mankind, it is well that it should be so. It is well that emotion and imagination should keep up in man a sense of a higher power than his own, before he is able to reason upon it. But is there, or is there not, what may be called a science of religion, as of other subjects of our knowledge?

What is the meaning of the word 'religion'? Is it not the tie, the *binding*, or connexion between the Perfect and the imperfect, the eternal and the temporal, the infinite and the finite, the universal and the individual?

Here, as in many instances, the derivation of the word shows its import, such as suits with our meaning, though scarcely does that meaning seem to have been attached to it, when originally so derived.

Religion includes a knowledge of the universal and particular, the general and individual, the perfect and imperfect natures which are within our ken, as well as a knowledge of the connexion between them. Indeed, it is obvious that this connexion can only be correctly appreciated in proportion as we understand the natures so connected.

The primary fact in religion seems to be the existence of an omnipotent spirit of love and wisdom – the *primary* fact, because it is the explanation of every other.

This gives us four words to explain, each of which is open to great misconception, and has been greatly misconceived; viz., omnipotent, spirit, love, wisdom.

By *omnipotence* we understand a power which effects whatever would not contradict its own nature and will.

By a *spirit* we understand a living thought, feeling, and purpose, residing in a conscious being.

By *love* we understand the feeling which seeks for its satisfaction the greatest degree and the best kind of well-being in other than itself.

By *wisdom* we understand the thought by which this satisfaction is obtained.

But, first, is religion a subject to be logically treated, or is there any truth in the feeling of deprecating, as irreverent, the sifting of what is true, as to religious belief, by the aid of the science of logic?

If religion is to depend upon evidence, not upon intuition or consciousness, a more comprehensive evidence is required than is necessary for any other subject. More faculties must be exercised for this purpose than are required in seeking after truth on any other subject. If a man is seeking truth in physical astronomy, the perceptive faculties alone will enable him to draw his inferences. But he will not know thus all that is to be known about astronomy, or the most important part of what is to be known about astronomy; for that most important part is its relation with religion.

If a man is seeking evidence concerning a nature which is love, his evidence must partly depend on his own nature being in some degree love; and, in as far only as it is love, can he judge of love in another being.

A London lady, speaking of a cousin who, on returning from the East, had remained some weeks in a foreign institution for training deaconesses, said, 'It is rumoured in London that Miss —— remained on the Continent for the purpose of recovering her complexion before her return to England'. Thirty years acquaintance with that cousin had not enabled her to draw any inference with regard to her nature. This is a homely instance of our meaning with regard to the study of the nature of God.

Is it an intuition, when a child feels a consciousness of love in another being, and gives love in return? Certainly, such a sentiment or emotion exists in a human being prior to any reasoning upon it.

But, love to God does not exist as an 'intuition'. At an early age, awe, admiration, or fear may exist intuitively in a human being towards a superhuman power, manifesting itself in nature or the events of life. But love or trust towards this superhuman power can have no true or firm foundation, except from inference.

The nature and purpose of God is a subject immediately connected, bound up with every subject of possible human inquiry. Truly, therefore, may we express by the word 'religion', inquiries concerning the nature and purpose of God.

All that comes by intuition (of that which is true in religion) is an emotion or sentiment of awe or admiration.

Reasoning will reveal the existence of a spirit of love and wisdom to a loving and wise spirit, but cannot do so to any other mode of being. Consequently, the evidence for *religion* requires the exercise of parts of man's nature, which are not necessarily exercised upon evidence for mere physical facts.

The confusion in which men are as to the nature and true sources of a real belief in religion greatly impedes its existence. Few, even of thinking and feeling men, have any true estimation of the present state of religious belief and religious feeling among mankind. Numbers are thinking they believe what they do not believe. Numbers have feelings towards beings of their own imaginations, or taught to them from the imaginations of other men.

This deplorable ignorance on the subject, which is connected with every possible interest and question which can present itself to man's heart or mind, will remain till mankind are aware of it; till they know and feel how to make some advance towards removing it. We say, *advance* towards removing it. No man – no number of men living in any age – can remove it. All men, through all ages of human existence, must unite to learn and to feel more and more (and yet not fully comprehend or appreciate) that universal Spirit. To learn and to feel Him perfectly requires perfection. Man and mankind are essentially imperfect; but they are to be workers towards perfection – towards that which, in the view of the All-comprehending, is the only true perfection, – that which has been attained by exercise.

Let the question now before us be, What *is* religion, and what the grounds of belief in it?

Religion is the tie between the Perfect and the imperfect.

By *the Perfect*, we mean His perfectly *right* thought, feeling, and purpose. Concerning *right*, we can only say this, – It is that thought, feeling, and purpose which produce, in the course of eternity, the most happy being possible, without involving the supposition of any contradiction.

The primary fact in religion is the existence of an omnipotent spirit of goodness and wisdom, whence spring all other modes of existence and all connexions between them.

Our evidence for this existence is the consciousness and the experience in man of goodness and wisdom in himself and his kind – the discerning certain phenomena of the same nature as those which spring from human thought and feeling – from purpose to promote human welfare, – but which do not spring from human nature – which would spring from human nature, if it had the power to call into existence such phenomena – the inference that other thought and feeling, more powerful for effecting its purpose than man's, calls the phenomena into existence.

Thought, feeling, purpose for other welfare than *that* of the individual who thinks, feels, and purposes, we recognize as *benevolence* (or wish for the well-being of others).

The pursuing a right end by the means adapted to attain it, we call *wisdom*.

The existence, then, of a spirit of wisdom and benevolence may be inferred in this way, – we trace the operation of a benevolent and wise will by the existence of the same *kind* of effects as spring from a benevolent and wise will in man; by effects which the benevolent and wise man would produce if he could.

The aim of the benevolent and wise man will be to help his fellow-men, by the improvement and exercise of their natures, to attain well-being.

Experience proves well-being to be attainable only in this way.

Thought, feeling, reflection, experience, agree that in no other way, without some contradiction, can well-being exist.

In this way, observation and experience will show ever-increasing evidence that a power superior to man's is ever promoting man's welfare.

Looking into the nature of human existence, questions arise as to the source or sources of the phenomena which we discern, some tending apparently to man's welfare, others to his suffering. Hence have arisen the questions, do these phenomena spring from a variety of wills? – from one benevolent and one malevolent will? – from no will at all? – or from *one* will?

Inference, arising out of conscious experience, may be found, tending to prove that (in proportion as we improve in being and increase in knowledge) we shall discern that present evil and suffering, as well as present good and enjoyment, essentially spring from *one* source, the omnipotent spirit of benevolence and wisdom, which is thus effecting human welfare, human progress towards the divine, through the improvement and exercise of the capabilities of mankind; these capabilities and this exercise arising from what we may designate divine laws – that is, from certain invariable co-existences and successions springing from the omnipotent spirit of benevolence and wisdom, who would have no existence, were anything other than it is, has been, and is to be. In accordance with his righteous thought, there is a way in which every law is susceptible of being kept, which will ensure human welfare – *i.e.*, human advance towards the divine. Human nature is, through law, constituted capable of discerning these laws, how they ought to be kept, how to incline human will to keep them.

To attain this, is the problem which the omnipotent spirit of benevolence and wisdom sets before humanity, supplying humanity with the means by which to attain it.

God's law is absolutely definite. One of its purposes seems to be to educate a divine capability into a divine existence, by the exercise of the capability of the individual and the race. Does not this purpose come home to our conviction as worthy of, consistent with, the divine nature? The definiteness of the means by which this is effected is complete and entire. If our comprehension could penetrate through the whole, we should be conscious that not the bending of a leaf this way or that – not the resting of a grain of sand in one place and not in another, is without a purpose, as part of the whole. All is connected with all so intimately, that the most minute difference in any part would alter the whole. In some minds there is a sort of struggle against this definiteness, as if it implied some necessity – *i.e.*, some yielding to need. But that would be to imply that it were to be wished that something had been otherwise, whereas of nothing can it be truly wished that it had been otherwise, for all has accorded with right.

The two great objects of a wise benevolence are secured, –

First, that man works for himself and his kind – he is not worked for, he being in a state of passivity, but he lives in the midst of the means and inducements which make him or which *will* make him active.

Second, that it is the eternal, the omnipotent spirit of righteousness, who is the spring of the means and inducements which will assuredly set in movement the springs of active will in each human being, so that he attain unto righteousness and knowledge. No satisfaction could there have been in beings moved like machines – none could there have been in ignorant and finite man being left without full guidance. All the suffering, all the privation in human existence, is because it is the education of mankind which is going on, so that his will shall attain to be right; not that he shall be driven at the will of another, his own being passive.

SECTION II

What is this age? In a sister country it is said to be the age of
atheism and despair. In ours, is it not a time of indifference and
unbelief? We do not believe in a type of perfection into which
each man is to be developed, we do not believe in social
progress, we do not believe in religious progress, we do not
believe in God. Our *political* progress is the only thing which we
do believe in; but as to any development of our Church, any
improvement in society which shall modify the two great ex-
tremes of luxury and poverty, we do not so much as imagine it.
In the last 300 years much has been gained politically, but what
has been done for religion? We have retrenched a good deal, but
we have put nothing in the place of it. It has been all denying
and no constructing.

SECTION III

We call ourselves Christians. If the word mean 'followers of
Christ', there appears to be scarcely anything in England now
which bears any resemblance to Christ, which would not surprise Him as something He had never thought of. Call us
something else – do not call us Christians.

The Roman Catholic orders, indeed, do follow, word for
word, what Christ said and did; *thus far*, therefore, either the
Roman Catholic orders are Christians and are right, or Christ
was in some things mistaken.

Who can wonder that this world is such a poor world as it is?
that it does not seem, certainly at present, worth the creating?
that Europe, Asia, Africa, and America should be so miserable a

contemplation? when nobody is interested in the one vital interest which runs through all other interests, and nobody is set free to pursue it. Here and there a man thinks a little for his amusement in his library; others do not think at all; they believe that they are to take their thoughts out of a Book or a Church.

Is the worship of the goddess of wisdom by the ancients more unreasonable than the worship of the God of the nineteenth century? We should not have liked, it is true, many things which that goddess of wisdom did; but a *really* wise God, what a grand conception!

The Greeks and Romans divided the evil among all their Gods; the Persians heaped it all upon Arimanes – their mode of purifying the one good spirit. The motive of all religions is to account for what men saw. The Greeks seem hardly to have cared to suppose their Gods perfect. It is not to be supposed that they could have called the things good which their Gods did. They were simply the explanations, after the Greek fashion, of the phenomena believed to be observed. But, since that time, in all *so-called* Christian religions, the God has been *supposed* to be a perfect man. Historically it might be shown that the perfection in fashion at the time was imputed to God.

I was much struck by the terror of death, felt by a sweet young girl of fifteen years of age, the daughter of an Unitarian, in her last illness. 'Save me, papa, pray for me that I may not die'. The ignorance in which the unorthodox leave their children is very lamentable; perhaps, as things are, they can hardly do otherwise. Religious instruction by the orthodox is given under authority. The Bible, the Catechism, or priestly instruction is all supposed to rest, *not* on discovery by human capability, but on more or less miraculous light. Those who do not believe in this miraculous light either think too little on the subject to teach, or they fear to teach what they are not sure of, or to disgust with what they know not how to teach. May we not look to see the possibility of a religious society, the religion of which shall not profess to be other than the discoveries of mankind through the nature God has given to man, and through the teachings of God in His universe *to* that nature? The principles of the Roman Catholic orders might, with modifications, be adopted, viz.:

I. In religion being the foundation and spring of the *life*.

II. In unity of religious belief among these associated.

III. In *regular instruction* in the principles of this belief.

In respect of youth, would there not, at an age when death can be conceived of so as to terrify, be capability so far to conceive of the ruling spirit of the universe as not to fear death? Grown-up people show such a stiffness in their ideas and prepossessions that it is easier to deal with fifteen years than with fifty, or even than with thirty or forty years. One says: 'I believe all you say to be true', yet continues to manifest a fear of death and of punishment for the sins and omissions of this life. Another stops short with, 'I must have a God who' etc.

Such religious instruction to children would be inexpressibly facilitated by the *life* being a constant exemplification or manifestation of what was taught. Could I teach my children what I think of God's nature and purposes, of man's nature, duty, destination, and then live after the fashion of conventional life, and turn them back from my lesson on religion to the same life? This may be done consistently by those who can call this life the 'state to which it has pleased God to call' them – who can bid their children pray, at morning and evening prayers, to be forgiven for having done nothing and omitted everything; but we, who think we ought to strive to fashion our circumstances so as to enable us, in *accordance with* the divine law, to do what is right, and *not* to omit what God calls us to do, how can we teach what we believe, and then send them back, as well as ourselves, when the lesson is done, to a life of which we *know* that, *in accordance with* God's law, the effect will be to make it impossible to live and to be in the spirit of that lesson?

SECTION IV

'What *is* the religion that people have now? If they do wrong, they say, Let us pray – pray for pardon and peace. If they have 'trials', as they call them, they say, Let us bear them patiently: in another world it will all come right. If they are well-meaning and conscientious, and they make mistakes, or fail, or are hindered by external circumstances, they say, God takes the will for the deed: in heaven we shall see our hopes fulfilled; – not, there will be no heaven for me, nor for any one else, unless we make it – with wisdom carrying out our thoughts into realities. Good thoughts don't make a heaven, any more than they make a garden. But we say, God is to do it for us: not we. We? – what are we to do? – we are to pray, and to mean well, to take care that our hearts be right. 'God will reward a sincere wish to do right'. God will do no such thing: it is not His plan. He does not treat men like children: mankind is to create mankind. We are to learn, first, what is heaven, and, secondly, how to make it. We are to ascertain what *is* right, and then how to perform it.

SECTION V

Why, with our certainty that all, through God's laws, will come at last to perfection, are we not happy? Is the man happy who dreams only of California, and goes up and down, finding no way nor means of getting there? I see, or believe I see, in a better future a relief from present poverty, but how am I to make my way into the new era, religious and social, which is coming? I have not the strength to create it. I have not resignation to wait for it. Many a man takes refuge with one loving heart, and so contrives to live till the time when the world will have brought in a new era of itself.

In this way he survives the present storm; and thus he learns, it is true, the soundings, most effectually, by the way his vessel has struck; but she will be too much damaged for a successful voyage.

SECTION VI

In this age, atheism and indifference are man and wife. In former times, atheism used to be the father of despair. But now people live without God in the world, and don't so much as know that He is not there: they are not aware of his absence. Formerly, the terror and the anguish of the sceptic testified to what he had lost, and were the truest witnesses to God and to his own *religiousness*. Now, the indifferentist is called the religious man, and the religious man is the heretic.

How do you know a religious man now? By his going to church. And going to church is considered as a duty, that is, as something *due* – to whom? – to God: something you have done for Him; He is flattered by your going to church. But it is not always done as a compliment to Him; sometimes it is done as a compliment to our fellow creatures. Mrs A is deaf, and cannot hear the service; but she always goes to church for the sake of 'example'. A great many ladies never miss going where they are known, for this purpose; but if they are where they are not known, they do not go. What a poor compliment it is to God to go, not because you have something you want to say to Him, but 'because Mrs A goes'. In a country church, if there is a wedding of any consequence, the church is always sure to be full the first Sunday the bride appears, in order to see her. 'To see the bride', is a very innocent amusement; but is religion come to that pass in this country that people go to a place, where they say they expect to meet God, to 'see the bride'?

In more civilized society, a woman scarcely ever leaves a breakfast table to put on her bonnet for church, without hearing a joke among the men and the inquiry, 'Shall *you* go this morning?' 'No, I don't like the Litany. Shall you?' 'Yes, I shall; I don't like shocking our hostess'. And when you meet at luncheon, 'Have you fulfilled your ecclesiastical duties? Oh! shocking; don't you consider it a duty? I did not know you were so bad'. Or, 'I counted forty-six people asleep this morning'.

And when one thinks that there are fifteen thousand sermons to be preached this morning, and more than fifteen thousand breakfast tables where similar jokes are making, – and this is called a Church, and this religion!

SECTION VIII

The prison which is called a family, will its rules ever be relaxed, its doors ever be opened? What is it, especially to the woman? The man may escape, and does. The cases where a child inherits its parents tastes are so rare that it has passed almost into a proverb. The son of a celebrated man is never a celebrated man. The two Herschels, the two Mills,[53] are mentioned as memorable exceptions. A son scarcely ever adopts his father's profession, except when compelled, as in the case of caste; and in the countries where caste prevails, the race deteriorates. How often a parent is heard to say, 'All that I have done will go to rack and ruin when I am gone. I have none to come after me who will keep it up!' It is said that the chances are 200 to 1, where a man's immediate descendants consist of three children and three grandchildren, against there being found one among these six who inherits his tastes and pursuits.

The law of God, it seems, is *against repetition*. Whatever the family, whatever the similarity of education, circumstances, etc., repetition is never seen. And is this extraordinary? In chemistry, the mixture of two substances constitutes an entirely new substance, of which neither the colour nor any of the properties can be predicated from a knowledge merely of the colour or any of the properties of the two original substances. So, in the family, though there can be traced, it is true, the family character, the family likeness, yet the children are all strikingly unlike each parent, strikingly unlike each other. Here the analogy with chemistry *appears* to cease, for the product of two chemical substances is always the same, under the same circumstances. But, such are the minute differences of circumstances which we never estimate, that the analogy may still remain; and, as it is said that there are no two leaves alike upon the same tree, so, and much more, there never were created two human beings alike. Now, what do we do with these *un*likenesses? The family strives to make them all do the same thing. If one of the family, as often happens, is superior to the rest, the rest, and especially the heads of the family, seem to want this one to be one with them, as we try to be one with God; he is to devote all his talent and genius to forward their ideas, not to have any new ones; to put their opinions, their thoughts, and feelings into a better dress, a more striking light, not to discover any new light; and, above all, he is not to find out any untruth in their ideas, or think he has any new truth, 'for there is no such thing'!

To help others by *living* – by being *oneself*, is not this the true meaning of sympathy, the true benefit of companionship? But, in general, we have to live by *not* being ourselves. And what a fatiguing way of life it is! When we are not afraid of being ourselves, when we suit the people we are with, when what we say and feel does not shock them or annoy them or frighten them, life is easy, life is improving, we make progress. Now, *how* often does this happen in one's own family, where one can rarely speak without implying blame of something, without knocking against some one's prejudices? And can it be otherwise when people are chained up together for life, so close in the same cage? It is often said that you are less known by your own family than by any one else. Is it wonderful? There is much of which you can never venture to speak. 'The extraordinary reserve which he (or she) maintained with his (or her) own family' are words so common that every one has heard them, and yet they are always uttered as if it were a solitary, or, as it is put, an *extraordinary* fact. 'He is so much more agreeable out of his own family', is another common remark. And how often you see 'his' countenance fall when he is speaking to one of his own kin! As long as the iron chain is drawn tight round the family, fettering those together who are not joined to one another by any sympathy or common pursuit, it must be so. It is often disputed what kinds of character like society. It is probable that those like it who can say aloud the things which they would think to themselves, if they were alone. But how few can do this at home! There is no tyranny like that of the family, for it extends over the thoughts.

SECTION IX

What blasphemy has there ever been worse than the blasphemy of the religious man of the present day? He tells us that God is angry, that He seeks His own glory, that He is revengeful, – sometimes, as a climax of panegyric, that He does not wish for the 'death of the sinner'. Could any one ever think He did? Do we take Him for a murderer? Him – the Creator?

Suppose you were to say of me that I do not desire the death of my child, but rather that she should turn from her wickedness and live – and expect that I should be admired for it!

It must have done much more good, in the days of the Pantheistic Greeks, to have gone down in the beautiful summer mornings to the river's brink, and thought of its benevolence and its beauty, and how much good it had done on its way, than it does now to go to church, and say the very same prayers over and over again to the Being whom *we* worship.

'Grant all this for the sake of Jesus Christ our Lord'. What a being not to grant it because it is right, if it is right to grant it, or because He loves us, but for 'the sake of Jesus Christ'! We cannot think such a Being good, though we tell Him that He is so. 'Have compassion upon thy children'. Is it possible that we can love such a Being? one who cannot, or will not, take care of his own children, unless he is begged and prayed. We love Jesus Christ for saving us from Him.

SECTION X

It is often said that the time is past for *individual* saviours (male or female) – that the rough machinery of many hands and many minds must now work out the slow results of regeneration; that the most enlightened despotism of mind or body (emperor or philosopher) will have a poor chance, even when Europe has burst her chains – that we have passed the days of enthusiastic saviours – we must be of the mob; that a J. S. Mill cannot ensure us of a single truth in political economy – that no two men agree upon whether ownership or partnership is to form the remedy for the labourer's misery – that neither a Pitt nor a Fox[54] could settle the best extent of the future suffrage, nor the best scheme of education – that no future president could settle the slavery question in America, – that single hands are non-co-operative, and when they have done their work, there comes a collapse.

Nevertheless the world cannot be saved, except through saviours, at present. A saviour means one who saves from error. But we do not think it worth while to dignify with this appellation one who saves from merely intellectual or scientific error, and therefore it means one who saves from moral error. It has been generally thought that Christ saved from *all* moral error, and that we have nothing to do but make 'faith', as it is called, in Him, 'effectual to bring down our pride subdue our selfishness, restrain our tongues', etc. Men do not see that pride is only the perversion of the natural desire (implanted by God in us) to be and to feel of importance. Every human being *is* of importance, and ought to be employed in a way to make him feel himself so. The 'bringing down' *this* feeling has been the origin of some of the most cruel perversions to which the poor human being has been made subject. But man does not know, first, what *is* pride, nor, secondly, how to save himself from it, and therefore he prays to God to make the faith of Christ do it, and then to give him his 'great and final reward'. He does not see that God will not give it him, because it is not consistent with infinite goodness and wisdom to *give* him anything, but that *he* must work it out for himself and for mankind, not in the shape of a 'reward', but of a state of well-being.

Now what are the saviours to do? Not to do anything *instead of* man. Still it is not intended that every man shall learn all the laws of God for himself. In astronomy, Copernicus, Galileo, Kepler, Newton, Laplace, Herschel,[55] and a long line of saviours, we may call them, if we will, – discoverers they are more generally called, – have saved the race from intellectual error, by finding out several of the laws of God. We do not say, 'don't look at what these men have done – they may be despots, enlightened despots of the mind – you must learn all the laws of God yourself from the beginning'.

In the same way, there may be, there must be saviours from social, from moral error. Most people have not learnt any lesson from life at all – suffer as they may, they learn nothing, they would alter nothing – if they began life over again they would live exactly the same life as before. When they begin the new life in another world, they would do exactly the same thing, and they must, till somebody comes to help them. And not only individuals, but nations learn nothing. Austria, four hundred years ago in Switzerland, was doing exactly the same thing which she is doing now in Hungary. She has learnt nothing. A man once said to me, 'Oh! if I were to begin again, how different I would be'. But we very rarely hear this; on the contrary, we very often hear people say, 'I would have every moment of my life over again', and they think it pretty and grateful to God to say so. For such there can be no heaven; in fact it will not be there for them to have till saviours come to help them. This *is* 'eternal death'.

124   *Florence Nightingale*

We sometimes hear of men 'having given a colour to their age'. Now, if the colour is a right colour, those men are saviours.

People think that the world is in the mud, and that it must stay there. *We* think it is in the mud too, but we are sure it is not to remain there.

SECTION XI

We are often told to find our solace in nature. To those who remain always children and to those who are still children, with whom the poetry of life is everything, nature may be all-in-all. But those who have attained the weariness and discouragement of middle life, of efforts which have been made and have failed, such require not so much the beauty as the wisdom of life; not art, but knowledge and strength. The intellect, left inactive, its powers without an aim; the heart, left empty, its *ennui* without an employment; the moral activity, left objectless, its appetite without food, – gnaw themselves; and the spectacle of life and beauty only excites and increases their torments.

The worst of inactivity is that it does not, with the faculties any more than with the limbs, lead always to activity through suffering. Though we detest the sofa which has become necessary to us, yet we dread the exertion which would save us, and of which we are perhaps become really incapable.

Suffering sometimes extinguishes us, sometimes partially paralyzes us, sometimes enfeebles us, sometimes, indeed, it enriches us, as nothing else can; but, in the first case, what *can* save us but a saviour? Only where suffering exercises our faculties, does it enrich us.

Pity a man because he knows too much of life to be happy? Pity those whose ignorance must one day be torn asunder like a curtain, and passing through an age of misery, must be transmuted into pure wisdom before they can be happy!

Many long intensely to die, to go to another world, which

could not be a worse and might be a better than this. But is there any better world *there* to go into? Has mankind yet made a better world ready? We are sure that it will not be there till mankind has 'gone to prepare a place for' us. Have we any reason to suppose that any other world is forwarder than this?

The 'kingdom of heaven is within', indeed, but it must also create one without, because we are *intended* to act upon our circumstances. We must beware, both of thinking that we can maintain that 'kingdom of heaven within' under all circumstances, – because there are circumstances under which the human being cannot be good, – and also of thinking that the kingdom of heaven *without* will produce that *within*.

SECTION XII

Christ's temptation is the epitome of all life, as it was, no doubt, the epitome of his own, which he told to his disciples in that form. A sensitive, noble spirit could perhaps hardly bear to speak of it in any other form.

Do not we live for 'forty days', often for as many years, in the wilderness, seeking bread and finding none? Have we not lived these many years trying to find bread in society, in the literary dawdling of a civilized life, in the charitable trifling of a benevolent life, in the selfish elegance of an artistic life? Have we not, in these deserts, these long, long weary years, tried to pick up food, and at last, craving and despairing of anything better, have we not eaten that which was not bread, applause and sympathy for that which is not good, the vulgar distinction of social praise, the temporary forgetfulness of excitement? Christ was never satisfied with anything short of the highest. He resisted the temptation, which presses so sore on weaker minds, of making stones into bread. Then comes the temptation to make the great leap, inconsiderately to disengage ourselves thoroughly and entirely from this life of starvation. With some this temptation comes first, with others later, as St Luke has it. But in all, it comes from a religious impulse, as it was from a 'pinnacle of the *temple*' that Christ was tempted to throw himself down. And it is in 'the city' – not of solitude, – that such resolutions are bred, from the monotonous superficialities of common-place intercourse. Women sometimes try to take the great leap; they long for a man's education at college, and sometimes even think of disguising themselves and going to Cambridge. They endeavour to enter institutions, to learn a charitable profession, in order afterwards to teach it in a better way; or when all other 'trades' fail, they try marriage with a good man, who loves perhaps his wife, but who initiates her into the regular life of the world.

Disappointment often costs the woman her life – by life is meant all spirit, energy, vitality – while the vocation, if gratified, as often becomes the angels' hand to bear her up, that she shall not dash her foot against the stones. If parents would let their daughters follow their vocations, when they have any, what different creatures they would be!

The 'devil' shows us the glory of the 'kingdoms of the world' – sometimes in the shape of the vanity of colloquial or literary or social distinctions, of reigning by the intellect or by the word, or by love; oftenest, to the woman, in that of power over a heart. It comes in the desert, is most seductive to those who live out of the common vanities of life; and it comes, with overpowering force, upon those who have long wanted for bread, and found nothing but stones. Christ resisted the vanitous devil; but how few do, when weary, faint, and wounded, having prayed every day for their 'daily bread', and found none; they see how almost any amount of reputation is to be made by cleverness, and none by wisdom, and yield to the temptation!

SECTION XIII

Going to church at night, when it is lighted up, reminds one of the times when they worshipped in catacombs and in dens and caves of the earth – they, of whom the world was not worthy, as St Paul says; one would rather say, of whom the world was so in need as saviours. It reminds one of the first churches – caves in the third story below the earth, in the catacombs at Rome, where, renouncing the beautiful light of the sun, they lived – a greater sacrifice than to die.

It was necessary, when man was still in the savage state of war, revenge, and barbarous life, that the Holy Ghost, the manifestation of the Father, should make itself forgiveness, mercy – on His part atonement, on ours humility, imploring prayer, hope. We could not apprehend the Father in *any* other way, then. The Father is at all times making Himself the Son, God becoming man to enlighten us. But how can we understand the Word, unless it is a Word that we can hear? How can the *Father* speak to us? We should not comprehend. He *must* speak through the Holy Ghost. Therefore, at that time, it was necessary to speak of 'descending' to us, to our weakness and unworthiness; of hope and peace offered to the sinner through a *sacrifice*; with all the poetry and love of the Christian epic. The Greek mythology was the deification of the powers or laws of nature. The Christian mythology was the deification of the spiritual laws or ways by which communication exists between God and a half-savage, half-corrupted man ('I am the way', Christ says) – a man who fancies to himself God offended with His own creation, and taking His revenge upon it. If Christ were obliged *now* to speak to the judges, magistrates, and staff of our criminal courts, where He heard the word 'punishment' used, must He not speak of the mercy of God to those whom He sees condemning criminals, in perfect good faith, to places where they must lose every ray of humanity still shining within them? For is not mercy the only goodness which society can apprehend, while we still conceive the idea of *punishment*, still have the word at all, instead of reformation? A Christ *must* speak of the forgiveness of God: society can conceive of nothing else.

Those who don't believe in reformation, in Sir Joshua Jebb, in Lord Shaftesbury,[56] and the ragged schools, have attributed the same impotence to God. He *can* only hang them, and put chains on their legs, as we do. 'The Court feels bound to pass a severe sentence', what does that mean? and the criminal 'is imprisoned for eighteen calendar months', what is that for? – merely to keep him out of mischief for that time?* or to deter others by terror? or to reform him? We know that the second of these objects is not attained, and the third is not even aimed at. Would it not be better to let him out? But no, 'the Court feels bound to pass a severe sentence', and God feels bound to give the sentence 'of everlasting chains under darkness'. Can He too only punish, instead of reforming? The idea of eternal damnation had its origin amid a society which exercised punishment; and as soon as mankind sees that there is no such word, that reformation is the only word, eternal punishment will disappear out of our religion: everlasting damnation and capital punishment will go out together.

SECTION XIV

What has 'society' done for us? What is the mission of society? of mankind? to civilize and educate us. How does it fulfil this mission? What does it do for 'fallen women'? Those who have committed indictable crime, it takes possession of, and ordinarily condemns to a place where they must lose all hope as well

---

* Serjeant Adams, at the Middlesex Sessions, complained that always the *same* criminals came before him, again and again, most of them young boys.

as all desire of reformation. One would have thought that society, which had done so badly for them in their childhood, would now have wished to re-model them. Not at all. That is not the question. To punish them is all that is wanted. They must go, where the poisoner becomes corrupted and the forger loses all feeling, divine and human. They must be punished by being deprived of all lingering claims, to being thought human creatures and our sisters. 'From him that hath little shall be taken away even that which he hath'. But if indictable crime has *not* been committed, what does society do? What protection does she give those wretched women? What constraint does she put upon those men who make them what they are? Does she even turn a shy look upon them? Not at all. On the contrary, she throws open her doors wide to them, vicious as they are, and like the beggars, whom she puts in prison, while she praises those who give to them (curious anomaly!), so she says to the woman, 'Get out of my path'. While to him without whom the woman would not have been vicious, she offers her drawing-rooms and her high-bred daughters. Society takes pleasure in stimulating passion in every kind of way, by early excess in wine, late hours, school-boy conversation and classical books, etc., etc., and then says, 'you must not gratify this in a legitimate way, under pain of exciting our censure – the illegitimate satisfaction is the only one we allow'. And then she gives these satisfactions, 'like lilies, with full hands' – and allows no difficulty to remain unremoved.

But, if a criminal is great, if, by some political trade, he has, like Schwarzenberg,[57] made himself useful to the designs of a government, of a sovereign, then he does not go to prison or to Norfolk Island at all; on the contrary the 'Times' writes of him that he will be remembered with gratitude, if not with love. Society punishes a Rush[58] and protects a Schwarzenberg.

And we who are not 'fallen women', we talk about mankind creating mankind, – what has mankind done for us? It has created wants which not only it does not afford us the opportunity of satisfying, but which it compels us to disguise and deny. It affords us neither interest, nor affections, nor employment. Society neither finds us with work, if we are too weak to find it for ourselves, nor with training to perform it, if we have found it – nor does it so much as suffer us to follow a vocation of our own, not even if there be one too strong within us to perish for lack of nourishment.

It has made rich and poor, without teaching the rich to use their riches, nor the poor their poverty. It says, if any one dies of hunger, 'you must not starve – so and so shall be punished if you do'; or 'you shall be provided for at the expense of society'. But it never says, 'you shall not starve spiritually – you must not want the bread *of life* – so and so shall be punished if you do, if you lack the satisfactions which are as necessary to the faculties and feelings as food is to the physical wants'.

SECTION XV

If we lived in a race which knew how to employ our strength instead of frittering it and repressing it, how different it would be! But now, when it finds one of its members with a great power of work, it is disagreeably surprised, it does not know what to do with him, he is something extra and troublesome, which it had rather were not there.

The will is not intended to be frittered away in little decisions about every moment. It is meant to have a great type before it – means and inducements for attaining that type – every day to receive some knowledge or training towards realizing it, every day to apply and test that knowledge by actual work. Repose, which is the employment of all our powers (of mind and heart) is found thus and only thus – thus it may be found in an external hell. This is God's repose – otherwise how could He be happy in the midst of all this wretchedness? There is always something repulsive in the thought of God's existence as solitary enjoyment, while his children are suffering all this – as if there were something selfish in it. But in His goodness and wisdom He finds His peace.

But, without a type before one of what human nature may become, how can any one work? There is a kind of vague belief that mankind goes on improving – that every generation is farther on than the last. There is, existing at the same time with the other, a vague belief that it is a kind of law that nations shall rise to a certain point and then fall, without any particular reason but that it is a law – and people point to the Assyrians, the Egyptians, and others, whose name is legion – and some say that England is come to that point, and must now decline. It is very true that nations have risen and are now fallen, but not because there is a law that so it shall be. Do we know yet what the type of England ought to be? Has any one a type before them in what they do? Do we think Lord Derby,[59] or any English prime minister, has a type of what are the nature and destination of mankind or of England in his head? The words are absurd. Lord Derby thinks of 'staying in' a certain time, of not becoming unpopular with the country, of not doing any serious harm.

When a young lady takes a poor child out of the village and thinks she will teach it, has she any type before her of what ought to be done, of what it ought to be by a certain time? She thinks, as the phrase is, that it is better than 'doing nothing' for the poor child, that some good will come of it, she does not quite know what, either for her or for it. She has no type.

And it does not appear at all certain that mankind *is* always making progress. Sometimes they are going forward, sometimes they are going back. It is very evident that Asia has been making retrogression, expecting the Chinese, who have probably remained stationary, perhaps the only people which has done so. Parts of Europe have been making retrogression, Greece, Italy, Spain – England and Germany have been perhaps advancing.

Women's life is spent in pastime, men's in business. Women's business is supposed to be to find something to '*pass*' the '*time*'. If young ladies are seen sitting round the table doing worsted-work, they are supposed to be appropriately and rightly employed, especially if one is reading aloud. But if men were to be discovered sitting round the table doing worsted-work, or even in the evening talking over the fire doing *crochet*, how women would laugh! The reason is that men are supposed to be doing their business in the morning, and in the evening, when their business is done, to be talking about something important enough to prevent their being able to do fancy-work at the same time. But women have never anything to say so important as that they should not be looking at their pattern.

When tailors and shoemakers are at their work we do not laugh, because they are doing their business; and tailors and shoemakers are generally reckoned among the most intelligent part of the community. It is only the regarding anything as a mere '*pass-time*' that strikes us as so ridiculous in a full-grown man; and why is it not so in a woman? Without the right cultivation and employment of all the powers, (and where do we see the woman with *half* her powers employed?) there can be no repose, and with it, as we have said, repose may be found in a hell, in a hospital of wounds, and pain, and operations, and death, and remorse, and tears, and despair. The effervescence of energy, which there is in every young being not diseased in mind or body, which struggles to find its satisfaction in the excitement of society, of imagination, of the vulgar conflicts of social life, will seek its true occupation, at last, in the anguish of real life.

Many a woman cannot resign herself to lead the life she has seen every woman about her lead – of composing parties, laying out the grounds, reading newspapers, superintending children whom she cannot manage, servants whom she cannot influence, schools which she knows nothing about, and seeing them all fail; and this unsustained by any real deep sympathy with her husband, good though he may be. He is thinking of other things; he does not cause her to partake his ideas and plans, except indeed his desire to have such and such a person at the house, such and such a disposition of the furniture or the garden.

Such a woman longs for a profession – struggles to open to women the paths of the school, the hospital, the penitentiary, the care of the young, the sick, the bad – not as an amusement, to fill up odd times, to fancy they have done something when they have done nothing, to make a sham of visiting – but, systematically, as a reality, an occupation, a 'profession'.

For such women what does the Church of England do?

But what should we have better, if we were to do away with the Church to-morrow?

We may well ask this question. Much mischief has arisen from its not having been asked long and considerately before every change has been made. But how can we answer it, solitary beings as we are? Numbers of men must consult together and discover their wants, and how to supply them, doing nothing hastily; for from these hasty destructions small good has ever arisen. In fact, the day of destruction is over. We must now build up. But to build up without much consideration is as unwise as to pull down without any. Luther saw the mischief of 'indulgences', and he, by the most colossal effort of the human intellect, set aside the idea of an authority which had never before been doubted. But, instead of one authority, he set up another. Instead of a Church he gave us a Book. Then his mind was incompetent to look what was to be done next; And the Protestant Church is, perhaps, little improvement on the Roman Catholic. In some respects it may be a deterioration, inasmuch as it expects to excite the same feelings while it has lopped off half the means. Yet we should not say that Luther had better have left the indulgences alone. Brutus killed Caesar, but he had not thought what was to come next; and there followed a worse than Caesar. In the same way the French knew very well that Louis Philippe's[60] government was an evil, and they overturned him without more ado; but they had not thought about what was to come in his place, and a worse than Louis Philippe is here. This is not saying that Louis Philippe was not an evil, and that they had better have left him alone; but that they had better have considered what they were about to place in his stead. We quite agree with those who ask, if we were to do away with the Church to-morrow, what should we have in its place? Mankind must consider – those of mankind who want something more than the Church, as she is. To take her away from those who are satisfied with her would be cruel.

And about everything else, people *do* consider and lay their heads together. Mr Hunt, of Herne Bay, writes to all the medical men in this kingdom to ask what has been their experience about the effects of arsenic as a medicine; and out of the experience of many men he deduces a result. People will do this about a medicine for the body, but they will not do it when it is only for the soul. They will do it to ascertain a fact; and when a fact has been ascertained, and people are interested in procuring means to apply that fact to their advantage, how they will work! Look at the Anti-Corn Law League,⁶¹ at the thousands of pounds which were subscribed in a few days when Lord Derby's administration appeared to threaten the return of protection!

But we are so little interested about religion, we are so little sure of our facts concerning it, that we never go to the same trouble nor exertion for its sake.

SECTION XVI

What a dangerous and hairbreadth speculation it is to bring up children on the plan of doing a thing because 'you like it', because 'it pleases you'. What does it signify whether I like it? what *God likes* is the question; not what He likes by an arbitrary fancy, as we often imagine, but what His laws, His eternal immutable laws, the expressions of perfect goodness and perfect wisdom, are for or against.

Let, then, the question be not what Mr A or Mrs B thinks, but what God thinks. Relations intermarry, or persons with scrofula or insanity in their families. In the whole family the question immediately arises, 'does E like it'? 'I don't think S does'. 'J I am sure does. He has quite got over all his prejudices against it'. 'And A, she was always inclined to it'.

The question never once presents itself to the minds of either bridegroom or bride, or any of those in authority over them,

does God like it? Is there a law of His or is there not which favours marriage between blood relations? or between persons with hereditary disease in the family?

People do not for these purposes investigate physiological laws, consult statistics, or make out what they can from the experience of those who have experience. They consult fancies.

Again, when a poor marriage is decided upon, neither bride nor bridegroom make the smallest calculation, how much bread, how much butter, how much house is to be had for 600*l.* a year. They say they will be guided by the wishes of their parents. Which of us has not heard that dutiful speech? Then, after- wards, they grow tired of being guided by the wishes of their parents, and quite amiably and respectfully 'think' they can marry, still without making the least calculation. The parents 'think' they could not, and disapprove. The poor girl grows thin and pale. '*Now*, don't you approve?' she says, or, if she does not say, she feels; and at last they are fain not to 'disapprove'.

The thoughts of children are seldom directed upon the question before them, but upon questioning the judgment of their parents; and this is not entirely their own fault. It arises from the views of authority and of their responsibility, taken by parents. They *assume* a responsibility they cannot have.

'I will wait two years for your satisfaction', says the young lady. It is exactly as if she had said, 'I do not know whether it is safe for me to go into that river or not, I have not examined the point, how deep nor how rapid it is. I don't know whether I shall sink or swim, but I will wait two years'; what for? 'for my mother's satisfaction, before I jump in'.

Is not this a true experience of what passes between parents and children in most families?

A young lady teaches at a Sunday school, and feels that it is all a sham and that she is pretending to do that which she is not really doing. She begs to be allowed to go to some place for a few months to learn to teach, and the mother answers, 'You teach quite well enough *to please me*'. The girl has a vague idea it is not all right, but knows not what to answer.

What a mistake that word 'indulgent', as applied either to

God or man, implies! If 'indulgent' means doing what love prompts and wisdom teaches to be right, God *always* is indulgent and parents ought to be so. But if 'indulgent' means giving something which may be a little hurtful, because you love so much, that is not true love, and God never is indulgent and man ought not to be.

SECTION XVII

What are we to do with girls? It is vaguely taken for granted by women that it is to be their first object to please and obey their parents till they are married. But the times are totally changed since those patriarchal days. Man (and woman too) has a soul to unfold, a part to play in God's great world.

Marriage is supposed to exercise a magical effect upon the judgment – for a married woman of eighteen has more independence, and is thought better able to act for herself than a single one of thirty-six. But it is not to be the first object for a man 'born into the world', nor for a woman either, when he or she is of age, to please the parents. There is a higher object than this for the being which is to be one with God. It is true the child must obey and ought to obey implicitly. The question is, then, *when* the child becomes of age. If this were left to the parents' discretion, they would, perhaps, with the best and purest intentions, declare that their children were never of age. Parents seldom think that their children are grown up, and the children who have made most advance, and are before their generation, will always be those whom conscientious parents are most tempted to restrain as 'geniuses unfit to judge for themselves in the common affairs of life', because, naturally enough, they cannot understand them. We see parents building up obstacles in the way of their children as zealously as if it were their sole vocation! It is almost invariable that, when one of a family is decidedly in advance of all the others, he or she is tyrannized over by the rest, and declared 'quite incapable of doing anything reasonable'. A man runs away from this, – a woman cannot. The one who ought to be at the top of the ladder is always at the bottom. It is not only against those esteemed physically insane that commissions of lunacy are taken out. Others have been kept unjustly in confinement by their well-intentioned relations, as unfit to be trusted with liberty. In fact, in almost every family, one sees a keeper, or two or three keepers, and a lunatic. Happy for the poor lunatics, if there are two of them in one family! They may combine. Those natures which have the strongest affections, and therefore cannot bear not to please the others, not to be in the same key with the others, follow where they ought to lead. It must not be left to parents' discretion to declare, when a child is able to act for himself. The law has not left it at the discretion of parents and guardians to decide when a man becomes of age. If it had, he never would have become of age. It has fixed this age at twenty-one. It has not said twenty or twenty-five, but advisedly, taking into consideration the experience of mankind, it has fixed upon twenty-one. Guardians are not left to say *when* a young man shall come into the possession of his property. If they were, some, self-interested, would like to keep him out of it for their own sakes; others, well-intentioned and conscientious, would think he was still a child and not fit to manage it. But the law says *twenty-one*.

Who is to decide when a young woman shall come into possession of herself? Not the parents, certainly. A woman of twenty-one ought to consider herself of age, as regards her own conduct. It may be too early for some, too late for others. The real age of regeneration varies, when the child, generated by the parents at the age of 0, is *re*-generated by reason and education. But in spite of the mistakes which will follow, it would be better for children if they no longer considered themselves under tutelage after twenty-one.

The connexion between parents and children, in its present state of transition, is a miserable one; yet we would not have it back to its old state, if we could. In former days, children called their parents 'Sir' and 'Madam'; in the present days, they call them, at least one of them, 'Governor' or 'Relieving Officer'; in former times, they did not sit down in their parents' presence; in these, mothers wait upon their daughters, and are vexed at once that the daughters do not do it for themselves, and that they are not grateful to them for doing it. In the last century, proposals of marriage for the children were made to the parents; the parents accepted or refused, often without the knowledge, generally without the consent, of the children; in this, a man asks the woman herself, without the previous knowledge, and sometimes even in the absence, of the parents. In the last century, the relation was therefore a much more definite and easy one. Implicit obedience was exacted and given; submission, not love was demanded; silence, not gratitude, expected. Then it might truly be said that the responsibility rested with the parents; for they undertook, and were understood to act, in the stead and without the co-operation of their children.

But now with whom rests the responsibility? The parents assume that they have it, but without any longer the rights to support it. Many a mother of this day would speak (if her feelings were put into words) thus: – 'My mother did not think of what her daughter thought; her daughter had no business to think, *she* thought in her stead. *I* allow my daughter to think, but I expect that she shall always think like me. This is the least she can do, in common gratitude, in return for all that I have done for her. I don't desire her to obey – no such tyranny can exist in the nineteenth century; but she is always to act as I should do. I don't wish her to submit; but I wish her to be, what I wish to be with God, one with me. I don't command her to be silent, but I expect that her opinion shall always be the same as mine. I am excessively indulgent, that is, I take immense pains (*my* mother took no pains of the sort) to make her happy, in my way; to please her, according to my taste; to do what she *ought* to like, not what she does like; to arrange what *I* think is good for her, not what interests her – and she is not grateful'. In these days, it can no longer be, 'Do unto others as you would be done by,' but 'Do unto others as *they* would be done by'. In the vagueness of all things which belongs to this transition-time, the relation between parents and children is as difficult to find as your way in a London fog. The parents take responsibilities which they cannot perform; the children feel that they are not performed. The parents feel that they are going through a great deal for their children; the children that gratitude is exacted from them for that which does not make them happy. Both sides suffer equally from disappointment, and both are alike to be pitied. The mothers are disappointed that they are not loved; the daughters that they feel no attraction towards the parents; for we can only love that which is loveable to us. An uncomfortable age! The last one was better. But no, it was not. We could not go back to that, if we would; and we would not, if we could. Still we know our daughters wish that they were married, as we did, in order that they may exercise at least some of their faculties and attractions. And no wonder; that is the reason why *we* married; and they will have to run the same chance with *their* children.

See what is expected of the poor unfortunate mother, that she should be able to respond to all the wants and tastes of all her daughters; the parts which twenty people could not play must all be acted by her; she must be a poet with one, a woman of business with another, an artist with a third, a thinker with a fourth, in order to develop the capabilities of each; and why? because they are shut up in a family, without free scope to find and exercise their natural inclinations and powers.

Yet daughters are now their mothers' slaves, just as much as before; they are considered their parents' property; they are to have no other pursuit, nor power, nor independent life, unless they marry; they are to be entirely dependent upon their parents – white slaves in the family, from which marriage alone can emancipate them. Mothers acknowledge this, even while feeling that they are the daughters' slaves too.

What we have to do is so vague that we are obliged often to keep our responsibilities, while we have lost the privileges to which they appertained, and which alone could enable us to perform them.

SECTION XVIII

Shall we not all allow that every one ought to have exercise for all his faculties, and that every one ought to come freely into contact with all others? But how *is* it? We begin by teaching something to our boys which we acknowledge, if it is to be learnt, will leave time for nothing else. Dr Arnold wished to introduce German into Rugby; but he soon found, if the boys were to learn Latin and Greek, they had no time for German or anything else. We teach languages and history. History consists of facts, which can be made no use of by the boy, because he has not yet sufficient experience of life to understand them; they may lie fallow, it is true, till he has. And yet there is not one of us but admits at once that *all* the faculties ought to have exercise and food.

As to mixing freely with all others, we mix (at least our women do) with the narrowest of all possible circles, – a family, where the chances are almost nothing that we shall find two persons who will have one idea or mode of action in common. For the law of God is against repetition. In so narrow a limit, you can scarcely find room for the exercise of one of your faculties; for everybody must do the same thing. It is well known what difficulties a genius produces in a family. We had much rather have a common-place person.

Monasteries, according to their original plan, were a much larger circle than the family. For there people did meet for a common object: those who had a vocation for work went into a house which supplied their kind of work – for contemplation, into a house of contemplation. Afterwards they degenerated into places of idleness and vice. But, in their original idea, they were places where people who liked to work for the same object, met to do so; and the enormous rate at which they multiplied showed how they responded to a want in human nature. Each was employed according to his or her vocation; there was work for all; but there is no such possibility in the family. *There* every one must be employed within the narrowest of all limits on the occupations least susceptible of any expansion − tied together, with rarely any common pursuit or interest, by the closest of all possible chains, and without a possibility of getting out, except by marriage.

Fathers are much to be pitied who, without any attraction for their daughters, are condemned to pass their lives with them in the narrowest of prisons, and cannot by any means escape from them. Many, who would never confess it, even to themselves, have a dread of being left alone with some other member of the family. I once knew a father − the best of fathers − who begged that he and his son might never be left in the house without some third person. There is a constraint, an embarrassment, which is the more painful the more excellent the person. Yet what can be more natural, nay unavoidable, in such a prison as the family? Open wide its doors, not only to your sons, but to your daughters also. Let them all have free scope and exercise, and room for all their faculties.

SECTION XIX

One of our most distinguished ethical philosophers says that he fears the present tendency to separation into assemblies of *the same*. 'We find', he says, 'the sick together in hospitals, the blind, the insane also. We find boys together in schools, young men in colleges, etc., whereas *the family*', he adds, 'which is Nature's work, presents variety − old, young, male, female'.

We entirely agree in the objection to that to which he objects. But if, by a family, he means the father, mother, and the children born to them, the evil is not thereby remedied; and it is plain that if it is desirable to bring together variety, *such* a family as this is by the very word pronounced against.

Such a family presents one man, one woman, the number of children uncertain, is generally said; but that word is inapplicable. Observation is indicating laws which regulate it. The tendency is to decrease in number, up to a certain point, with full exercise of faculty and sufficient supply of food. But take the family as it is now. Perhaps there is one boy, three girls, perhaps there are two girls; perhaps, four boys, four girls, or say one boy, one girl. What that we can call companionship in life and work springs up from this? The father and mother have had an education from life and circumstances different from the children. The father, where he is earning his bread, necessarily spends his time apart from the mother and children. What sympathy in life and work is there, in general, between parents and children, however good and affectionate each may be! Then, as to the children, does it not come, in the family, to this, that the boys go forth to the work, the girls are left at home together? A *small* assemblage of *the same* is presented by the family in the *girls*. This is all the difference (if we come to the consideration of parents and children in family life) between the family and the assemblies of schools and colleges.

We agree so much with the principle laid down by this ethical philosopher that we should wish for a different organization of life and society. We are not satisfied to see father, mother, and children living and working together. This was on our lips to say; but, in fact, we never do see it. We see father, mother, and girls living in the same house, and boys occasionally visiting them. We want to see all ages and both sexes really living and working for each other; each contributing what the other has not to the great existence, humanity.

We never have to *root out* feelings or opinions. We have to make them more comprehensive. We want a family which will really live and work together in sympathy, and efficiently. Whoever has *that* in parents or children, let him work on; it is well with him. But if he have it not, however dear and good his parents or children, his brothers or his sisters, – or if he see others wanting it, let him, in all love, look whether God did not intend mankind to use their means to obtain sympathy and efficient work and help among the varieties of age, sex, and character in the world. God knows we want to break no tie. We want to strengthen and enlarge ties.

PART VII

SECTION I

It is acknowledged that daughters are brought into the world without the possibility of asking their own consent. It is acknowledged that they have then but two alternatives. There seems to be no doubt that marrying a man of high and good purpose, and following out that purpose with him, is the happiest; but the mother must say to the daughter, 'I cannot ensure your meeting such', and the daughter cannot go out seeking them for herself. The parents must show them to her. 'If I can show you one such it will be a great deal; if I can show you two or three such, it will be an extraordinary thing indeed, and out of those whom I can show you, it does not follow that all will want to marry you or you them'. How many, then, are the chances against the woman embracing this alternative!

The other is, as we have said, to adopt the way of life which her parents have adopted for themselves from necessity or inclination, necessarily without any regard to her vocation, or capabilities for it, before she was born.

And why do the parents wish this? Not selfishly. There is really no selfishness in it, for it would rejoice them, as we have said, beyond anything, if the daughter could marry as *they* like. It is because they are afraid of what the *world* will say; of how they will judge a daughter who should leave her 'duty to her parents' and 'fly to other duties', who should forsake her 'home sphere' for 'strange fancies'.

To the *world*, then, I appeal. Is this right or is it wrong?

Men are so well aware of the fact that it is very important that a woman should marry – that she is anxious to try whether she cannot find more of interest away from home – that they take for granted, if they have means, that a woman will be too glad to accept them.

'Yes', we ought to be able to say, 'it *is* very important that a woman should marry, but not that she should marry you. She has a vocation. She will not marry, unless she finds a man with whom she can unite in high and holy purpose to serve mankind'.

Now, in the ordinary course of an ordinary woman's life, she is asking people to marry her all day long. Men only ask once and occasionally. It is true that, when a man asks, he must take his answer; if it is in the affirmative, he must stand by it; but a woman may ask, and if she gets her answer, she may draw back (which a man cannot do), and say, I meant nothing by it.

There are three things on which marriage is generally founded, – a good opinion of a person, a desire to love and be loved, and a wish to escape dissatisfaction at home. Any real attraction is difficult because there is so little choice, for there must be similarity of means and age. There must be acquaintance.

Will it be said, we do not take love into the account? We hardly ever saw it, and therefore cannot well tell what it is. We have seen women asking men to marry them, as we have said, all day long, and men asking women occasionally once. If that is called love? We have seen married people consulting together about whom they shall ask to dinner, or how they shall lay out the grounds. If that is called love?

What, then, *do* we call love?

The highest, the only true love is when two persons, a man and a woman, who have an attraction for one another, unite together in some true purpose for mankind and God.

But it is said, and said truly, that few people are capable of such a purpose. And are such capable of love?

We have seen women 'in love', as it is called, and men too. We never felt, 'Now *that is* love'. Mr and Mrs —— unite together to keep up a political 'party', and that is really more like love than most marriages, though it is only for party politics.

SECTION II

How is duty to be shown to parents? By destroying one's self? They say they want you to stay at home to take care of them. The whole thing is a falsity! They don't want you to stay to take care of them, they don't want you to stay for their sakes, but for your own sake, for fear the world should think evil of you. That is the first falsity. And you can't benefit them by cramping yourself any more than a slave can benefit his master. That is the second falsity. An injury to any one person is an injury to all the world. That parents should fancy that they can be benefited, or that anybody else can be, just by the cramping of the daughters!

The parents don't want the services of the daughter; but they are obliged to pretend to do so, for fear of something unfavourable being said of her by the world – out of kindness to *her*, therefore, and for *her* sake. The parents are really as much to be pitied as the daughters.

Daughters can do nothing but what their parents approve. They may, it is true, play at one hour and draw at another, as they choose; but they must come down to the company which the parents have invited. They cannot make even of their drawing a pursuit, for fear of appearing singular, of not performing what are called the 'social duties'.

They can only have a choice among those people whom their parents like, and who like their parents well enough to come to their house, and among those few, if one suits you, well; if not, not so well.

Christ did not marry; He was so devoted to God and

mankind that he appears not to have wished for marriage. We profess, but it is only a profession, to take Him for an example. Yet no one out of the Roman Catholic Church recognizes Christ as an example in this particular. Even the idea of marriage, in connexion with Him, offends, from the confusion of His divine and human nature.

There are two alternatives, either of which might be a happy one, a good marriage or this devotion to God and mankind. But we say, she shall not be devoted to God and mankind, she shall be devoted to doing what her parents do, whether it suit her or not.

What parents ought to do is not to approve what their children do, but to approve that their children should do what they think right, to bring them up till they are 'of age', so as that they shall have power to judge what they shall think right; and then, when they shall have come into possession of themselves, cordially to acquiesce that they should do what *they*, not their parents, judge good; but parents never think children 'of age' *till* the children think like them. They want the daughter to have her own peculiar genius, in order to think their thoughts, to advocate their opinions, and say what *they* think right.

Children cannot give love and duty for binding them down, for crushing their heart. They may recognize the good intention. We never see children in the street without thinking, 'why did you come into the world'? because it was convenient or agreeable to Mr and Mrs ——— to marry, or because it satisfied the passions of B and C to come together, for no other reason.

How is it, it is sometimes asked, that women of the upper class have nothing to do, even if they are set free – that they never desire nor look forward to anything but marriage?

Very few people live such an impoverishing and confusing and weakening life as the women of the richer classes. What is it? They have made up their minds to live in public, never to have any time to themselves. If one of a higher stamp joins them, she will not help *them*, but they will all go to the bottom together. Their brains all become muddled in company. They will go on impoverishing and getting worse to the end of their lives, and she will too.

It is the most confusing life. They have all cultivated general literature. Everybody is reading aloud half a page out of her own book. The mother has a sort of pride in her daughters being literary ladies, in their having five books lying upon the breakfast table at once, and quoting from a heap of authors. She says, with a sort of half pride, half regret that there is not more done, 'You know they are literary'.

You cannot bring forward an opinion without exciting a storm of words. You have made up your minds to live always in this whirlwind. What can be so confusing?

We pity the mothers quite as much as the daughters. The impossible is demanded from a mother. She is expected to undertake all, to sympathize with and understand all her children, among whom are the most dissimilar characters, the most unlike her own. Yet, by our method of imprisoning in families, she is to supply all these different kinds of characters and wants with sympathy, instruction, and help. It is like having no division of labour. The end is, a mother does nothing well, only interferes with everything, looks for the faults in those she deputes, and painfully feels, if she sees the faults, that she knows not how to prevent them.

Let a mother, when her daughters grow up, tell them the truth, as to independence of time, faculties, money, which women ought to have at 21, allowing that age to be too young – but considering a *too young fixed* time better than an unfixed time to be regulated by the opinion of each individual parent.

But, if a daughter wishes to do something flagrantly imprudent, to marry upon nothing, for instance, is she to be free to do it after 21?

The parent has then to say, 'You are free to do so, but I am not free to take a part. I cannot receive your meetings. You may correspond and meet elsewhere, if you have other friends who approve that course. That which would be spent upon you at home I lay by from the moment you cease to spend it at home. I cannot, in duty to the others, give it into your hands. I keep it,

because experience shows that you are undertaking what will
probably require more than your share of that common fund, of
which, in the present state of things, I am the guardian'. Greater
liberty than this could not be, because that could not be called
liberty which would trench on the rights of others. Women
ought to be free to follow any pursuit, or to marry, irrespective
of parents' opinions, so long as they can show, on experience,
probability that they will not trench on the shares of others;
money for the others standing for means, in like manner, to
follow *their* wishes. If they do not wish to spend their share of
means like the rest of the family, they ought to have that share
for their own purposes. This liberty is alike at all ages after 21,
never less, but never more, while the parent lives as guardian of
the means of all, because at no age must the rights of any be
trenched upon.

SECTION III

In thinking over life as it is now, practically, it is very desirable
to understand, to feel truly as to our *possibility* of sympathizing
with each other. Sympathy must and ought to be a want to man,
since the essential nature of mankind is to be one. We should
not wish, even if without it, *not* to feel the want of it; the evil is,
that people throw themselves into the outward, so that they do
not feel the want of it.

Very few people, for instance, *can* sympathize with each other
in any pursuit or thought of any importance. If there have not
been the means to learn, if one knows nothing on a subject, to
pretend or to try to sympathize is more balking than to give it
up. If people do not give you thought for thought, receive yours,
digest it, and give it back with the impression of their own
character upon it, then give you one for you to do likewise, it is
best to know what one is about, and not to attempt more than
kindly, cheerful, outward intercourse, or occasionally each

giving *information* to the other which the other has some pleasure in receiving, though not able to make much of it. This is well as far as it goes, and it is better not to fancy it can be more.

Let us think of the sympathy we don't have, as merely *absence* of sympathy, not fault in others (who often would gladly sympathize if they could), nor fault in ourselves (who also gladly would if we could).

Solitary confinement! Should we be afraid of it? It *is* solitary confinement. What are we all in but solitary confinement? To be alone is nothing, but to be without a sympathy in a crowd, this is to be confined in solitude.

Some of the most painful suffering in women of the richer class arises from not understanding that sympathy cannot be *willed*, cannot be given at will, nor attraction felt at will. The want of sympathy is painful enough, without the aggravation of blame to oneself or others. Some find amusement in the outward, do not suffer inwardly, because the attention is turned elsewhere. When this is not the case, and there is this want of sympathy, of attraction, given and returned, must it not be a feeling of starvation? Sympathy being one of the essentials of the human spirit, must not the human spirit be famishing without it, as the human body without food? No, we can feel what is to be called happiness, without attraction or sympathy, in certain exercises of the nature, where God has had a part.

In certain diseases there is no remedy known for acute and constant suffering, and it is right that it should be so, in order to bring about circumstances in which the causes of such suffering shall be removed, in which man shall attain a right physical state. Disappointment always springs from want of wisdom. Let us not, in a cowardly spirit, shrink from the pain of disappointment, but let us seek the wisdom which will prevent disappointment. It may often be that it is not in our present possibility to prophesy aright, but when this is so, we would wish for the consciousness of its being so, which prevents disappointment. It may be wise to try that which will fail, but not wise to feel disappointment in failure. Hardly any class suffers more from want of sympathy than married women, even those who are loving and loved. In some sorts of attraction the woman does not want sympathy; she only needs to satisfy the want of 'his' presence, the want to supply *his* interest, or amusement, or comfort, to feel what he is feeling, and fulfil his consequent desires. But this is by no means the highest, certainly not the most improving kind of married love.

To work at one or more objects interesting in the view of God, important in God's purposes for man, to work with one or more between whom there is a mutual attraction, and who are mutually interested in these objects, not only for each other's sakes, but from their own natures and for God's sake and man's sake, this only is human happiness, Who has it?

While unhappy, we can do comparatively so little. Let us look carefully to experience to make out whether there is to be nothing which can be called happiness, while this is impossible.

The want of all this ought to be recognized as a want, but it is not essential poverty, misery; such a state admits of partial riches, of partial happiness, even with a sense of want and suffering.

Oneness with God, kindness, sympathy (even if not mutual) with the feelings of others, and such exercise of the faculties as life affords, together with attention to the idiosyncracies of our own nature, will, in many cases, prevent the suffering which paralyses and impoverishes, will turn suffering into a species of happiness, which is the only right way to suffer. We must not desire to be unconscious of it. To faint away, or to be paralysed, or to have the attention so turned away as not to be conscious of the truth, are not desirable modes of escaping sense of suffering. Yet neither is it desirable that a phase of life and experience should pass unattuned to all possible enjoyment of right kind which circumstances admit of, for this enjoyment is in accordance with God's pleasure. Will it not answer our purpose of stirring us to *seek*, if we are conscious of greater happiness to mankind from a supply of what is wanting, without actual suffering in the want?

It has long been a practical question whether we can be

happy without sympathy, whether it would be well to be without the inward cry for it. If that inward cry has made us conscious of the want, it will be well for us to find happiness in oneness with God, and striving to do one's part (even if a little one, though ever striving after a greater one). Need we be impelled by suffering? May not the bliss of God and wisdom and righteousness attract us onwards and upwards? We cannot live on suffering and poverty. We often try. We must find peace and joy if we are to be or to do anything.

There are so few means of learning to do anything well, people's attention is so little directed to good objects, is so spent on many small objects, and we are so little thrown upon the variety of mankind for associates, that even the want of sympathy in good work, one of the essentials of well-being, is little recognized. The other essential of well-being is oneness with God, but of this, too, few have the consciousness.

Love God, and love thy neighbour. How Christ resumed the whole science of man's well-being in those two sentences!

SECTION IV

Why are mothers so much to be pitied? The Church of England is not the only power which declines as it becomes moral. Parental power declines, in proportion as a door is opened to opinion. Neither the Church of England nor the parent having any real foundation for power, they lose it as soon as it is questioned. But the parent, like the Church, must allow for varieties of character, *whilst* he retains his absolute authority; otherwise he too will turn out John Wesley, instead of being strengthened by his earnestness and zeal.

'The mother at home!' There is no desert for the heart so oppressive as that of the 'mother at home' in England in the 19th century, at least as some of the deserts which she has to pass through. Perhaps that of the 'daughter at home' is

sometimes as much so. Many have passed through both, with
excellent parents and excellent children. In both, we long to
love and be loved, to sympathize and be sympathized with. In
both as to participation of the thoughts and feelings most
interesting, it is no exaggeration to say that we should not have
been more alone in any African desert. There is (in both) the
appearance of food which disappears whenever you stretch out
your hand to take it.

To excite us to remedy evils, we must see things in a bad
form; to show their imperfection we must see them in a
comparatively good form.* When we see a bad school, we think
a good one would supply man's education. When we see a
perfect one, like Mr Brookes's in John-street, we most strongly
feel that it cannot. When we see a family with obvious deficiencies *as a family*, we feel that a well-regulated family might afford
satisfaction. Taking for granted that what girls in the richer class
are supposed to aim at *is* the right thing, how much there is
which is satisfactory! They are indefatigable at their music,
drawing, reading; they really like one another, companionize
each other in their reading. They have all possible liberty. Their
father is generally an affectionate and enlivening element to
them; they are good and well-intentioned. Yet what poor work
it is for human life! The mother has hardly an interest in
common with them. Though they mean and feel so rightly to
each other, they can do scarcely anything for each other. Yet
there is so much of good in their lives that they will never know
what its wants are; they will feel 'ennuyées', will look to loves
and friendships and to outward things for relief, often in vain. If
a real attachment and a good one comes, they will embark in the
same sort of family life, enter upon its evils and deficiencies, will
live over again (unless they be some rare exception) the old
story of thinking their children, their difficulties 'peculiar'.

When will be revealed (by suffering falling upon a nature
capable of distinguishing whence it comes, and a remedy for it),

* The same principle holds exactly with regard to religious orders. It is only by seeing a
perfect 'superior' of such an order that its essential defects are made visible. (I speak from
experience.)

when will be revealed a glimpse of human nature's wants? We see no tendency to such a revelation.

If it is to be that I leave this world, seeing nothing done as to these objects, I hope I shall be able to die trusting and remembering that there is eternity for God's work. But looking to probabilities as they can be estimated, if nothing is done now, all seems as though there were no other salvation in sight.

Neither do we see any tendency towards a revelation to thinkers upon religion. Some blind clergy and methodists will preach what will go against their reason. This is the only influence at work directed to them.

To return, however, to the question of sympathy. Mothers, though living among the good and feeling, may be like John the Baptist living in the desert, as to absence of sympathy. In return they give none, for it is true that they generally know and care nothing about their children's objects. This the children must feel a want. Some mothers have learnt not to blame their absence of sympathy, but daughters cannot have learnt not to feel the mother's absence of sympathy to be a deficiency which they have to complain of or regret. Mothers have longed to know about machinery and natural history in order to sympathize with their sons, but they can't, and without knowledge they can't care for these subjects, much as they care for the sons. They can't care at least with such a sympathy as the sons ought to like to accept.

But oh! the wretchedness of these family parties – of this do-nothing life! Try to keep your head above water for the possibility that you may bring some light to the weary sufferers who know not why they suffer. Those who can only bear to the end may believe that all is well, that not one moment of sorrow is felt, which is not essential to the perfect whole; that even these helpless hands and this weary heart are working indirectly at that whole. And this is comfort.

SECTION V

Why is there all this new question about the relation between
parents and children now?

The question concerning our relation to God and our relation
to our parents arises naturally, or rather *necessarily*, in these
times. Hitherto (at least in principle, if not in practice), the
nature of both relations has been taken for granted, though
somewhat vaguely. In both cases power above our own was
recognized and acknowledged. In mankind's earlier ignorant
state, questions are not searched into by all or by many. A few
who think more closely, or feel more strongly than the general
run, are listened to as oracles. 'Fear God', 'honour your parents',
were acknowledged precepts, and largely governed practical life.
Those who did not conform to them dissented, – *not* because
they had thought out something else which they felt more true,
but because they were self-confident or self-indulgent.

In savage life, and for many steps beyond, the perceptions are
the part of the nature most cultivated and exercised. When the
perceptions are much exercised, general laws not understood,
and the intellect little cultivated, fear of a higher power naturally arises.

The next step to this is, that intellect becomes cultivated by
the few, while the many are 'hewers of wood and drawers of
water'. These few see the folly of the fears of the multitude, and
some become unbelievers. But a higher power manifests itself to
the learned as well as to the unlearned. Human nature is
adapted to venerate; and though some scoff, many acknowledge,
and the religion of the cultivated undergoes various phases.

No other religion, perhaps, ever died out so entirely as the
Greek and Roman Pantheon. In Asia, and to a degree in Africa (?),
(though we know, perhaps, too little about Africa to judge,) the
old religions either remain, as the Buddhist, and the Chinese

still do, or modify the present, either there or elsewhere, as does the Egyptian, at least to a much greater degree than do now the Greek or Roman or the religions of the north. These religions, we may say, expired; they left traces of themselves, in ceremonies and practices adopted from them by the Christians; the abstractions, virtue, goodness, etc., come from the Epicurean and the Stoic philosophers more than from the Christian; the worship of the Virgin, of a female divinity, by the Roman Catholic, owes its origin, perhaps, to the worship of Diana. All this may be granted. But still nothing of the *character* of the heathen deities appears in the Christian objects of veneration, neither in the Father, the Son, the Holy Ghost, the Virgin Mary, nor the Saints.

The Father was the God of the Jews receiving Europe into His jurisdiction. The essence of the religion of Moses was to deny more than their one God (at first, because, though others were acknowledged to exist, *He* was a jealous God, and where He was acknowledged, would admit no other).

The Christians, therefore, in adopting the Jewish religion adopted this principle, so strongly laid down by their first teachers among the Jews. But it had been necessary to force their doctrine upon the Jews. It did not satisfy the nature of men, in general, though it elevated a few, as it seemed, supernaturally, who were of high nature. Europe would not have accepted it. But Christ, deified under a character of love and self-sacrifice; the Virgin Mary, with all her loveliness and tenderness; the Saints, with their heroism; the doctrine of the Atonement, so consolatory to man, who felt his weakness, his sin, his danger; these doctrines, containing so much of truth and beauty, so much to engage the heart and imagination, took a strong hold on the thoughts and feelings. And so long as *power*, not to be questioned or criticized, was acknowledged in Heaven and at the head of the family, these doctrines remained in force.

People are hardly aware of the very great importance of the present phase of religious and domestic life, of the change going on, of the want of a Saviour, for this hour of peculiar trial. When religion expired in Greece and Rome, the Saviour, who appeared in Judaea, spread his influence to raise it from the dead.

These two questions of religion and family are so intimately connected that to ask concerning the higher power or powers acknowledged in heaven and on earth is one.

There *has* been an actual veneration for power, and readiness to acknowledge it, in mankind, without inquiry whether it consisted in the righteousness, the truth, the goodness, the wisdom, which are the *essentials* of all *permanent* power.

No reason is felt *now* for venerating or yielding to the powers which formerly influenced men's minds, from a sense of fear or of duty. The changes, which we now must bring about, are the substitution for *authority*, which cannot be replaced in heaven or in the family, of sense of truth and right, of *accordance with right*. No longer can it be *duty submitted to*, but *right accorded with*, which must be the spirit of mankind.

And an awful phase it is, while the former is a waning influence, and the latter can scarcely yet be said to be a waxing one.

Man used to throw himself under the wheels of the divinity's car. Now, —

> . . . he'll not lose a cup of drink for thee:
>   Bid him but temper his excess;
> Not he: he knows where he can better be,
>   As he will swear,
>   Than to serve thee in fear.

God surrounds us. His law is ever at work, bringing about the right, so all will be well. Without this conviction the present would be fearful, for, in the errors which are dying out, it is difficult to distinguish the germs of truth which are growing up. Truth, in our relations both with God and with man, must come in this substitution of *accordance* of the whole nature with *right* for *authority*, vaguely acknowledged from fear or duty. Let us do justice to these passing influences, to their good effects, imperfect and erroneous as they were. They were better than the phase which *is* now, though this phase will lead to better than they. Oh! that we could help ourselves and each other out of the present selfish, cold, self-satisfied views, poor and narrow, while supposed to be new and improved lights!

SECTION VI

Mistakes with regard to the relation of God to man, and of parent to child, arise from mistaken ideas concerning those attributes which are common to divine and human nature.

Power, as we have said, is the attribute most universally recognized, both in the divine and the human author of being. In the earlier ages of civilization it is acknowledged that *might* is *right*, and the ideas of the parental relation, both divine and human, are much modified by this acknowledgment.

Now, when we say *accordance* with *right*, we do not mean the right of might; right has come to have quite a different meaning; right probably comes from *rego*, I govern, but governing by the right of governing, and governing by the principle of right, no longer mean the same thing. We are tending to the discovery that *all permanent power arises out of wisdom*. Thus the *nature* of the Supreme, the source and spring of all other natures, seems to determine.

Under the idea that might was right, men worshipped deities, in whom was no goodness, consequently no wisdom. They yielded to a master (whether the king, the master of a nation, or the father, the master of a family,) whatever his character, unless he were weak, and thus forfeited his characteristic of power.

But now it is coming into view, though indistinctly and unconsciously, that the divine and human parent must excite in us the consciousness of love, goodness, wisdom, righteousness; then we shall love and revere, trust and sympathize. But if the human as well as the divine parent is not in the state of being to *call forth* these sentiments, and if the child is not in the state to *admit* of them, there will be no relation between the divine or the human parent, and the child except the latter yielding when he cannot help it.

This beginning to be recognized causes the uneasiness of the present phase of domestic life, especially in this country and in the richer class, and when we look into it we are not surprised that it is thus uneasy.

While God's power was acknowledged to be in *itself* an object of reverence, and duty to be owed to his power, a family united in worship to him. While they had more practical work to do, there was less time and occasion for the present uneasiness in families of the class whose practical work is now done for them. And while the right of the parents to direct was acknowledged without examination, whether they directed wisely or not, there was merit in submission and wrong in resistance. And *that* was a more peaceful, a more unselfish, a more conscientious phase than this, though this will develop into a phase much more so than that.

But now the parent is getting more and more into an anomalous and difficult position; more and more does any relation between his child and himself depend upon the love and wisdom with which he fulfils it. As civilization and luxury advance, he undertakes more and more for such wisdom as he may have; he, or rather she, (for these difficulties chiefly concern the mother – the father escaping them, as his employments of work or of amusement lie chiefly out of the house,) *she*, then, is to direct the servants, who are to provide conveniences and luxuries not thought of formerly. She has never learnt and does not know how, but she must take care to provide them. She must superintend the nurse and the governess of her children, though she knows nothing and has learnt nothing of the nurse's work. And the governess, whose time, if she prepared herself to be a governess, was spent in a poor little back room out of sight of human kind, excepting of her masters of music, singing, drawing, or languages, (or as many of these as time and money would allow,) what is she to do? *She* must direct the characters of her pupils. How is she fit for it? If she were not expressly *preparing* in youth for it, she comes out of difficulties perhaps little suited to prepare her for this work. Over her, so little prepared, the mother, so little prepared, is to preside. Over the *society*, the duties to the rich, the duties to the poor, the poor mother is to preside, and, naturally, she presides so imperfectly over some, if not all of these duties, that the daughters soon begin to criticize. In youthful spirits, knowing little of difficulties – in the 'irresponsibility of opposition', they do this. She is one – they more than one, banded together in this criticism and opposition. The more in her maternal affection or conscientiousness or in her ambition that they should excel she has striven for them, the more capable they will be to criticize. And here, without blameable intention, either in parent or child, is where we are now, in families in *easy* circumstances. Much power still remains with mothers if they like or think it right to exert it. Whether they do or do not, their position is anomalous and unsatisfactory.

We have heard something of the difficulties of a 'daughter at home', – these are the difficulties of a 'mother at home'.

SECTION VII

What was the original meaning of *authority*? Does it mean the tie between the Author and those of whom He was the Author? The Author has power over what He has created – God over the universe – man over the family – and *might*, as we have said, was *right*, in early days. Was this the pedigree of 'authority'? But reflection brings into view that might is not right. Is there any permanent power, any real power except what arises out of wisdom, truth, goodness, as we said? The tie comes into view that the Author shall make the existence he has created a blessing to the created.

The more man's nature is rightly exercised and develped (*i.e.*, improved from imperfection towards perfection, from ignorance towards truth), the more will he appreciate the right and good, love the loveable, sympathize *with* the right in respect of the wrong. His real ties to his parents and to his children will be stronger and stronger. His ties to the Author of the universe will be stronger and stronger. More and more, in proportion to his own improvement, will he love, venerate, trust, sympathize, and *work* consistently with such feelings.

But this applies, it will be said, to his relation with all men, with whom circumstances throw him into relation. What ought there to be peculiar between parent and child? is our question. Undoubtedly the parent has *power* over the child. At his call comes into the world an utterly helpless being, who, without some care from him, would soon cease to be a *human being* (though that which is will never cease to be in some mode; nothing that exists ever ceases to be, *i.e.* to lead to some other modification of being). Immense might be the power of the parent over the child for good, if he had wisdom.

However, in proportion as the parent has wisdom, goodness, righteousness, love, and as these develop the same attributes in the child, will the tie be strong. The parent having peculiar power over the child will, in the exercise of these attributes, call forth the love, the respect, the trust, the sympathy of the child, more than others who have not that peculiar power and influence.

It is certain that there *are* to be families, *i.e.*, there are to be parents and children, brothers and sisters, and cousins. One remark we can at once make with regard to these relationships, that the relation of marriage is, by God's law, not to take place between brothers and sisters and cousins. The tendency of this law is separation. Marriage thus breaks up families, separates parents and children and sisters. Brothers go out into the world, and in general are separated, whether married or not. There is felt something almost unbecoming in a son living at home after he grows up; he sometimes leaves home and lives elsewhere, for no other reason scarcely. God's laws seem to point to dispersion of families. Man accords, with regard to marriage, so much as often to seek or agree to marriages which are undesirable – accords with regard to the desirableness of sons going out to work in the world; to daughters doing so, who have to maintain themselves. But daughters, who are not *obliged* to maintain themselves, must *not* do so; they may not leave the paternal roof, except to marry. To try to find out whether this is right, let us go back to the nature of the relation between parents and children. It begins with that great point which we have already mentioned. The parents call the child into existence. Let them take care that they can prophesy that the existence to which they summon him will, in probability, be one in the direct road to being *worth* having. All existence is essentially worth having. God takes care of *that*. But one of the means by which He takes care of this is, by man seeking the right; by presenting means and inducements to man to seek the right. Till man has an appetite for the right, he is under liability to suffering and privation; till he has attained how to find the right, he is under liability to suffering and privation, which are among the teachers of mankind.

The parents, then, have to try to be able to prophesy that the being whom they summon to human existence, shall find human existence worth having. This principle is, *to a degree*, acknowledged and generally acted upon in the educated classes. The class in which women are able to live without working for a livelihood, takes it for granted, however, that 'to be *worth having*' means, 'to live without working for a livelihood in the way which well-disposed parents have fixed upon'.

So far we have come, then, that the tie springs from the parents, who, if they are in a right state, will feel a repulsion, not an attraction, to summoning this human existence, unless they can prophesy a probability that it will be worth having. Before we inquire what the being 'worth having' means, let us inquire what will be the tie of children to parents, and what its nature.

Parents have a greater field of influence than others. They ought to provide life, and what is desirable in life, till the child can provide for himself. Money answers to means for all that is desirable. Without means for food, clothing, shelter, sleep, man

cannot develop and exercise his faculties for perceiving, thinking, and feeling. Money, or something equivalent, is essential as
a mode to enable man to work with man in such development
and exercise.

Does, then, a parent's power, his means for influence lie in
money? and ought it to be exercised only till the child can earn
money for himself? Partly, but not entirely, his influence is in
money. In theory, the parent has wisdom and goodness beyond
the child. If he has not, he ought not to be a parent.

In proportion as a parent has wisdom and goodness to fulfil
the part he has undertaken, he will, naturally and essentially,
have the affection, the respect of his children. But, if circumstances are such that present wisdom and goodness *cannot* exist
in the relation of parent and child, the parent must not expect
respect and love. For instance, suppose a parent, in ignorance,
undertakes the relation of a parent, and is not conscious that,
not having learnt, he cannot teach, or superintend the teaching,
of a variety of things necessary to well-being for his child. If he
finds that the arrangements of society, and the wants in himself,
or rather *her*self (for all this applies much more to the mother),
of which she was not conscious, impede the well-being of the
child, let her see *this truth*, viz., that it is not possible for the
child to love and revere her, though she be good, and would
gladly do anything possible to her, in the way of active work or
passive self-sacrifice and endurance for her child. Let her find
comfort in accordance with her God, in the lesson she has
learnt. There is still a possibility of wisdom and righteousness
for her, relative to her circumstances, though perhaps not one
which will engage the affection of her children. What has been
said is true in reference to *most* families of the upper class now,
though, of course, it varies with individuals.

If it appears that mothers cannot teach, nor superintend the
teaching of, nor regulate life for, their unmarried daughters, let
us look what *should* be the fate of these. As things are now, at all
events, they cannot go out alone into the world as men can.

This brings us to the difference between men and women,
which would lead us too far. But thus far we may safely say, that

the difference is physical; that the woman, in consequence of this, required help and protection from the man; hence the difference has resulted. But man is not to work for woman, merely as a personal defender – one man for one woman, or one man for a family. This was so in earlier times, but cultivation of the whole nature is to do the work which then was for the strong arm. It is the remains of uncultivation, of want of good exercise, in consequence of which woman cannot go about freely, where man's arm is not known to be ready to defend her.

Any way in which the daughter can be helped to facility in doing well that, or those things which she has a natural attraction to do, will lead her to happiness, provided, however, that her whole nature be so cultivated and exercised that what she does, she does *in sympathy with God and man*, or, at all events, in sympathy *with* God and *for* man. If she has this, she may live for the present without sympathy *with* man (though this is sure to come in the course of existence; the other is food to live, this may be waited for).

But is it possible to provide the circumstances, the exercise of the nature for a daughter, which will do this? We know not, we can only say, without this the essential of well-being is wanted. We would *tend* to this as much as possible, if unable to realize it. There are institutions which would seem direct means for the practical part of such an object; they should be accompanied with an endeavour to engage the whole of man's nature in a recognition of the God, who calls upon us to accord and to work with Him. By appealing to the reason, to the feelings, to the conscience, by practical work in accordance with the appeal, we would, if we could, strive to make the daughter 'one with man and with God'.

SECTION VIII

Why should any one be shocked at this? What we have said amounts only to this, that unmarried women should have every facility given them by parents to spend their time and faculties upon any exercise of their nature for which it has an attraction, which can be pursued in harmony with God, which can answer, in short, any good purpose. To know how to do well anything which has, or which leads to a good purpose for man, will be security for an existence worth having. To facilitate such an existence, then, should be the object of a parent. Many difficulties arise in the consideration of this question. What is good purpose for man? will be one of these questions, one where the parent and child will be apt to differ.

The parents have the child's education in their hands before the child can form any opinion for himself.

Educations may be comparatively better or worse, but no means exist now for a good one.

Let us consider children in the upper class of life. What is their education?

Ennuyés in the nursery, obliged to remain without any object but the amusement of the moment, as far as they can find it in their poor little selves, obliged to remain (a very limited number of children) always together, whether suited or not in character – who is their guardian and directress? Is it some one who has studied human nature to whom is given this most interesting and important charge? Has she an attraction for this employment? Is she wise and experienced in it? Have her heart and conscience sought it? No, it is a couple of nursery maids (making and mending the lady's or the children's clothes,) who sit there to prevent the children hurting their bodies. They are to jump up if a child is in danger of falling or burning itself, or otherwise doing itself or its companion bodily harm. But if, with nothing to do, with perhaps unsuitable dispositions, these poor children quarrel and mar their *dispositions*, the two nursery maids had generally better sit still, for in such circumstances the children *must* be cross and tease one another. Interference on the parts of the nursery maids would only do harm, they had better mind their work, in extreme cases only calling out, 'Master Johnnie, don't teaze Miss Eliza so'. These innocent helpless victims to ignorance, they *could* love, they *could* work, and how happy they might be; not in an infant school, with faculties stretched all alike, or nearly so, and for no object for which they themselves have shown an attraction, though this may be better than the nursery.

In the nursery nothing was taught, but afterwards comes the time for lessons, which lasts till children are said to be 'grown up'. What do they learn? What have they learnt when they are grown up? – when *re*-generated they *should* enter into possession of the conscious direction of a human being (till then more or less directed by others with more or less of conscious participation on the child's own part). When they enter into this vast possession, what have they learnt of God's laws, of the nature of God, of the nature of man, of his destination? Have they learnt to do any one thing well, with a comprehensive understanding of its nature, of its purpose? They know a good deal of history – but is it the philosophy of history? of languages – but is it the philosophy of language? they can play and sing – but does their music elevate either themselves or others, or send them forth to good things?

While direct teaching and the indirect teaching of circumstances is what it is, it seems of little use to speculate on what ought to be the vocations of women. Generally speaking, they have no vocation, no desire after anything; they read and play, and draw and talk, and are religious, and go to see sights, and go to church, and to hear music; they are dissatisfied, but they seek nothing better, and have no desire to seek anything better.

We are inquiring into the nature of the relation between parents and daughter, but while education or the want of it, *i.e.*, of *real* education, so fetters the nature, how can we judge of this relation, of what it should be?

It seems that part of the parent is to make worth having the existence which he is the means of beginning, and that a human existence worth having means one in which the person knows how to do well something which he has an inclination to do, which is in harmony with God's purpose of man's well-being. But literature, music and drawing, and fine needlework, do not answer this definition, nor visiting, nor sight-seeing, nor parish or school business, as *usually* done. Any of these objects *might* be pursued so as to make a life valuable to one who has an attraction for them, but not as they are superficially taught, not if so many of them are pursued that none can be done thoroughly, not if they are pursued for the purpose of mere selfish amusement – a *resource*, as it is called.

But what *can* the parents do? How can they help this? The means of teaching better do not exist. Many parents would eagerly grasp at them if they did.

He who would be a saviour to mankind must offer these means for instruction and for living a true life.

And when children *are* 'grown up' with their wings clipped, – their ideas, their instruction, the examples before them, all leading into the same path – is it likely that they should look out for any other? even if discontented in this? This is not satisfactory to them, but any other would be still greater dissatisfaction. If here and there one among parents is found who wishes something different, his children and society are against him. If here and there among children is found one who wishes to work at what he or she likes, and to learn how to do it, though in the sight of God it be an unobjectionable or valuable employment, society and generally the parents are in opposition to the child.

And what else can be expected of the parents, brought up as they were?

Another state of things quite as common as that of parents refusing to sanction the 'vocations' of their children – I had almost said more common, because fixed and defined vocations are comparatively rare in the present phase of life, is this:

Some young people have such determined sociability that they will contract friendship or marriage with any one, however inferior in moral or mental quality to themselves, rather than with none. There are young men who will marry any woman who chooses to marry them. Now, the best woman is certainly not she who chooses to marry a man; and, therefore, such a marriage is *sure* to present a wife far inferior in moral quality to the husband. There are young girls who will look forward every week of their lives to seeing some friend who as regularly disappoints their moral sense; yet *having no other friend*, they periodically hope and expect anew, and anew are disappointed. They marry in the same way. For such characters there is nothing but showing them a choice in variety, in order to save them from such deceptions.

There are 'vocations', if you choose to call them so, for sociability, friendship, and love, and marriage, just as much as there are 'vocations' for science, art, and administration.

Both kinds are often equally disregarded by the best parents. A mother incapacitated by ill-health, over-work, or a retiring disposition, maintains almost a solitude in the home. Sons who are in business or a profession are often just as much dependent as the daughters, upon whom they see at home, for whom they shall marry. It is impossible to say, the mother *ought to* 'take a house in London', to go to 'parties', to 'make society', for which she has such a distaste, and which is, without doubt, in itself so unsatisfactory, in order to enable her children to have friends and to marry. Yet not the less true is it that her children are cut off from satisfactory loves and friendships by her way of life, which virtually determines theirs, just as much as if they were forced into convents. What is natural to her they must adopt, however unnatural to them. The children's 'vocations' are as much baulked in the one case for marriage, as in the other for employment. I know not which is the more unsatisfactory aspect of the family; for the better mother is generally the one we have now described; and to see the imperfection of a mother's relation, we must, as we have said, see her in a good form. But no mother, however good, considers her children as anything else but her property. If she would have permitted their 'vocations', and they have none, she says, how *she* is disappointed. If, on the other hand, they have 'vocations', and she will not sanction them, she says, what can they want more than she has given them to make them happy? The mother's feeling is, more or less, always a selfish one; she refers everything back to herself. The child is her *thing*.

It is often said, we do not know what a wife's and mother's feelings are. I say *they* do not know what ours are. They do not know what it is to give one's life's work for man, and never to look for a return of affection, nor even to wish that one's labours should be acknowledged by those they were for.

To return. The good Roman Catholic 'director of conscience' is much more awake to the fact of what he terms 'a vocation for the world' (which 'world' does not mean that which is worldly) than we are; and he takes care neither to thwart nor to neglect it, nor to leave it unguided.

There are different ways of finding fault, both with oneself and with other people. To see the truth must be desirable; but we know that, whatever is – evil as well as good – is through God's laws. Most inconsistent with such a belief would it be, while disapproving, to condemn, to feel harshly towards those who, in ignorance, wander in the dark, though the sun is in the sky, who take sickly food, leading to numberless diseases, though the food is within reach which would supply the joys of health.

If all this evil were not, God would not be the object of our love, our trust, our veneration. His nature, His will which springs from His nature, His law which springs from His will, would not be, as they are, perfect – perfect in willing that mankind shall attain excellence of nature and consciousness of truth by exercise, His law furnishing the means and inducements.

Let us rejoice and bless God, with our eyes open to the evils around and within us. All we suffer, and see suffered, all the melancholy privations we feel and see, are voices telling us these things.

SECTION IX

Concerning the relation of parents and children, it seems impossible to say anything comprehensively true, which refers to general arrangements of society, founded upon such a narrow view. The only comprehensive view of what the various relations of life ought to be, in order to effect the well-being of mankind, must come from comprehending the nature and purpose of the will, whose manifestation is the universe.

What, in His view, *is* the well-being of mankind?

How, in His view, can it be effected?

When men and women set about a mode of life, or relations in life, do they refer to these questions?

In the 'lower classes', the men and women seek a livelihood, if single; if united, the objects are – for the man, a wife to help and make his house comfortable; for the woman, a homestead; at the cost of having children, whom they must maintain till these can maintain themselves. Some vague hopes and fears of religion, some affectionate feelings to each other, are intermingled. But, to these poor people, can there be any type of life which they are aiming to fulfil?

The 'higher classes' are as little pursuing any type, as little inquiring after the purposes of God in human life and society. To live in as high a degree of the conventional life, in which his purse and his circumstances place him, as that purse and those circumstances will permit, is taken for granted as the object of a man in the higher classes. He varies it in some slight particulars, but, in the main, conventionality lays down his life, spends his time and his money for him. Religion and the affections and benevolence have a part, but conventionality, we might almost say, settles *what* this part is to be in his life.

In whatever science it is, if we start from a fundamental law, progress is made. It took six thousand years to discover the law of gravitation, but to what discoveries has it not led? The source for the organization of social life is knowledge of the nature of God, which leads to knowledge of His purpose.

And where is this knowledge to be sought? In the Bible? In the Church? In the Fathers?

In the history of material phenomena and of consciousness, which will reveal to us the nature of God and His purpose, which purpose it is for us practically to realize.

But we must have some general idea of what we are

attempting to realize. The ants on an ant-hill look to us as if running to and fro with no purpose; but each has his purpose ingrained into him by instinct. We are, as to man's view moving about with the will of the moment; it may be with purpose for the day or something more; but with no purpose springing from a principle, that principle springing from eternal universal truth. To the view of God, indeed, there is purpose in all man's movements, as much as in the movements of every ant on an ant-hill. For the movements, which are ignorant and purposeless in man, are organized by His law to lead to knowledge of truth and to right purpose.

The question, what is the relation between parents and daughters? must lead us very deep. It is easily answered thus far.

The parents summon the daughter into existence.

It is their part, as we have often said, to facilitate to the daughter whatever will make her existence most worth having, in *the view of God*, – for this must be most really worth having.

But this is saying little in general cases, – for daughters, brought up in conventional life, seldom wish for anything else. A few of peculiar nature, or peculiar circumstances, mothers or daughters, are urged, either by suffering from the trammels of conventional life, or by feeling the want of opportunity to learn what they would do, if they could, to wish for something springing from a truer foundation than conventional life.

It is for these sufferers to lead the way, if they can. It is not necessary for *all* to suffer. Some through suffering must find out truth; but, when found, its loveliness will attract others.

If life, springing from the true principle, from knowledge and consciousness of God's purpose, were presented in practical existence, it would be so congenial to human nature that it would attract those who are feeling dissatisfied, though they know not why; and thus truth in life, in the organization of society, would advance. On that foundation only can it make any real or important advance. In vain do fathers and mothers suffer and complain of their children, in vain do children complain of their parents, masters of servants, servants of masters, husbands and wives, of their unsuitable wives and

husbands; all these disappointments and sufferings in the relations of society must continue till society springs from a true
foundation, *the nature of God*, – till it pursues a true type, which
the comprehending and feeling the nature of God will reveal.

The partial improvements which are made now cause the evil
to be more felt which lies at the core. More teaching (we will
not say, better education), is given to the working classes; but
they have no fundamental principle opened to their view. They
can read and write and understand grammar and astronomy,
and political economy. This last does give some principle as to
the nature of life, but not a sufficiently comprehensive one, not
a divine one. All this makes them ambitious to rise, as they
think. But where? What *is* rising? Perhaps there was more
conscientiousness, less selfishness before, except where sensuality got hold of a man. There is now less drinking, more ambition
to rise (as rising is understood) in society, than formerly. In the
'upper classes', people are infinitely better taught various things.
But the better things are taught in detail, without a principle
being understood or felt. *For what purpose are they learnt?*

The schools of design? The teachers dwell much on the
progress of the women especially. They have greater aptitude. It
was expected that, though they *began* better, they would fail
somewhere in their course when compared with men. Teachers
do not admit to this. They think from their experience, that all
can learn, if well taught, though, of course, with decided
differences of degree in aptitude for learning. Most decided is
the progress in the means of teaching drawing to women. Here
is an improvement which cannot be doubted, viz., the drawing
from models and from nature (not from copies), of which mode
of instruction, 100 years ago, there was not, perhaps, an instance for women, and which is now to be found organized in
almost every large town in England. What does this portend? It
might lead to the spiritual. But, at present, it has not, in general,
any connexion with it.

Such improvement is but urging on an evil crisis, resulting
from the want of a principle, an evil less felt while people had
less capability.

We have been sick at heart with our own faults and those of our friends. We feel more and more how such faults are the natural growth of the soil. Modify it, its productions will vary – will be better or worse, according to the soil whence they spring. Thus God gives power to man.

It is curious to consider each man's *possibility* at any given moment. He has certain physical possibilities. A certain weight (not an atom more) he could lift. With a certain degree of speed (not the unimaginable part of a degree more) he could run. As definite are his possibilities of thought, of feeling. What do these last depend upon? It signifies little whether we say, 'brain', 'nerves', or 'we do not know'. If it is brain and nerves, still we do not know. Because we know something about muscles, etc., in the physical frame, still we know not how these bring about the effects which are brought about.

The only real answer to the question, 'On what depend each human being's possibilities of every kind at any given moment?' is 'the laws of perfect wisdom, goodness, and righteousness'.

To return. A true understanding of the nature of God and man, of our relations to God and to our fellow-creatures, depends upon, requires the right exercise of, the whole nature of all mankind. We can only have such right exercise by a right organization of society, by mankind arranging circumstances so that they will have employment, work, suited to their natures, suited to call forth their natures into right exercise.

But, through the wisdom of God, man has all this to find out for himself, with such help as the laws of God supply, which is all that it is possible for the God who is wisdom to do for us.

These objects, which we have to find out, mutually help each other. To understand the nature and purpose of God will assist us rightly to organize society and to arrange its work; to understand the nature of man will also help us in organizing his social arrangements and his work. On the other hand, in proportion as man's social arrangements and his work are right, God's nature and his own will be more and more revealed to him, better comprehended, more truly felt by him. We must work on, recollecting that we *must* see and know imperfectly

God's and man's nature, while our social arrangements are imperfect, – that our social arrangements *must* be imperfect, while we know God and man imperfectly. Hence we must be careful not to dogmatize, remembering that the light by which we work is imperfect, though more and more is attainable, whenever we work for it in a right direction.

How great is Thy wisdom who keepest silence, excepting in the never-silent voice of law, and excepting in those voices, those human voices, inspired by Thee, in accordance with law! If we complain of want of companionship, the want is only temporary, and, like all other wants, may be supplied by our own work. As, in the course of eternity, we improve ourselves and our fellow-creatures, God will more and more dwell in us and in them, will speak to each through others; for no two are alike. Each, therefore, will be able to give and receive, to give to others some light from God which others have not, to receive from others some light from God which he has not. We are to have the voice of the One Perfect, ever the same; the varied voices of all mankind; but for both we are to work. Both will be heard, only in proportion as man works; and, in proportion as man works aright, one and the same God will be recognized by all; for truth is one.

While our God is taken from the Bible, a collection of books, written by different people, – from the Church, composed of different natures, living in various circumstances, the notions of religion must vary. The old Mahometans,[62] perhaps, varied little, for they went by one book, written by one person.

When we go by the revelation God makes of himself, we may differ, indeed, as astronomers differ, while reading, by imperfect light, the book of God in the heavens. But more and more of indisputable truth will be revealed.

In religion, which comprehends all truth, as in the various kinds of truth which compose religion, there must be teachers and leaders. Every man will not go to the fountain head to work out his own religion. It will not suit all natures to do so. No man can feel for another, or think for another vicariously; but one must supply for another that which will call forth thought and feeling. How carefully, how earnestly, then, should those work who have the nature which disposes them to work out what religion is!

These are difficult times, certainly, in which to work at spreading a truer revelation of religion than exists, and at improving the organization of society; for there is no loud or general call for either. There is an inclination to go back to the old forms of religion in Roman Catholicism, or to stick to the ease and well-doing of the English Church, and to keep up protection by Articles; or, because to some the error of these two courses is evident, to throw off all religion.

It is true that speculation is going on, as lists of books show, but not with much earnestness, as if life and hope depended on it. With some exceptions, it is more as an intellectual interest.

And the same of social arrangements. There is much discontent, though no definite demand for a better thing, which is looked upon as impossible.

The improvement of religion and society must go together. There can be no high tone and object in society, except from a true understanding, a true feeling of Him who brought man into life, of what His object is, His law for effecting His object. Nor, while we live poorly, can we comprehend the nature and purpose of the Highest, nor our own.

To offer, whether by words or work, help which is not sought, is difficult. Each family, or, at any rate, most families, suffer more or less, but not enough to make something else than the life which they live, sought for; besides, most find relief and pleasure in the outward. But a mother's situation now requires the impossible. Before she was a mother she had no means of learning how to fulfil its requirements, and, if there were means, to learn or to practise all would be impossible. What is she to do? Her best plan would be to have a pursuit of her own; with her family, if any of them like it; without them, if they don't or can't do it, like Mrs Fry or Mrs Chisholm.[63] But then what a cry the world makes!

SECTION X

All this is indefinite.

For no question can be studied comprehensively without embracing other studies, with which, in the nature of things, it is interlaced.

The nature of God is at the foundation of every subject. None can be rightly appreciated, none rightly applied in practice, unless the understanding and feeling of the nature of God is at the foundation of the study and practice of it. But we must study the nature of God in other natures, in which He has manifested and revealed His own. Thus, our ignorance, our want of feeling of the nature of God checks our improvement in social organization, makes our social habits wanting in a principle, in a foundation. What fundamental principle *can* there be but a reference to the nature of Him whose nature constitutes what well-being *is*, – to the law of Him, through a *certain manner of keeping whose law* alone well-being can be? By a certain manner, we do not mean an arbitrary manner; we mean *the* manner which is in accordance with wisdom and right. As certainly as from the invariable law of gravitation, if kept by a man in one way, he is dashed down a precipice, if kept by him in another way, he stands in well-being firmly on the earth; so certainly is his well-being regulated, with respect to every part of his being, by the *mode* in which he keeps those laws, which *not* to keep is not in his power.

The relation between parents and daughters, its nature, and how practically it should be worked out – how is this to be referred to the nature of God? How are we to find answers to the questions, 'What is this relation in principle, in theory', and, 'How is it practically to be worked out in life' from a study of the nature of God?

A mother was heard to say, when it was a question, whether

one of her daughters should go to a distance, for the sake of prosecuting a work upon which she was intent, 'It cannot be, because it entails the other staying at home, if I am not to be left alone'. *If she is not to be left alone?* If the purpose of God in bringing female children into the world is, that one woman shall not be left alone, then she was right in saying this, and this way of thinking was just and correct. But since then she has widely altered her views as to the purpose of God in causing that a woman 'be born into the world'.

Granted, that we discover, from observation and from experience, that, whatever is, is according to invariable law; that this law bears the impress of an invariable will; this will the impress of an invariable nature; granted, that we trace this nature to be benevolence, love, wisdom, righteousness, – we have then to inquire, not merely 'what do people say and do?' or, 'what do books say?' but how far is what people say and do, what books say, consistent with the purpose of benevolence, which wills well-being to the sentient part of the universe, which wills that the non-sentient part of the universe should be adapted by the sentient to its well-being? and what, that has not been said by people or books, may yet be consistent with *that will*?

Man must, then, come to observation and experience, to reveal to him what this relation between parents and daughters should be, in order to be thus consistent. What are the laws of human nature? In accordance with what mode of keeping them is human nature's well-being?

Observation and experience will reveal to him that the exercise of the faculties of the human being in *certain modes* constitutes happiness; he will discover how the benevolence of God works through and by human nature (thus giving human nature the happiness of such work), yet leaves it to human nature to discover what the work is to be, and how to do it. Otherwise there would not be the exercise which, in the view of wisdom, constitutes happiness. Thus he would see the parents constituted guardians, that the daughter shall have the organization, the development, the education, the opportunity, to exercise her faculties aright, *i.e.*, according to the nature of the human being and of her own individual idiosyncrasy. Thus, in the general, would be revealed the relation of the parent to the child.

As to the relation of the child to the parent, it would be the natural flow of sympathy, affection, gratitude, respect, appreciation for the parent for the right exercise of that guardianship.

This mutual relation would not involve that the parent and child should live together, work together, or that they should *not*. This would be according to their characters, their circumstances, according to whether or not they mutually found the best exercise for their faculties, the best purpose for their faculties, in living and working together. *Neither* would wish it, if it were not so. *Both* would wish it if it were. But the love, the reverence, the gratitude would exist from the child to the parent, whether they lived and worked together or not. The child's wish to promote the happiness of the parent would be one of the wants, the appetites of his life; but he would know that he could not promote the parent's happiness except by right and appropriate exercise of his own nature, for a purpose in sympathy with God's nature. The nature of God involves that this guardianship shall belong to the parent, that the response to it shall belong to the child.

Does not my son at this moment make me much happier than if he and I tried to live and work together? Does not he love and respect me more than would be the case if we tried to do so? This is admitted in the case of sons, but not of daughters. It is almost a proverb that sons and mothers 'get on the best together'.

But as things are now, few daughters *will* wish not to live with their parents, in order to have the saving of trouble, of effort, of responsibility, which prevents certain *dis*-satisfactions, if it does not give satisfaction. And the difficulties for a woman to exercise her faculties up to the best of her possibility, and for her best purpose, are great, even if both parents and daughter desire that she should do so, while society is regulated by conventionality, not by reference to the nature and purpose of God.

If mankind were set upon organizing society by such reference, modes of life would be almost entirely different from what they are now.

As to the present, all that the parent can do is to give all possible facility to the daughter to learn, if she is inclined, some mode of exercise of her faculties, which will be in harmony with God's purposes, and which will be in harmony with her own individual idiosyncracies (by which God marks His purposes), and afterwards to facilitate as far as possible her practically using what she has learnt.

'I have been a daughter living with parents whom eternally I shall love with the tenderest affection, whom I shall honour with sincerest respect; they were unselfish, conscientious, religious, had excellent abilities, most affectionate hearts. I was by nature conscientious, religious, affectionate; both they and I had active spirits for work, loving spirits towards God and man to lead us to work aright. How was it that we made each other unhappy? Will it be permitted to us again to come together, and to prove our love? To make them happy was the ideal of my childhood; as to have a good influence on my children to make them happy, to love and be loved by them, was the ideal of my womanhood. I can do little for them, I can be little to them. They can but little love me. I would work, I would love, but I must live in solitary confinement with every appearance of social life and liberty around me. I say all this in love to all, especially to my dear and good parents, and husband, and children'.

Is this a fiction? Is it an unknown case? Is it a solitary case? or has it been said by hundreds and felt by thousands of good women in this generation?

Few indeed will be able to say or to feel what follows, though it is the truth.

'God is the source of my suffering, and I bless Him for it, – I know it is all right – I will try to learn my lesson'.

SECTION XI

We want to give that which the family *promises* to give and does not. We want to extend the family, not annihilate it. We want 'not to destroy, but to fulfil' the hopes it holds out – to supply the sympathy, the love, the fellow-feeling, the tenderness which it offers to supply and does not. Where is there such rudeness as in a family? Everywhere but in our own family our feelings are regarded. Now, we want to make a family where there shall be companionship in work, mutual attraction, love, and tenderness, we want to make *God's* family. We would not take away *any*thing, we would enlarge and multiply.

But where is there such absence of tenderness, such constant contention as in a family? and the oddest part of the thing is that everybody thinks it peculiar to themselves.

No, certainly, family does not answer its purpose, – (nor is it likely it should among five or six,) we want to make it do so.

The law of God seems to be to scatter; 'go forth and conquer the earth and possess it', He says. Marriage does this, sons do this. The only exception to this rule seems to be the unmarried daughters. *They* must stay at home – because in a half savage state of society it is taken for granted that men have injurious feelings towards women, therefore women must remain at home till they are married for the sake of protection, or till society is in such a state that they do not want protection. The only exception to this rule is when they are obliged to earn their own livelihood; then, when they have something to do, they are allowed to go forth, that is supposed to be a protection.

But the Exodus should always follow the Genesis. Generated by the parents, they should, when they are supposed to be *re*-generated, go forth, – but unfortunately then comes the Leviticus, a number of rules and laws must be laid down, because they always misbehave when they have gone forth.

We don't wish to force them *out of* the family, we only wish them to be where all their faculties will be best exercised, *wherever that is*. Surely it cannot be denied that these two things are necessary, viz., that we should come into free communication with mankind, so as to give us room for our sympathies to find a response, *and* that we should have all our powers called into the highest exercise. If these two things were, there would be happiness, because then we could find work and sympathies for ourselves.

SECTION XII

Daughters come into the world without their own consent. The law gives them nothing. God gives them their time and faculties. May they not have these? And if the life, which their parents and the other members of their family lead, does not interest them, does not exercise those faculties and employ satisfactorily that time, may they not use them elsewhere than at home, or would they be wrong if they sought to earn their own livelihood by them? It does seem unjust that, whereas, if they were to marry, their fortune might consist of thousands, they are not to have a farthing (*because* they don't see any body who tempts them to marry) till their father dies. The days of our years are threescore years and ten – and if, by reason of strength, they be fourscore years or fourscore and ten, the daughters may be fifty or sixty years of age when the parents die. And is it not hard, because the customs of conventional society forbid their earning their bread with their own faculties and time, without losing their caste, – and because they may not see any body whom they like well enough to induce them to earn their bread by marriage, that therefore they should have nothing, no kind of independence till their parents' death? Is this not a premium upon thoughtless marriage?

It will be said that marriage does *not* give the woman

independence. Thousands may be given her at her marriage, but the law gives it to the husband, *she* will not have half-a-crown of it; a married woman does not exist in the eyes of the law; she cannot sue or be sued; her husband gives her a cheque when he thinks right, or rather not when he thinks right; he *never* thinks it right – but when she bothers him. This is true, still has a married woman the command of money more or less than a 'daughter at home'? The law may be against married women, still they *have* very much of the disposal of their husbands' incomes, and daughters have not, of course, of their fathers', during their mothers' life time.

A daughter at home cannot even tacitly disapprove her parents' life, by not joining in it, for, if they disapprove *her* way of life, they will probably wish to discourage it in every way, even by disinheritance. Now she *ought* not to give up her share of what her father will distribute among his children, when he no longer wants it himself, viz., at his death, and, if he believes her wrong, he will probably think it right not to leave her anything. But, if she is *not* wrong, that will not be fair, and she is not justified in being *willing* to give up whatever share he would otherwise have given her. Therefore should not parents ask themselves, 'are the following facts true or untrue'? We have adopted the mode of life which suits ourselves, before our daughters exist, or before they are capable of having a prefer-ence one way or another. Perhaps this mode of life gives no interest to them, or perhaps all but one would choose it by preference, that one alone cannot. Are we to alter our mode of life to suit that one or anyone of our children? Certainly not. Are any or all of our daughters to be condemned to our mode of life which may exercise none of their faculties, and to be entirely dependent as long as we live, which may be till they are fifty or sixty years of age? Whatever parents intend to give their daughters if they marry, why should not they have when they come of age, deducting from it the cost of their maintenance at home, *if* they choose to remain at home?

But parents live in such a way that they *must* say, 'We can spend 300*l.* a-year on a house in town, but we can't give

anything like that to our daughters; it would be very incon-
venient'.

Yet perhaps for one of them the life in London has no
interest. Is *she* to have nothing because she cannot like what the
others like? The ordinary course of things is this. The parents
provide a common home, if the children like what is there –
well – if not, they have no resource. It often happens that one
daughter, who chances to have the same tastes as her mother,
may spend anything, because it falls in with the spirit of the
family; and another, who has a somewhat differing turn of mind,
nothing. Her life may be full of interests, but if she have not
those which her mother and sisters have, she must have none.

It is said, first, that it is much better for a family to bear and
forbear themselves, and if one *is* a little different from the rest,
the lesson of self-denial is the best exercise which can be given
her, better than 300*l*. a year. Can *any*body follow his own
fancies in this world? Secondly, that not only the daughters will
be all the worse for the money given them, but everybody else
too; they will build almshouses, perhaps, or something worse.
And thirdly, that the scheme is an impossible one to carry out,
for any income, however large, would be broken up in this
manner.

Yet if a daughter wished to build an almshouse with her
share, more shame for the parents not to have taught her better
political economy; but they would have no more right to
prevent her than if she were a married woman, *so long as* she did
not trespass upon her sisters' right. If indeed *one* should have an
object, which was so heartily recognised by all, that all should
wish that a large sum should be given to it, *that* again would be
quite fair. But otherwise, each must keep within her own share.

But the real difficulty is this: there are not three women in a
hundred who have any object. Women are like the slaves; they
do not wish for their liberty, and they would not know what to
do with it, if they had it. They are very uncomfortable, and they
don't know why, and think that they would like to marry. Few,
if they were set free to-morrow, would know what to do with
themselves. One might be an artist, for which she has all the

powers; another a moral philosopher; a third a sister of charity. But as to most, – if they *had* their time and their faculties, what could they do with them? First give them their faculties; for, at present, how many women are taught well enough to do anything?

But *how* is a parent to make an unmarried daughter independent? The Duke of —— gave his daughters 10,000*l.* when they married, that is 300*l.* a-year; they probably each cost him very nearly that at home. Deducting their dress and maintenance, what would they have had left, even if he had given his single daughters the same as his married ones? Another rich man gave his daughter 5,000*l.* when she married, that is 150*l.* a year. If he had given her this when she came of age there would have been *nothing left, after deducting 100l.* a year which he did give her for her dress, and what she cost at home. Most girls actually cost their parents as much at home as they do when they marry.

But is it not extraordinary that parents should like to live in such a way that daughters *must* marry, or wait till their death, in order to carry out any of their plans which require money, or to be independent at all? Daughters cannot, however, *claim* the money. But their time and their faculties they *ought* to claim. What objection can there be, in the minds of good parents (the only case we are now considering) to their having these?

But they would not know what to do with them, when they had them. If parents did not make their claim upon the whole time of their daughter, to dictate how it should be spent, in entertaining the company, sitting in the drawing-room, driving out, reading aloud, cultivating accomplishments, visiting the poor people, what would she be doing? Her drawing, her music, her intellectual work, her interests (not very deep) in the people around her, her flirting, her reading to herself, and her outward things. She had better fritter herself away, as 'the law directs', (that is, the parents), than as she herself directs. There is less of the selfish element in it.

Let us look at the relation of parents and child. When people marry, they summon human beings from the Unseen World into existence, – no power existing in the hands of the latter to accept or refuse it, – consequently no stronger bond of responsibility (to make that existence a good to the child as far as lies in the parent's power) can be imagined than that between the parent and his conscience, his feeling, his sense of what is reasonable. Now it is taken for granted that an unmarried daughter, when grown up, is wrong not to devote her time, her capability, to the life, the circumstances, arranged by her parents before she was born, or while she was still helpless and incapable of forming a wish. To marry, or to devote herself to these circumstances, are the only alternatives in which she can enjoy the approbation of her parents. Parents, in general, are sincerely and earnestly desirous of the happiness of their children. If a marriage, which they think for the good of their child offers, they rejoice; they would be shocked at the idea of refusing it, in order that their daughter's society or work might not be lost to *them*. But with anxious interest for their daughter, they refuse her pursuing any path of life except that laid out by them (if she does not marry), because they fear for her the condemnation of the world, which takes for granted that to follow her parents' path of life is to do 'her duty in that state of life unto which it hath pleased God to call her', for 'God' substituting 'Mr and Mrs ——'. The parents plead with *her*, indeed, the hardship of her not giving them her society, her co-operation in carrying on, in the way they approve, the details of the life they have established. They are disappointed, complain that she is discontented, if she does not enjoy this life.

Let us look at these two alternatives, marrying, and living a life, the details and interests of which are regulated by her family.

God has instituted marriage, but apparently as matter of choice. It is not to be concluded that every human being will feel the desire to marry. He whom we love and revere above all mankind, whom we *call* our example, lived to mature life without marrying, and does not appear to have desired it. God and mankind so filled his soul that he appears not to have wanted more particular and individual interest.

To the generality of mankind, however, it will not be

doubted that married life will and ought to have most of interest and enjoyment, provided it be a marriage of attraction, of suitableness on both sides.

But, for a woman of high nature, for one who *has* sought to make an example of Christ, in devotion to God and mankind, what will be the opportunities of marrying, with suitableness of purpose in life, with attraction to pursue that purpose together? Whom will she see? Those whom her parents like and who like them sufficiently to visit in their family. How will she see them? Not at work, where his and her capabilities are drawn forth and attractions manifested. Men and women (unmarried) meet *only* in idleness, in the present age. Where will she see them? Under her parents' and companions' eye, where the eager game of marriage is played, where, in the thoughts of many, it is uppermost, as she knows, and where there is no work interesting enough to divert their thoughts from it.

Let us now suppose the other case of a woman living with her parents and brothers and sisters. It is not, *a priori*, to be calculated upon that their tastes and interests will coincide, like the triangles of Euclid's fourth proposition; and for this reason, that the law of God in the characters of mankind appears to be variety, not repetition. There is, therefore, the strongest reason why a family cannot develop itself to perfection within the walls of one home. With sons it is thought out of the question. Three or four living at home all day is a state of things never seen, never desired. Each must follow a career of activity out of home. But what an alternative it is for a woman!

The ordinary expectation, the eager desire of most mothers is that the daughters should find other homes by marrying. This desire may be suppressed and concealed by the mother, perhaps even from herself; but there is no excitement so strong to a woman as that of marrying her daughters, except that of marrying herself. And this, whether she be a good and affectionate or a worldly and ambitious mother, is a mother's first interest. In the former case she generally feels the insufficiency of home to satisfy the yearnings of the young nature, for which she has perhaps unthinkingly undertaken to find food other than the daily meals; in the latter case she desires it, because it is the only field where she can exercise the talents and desires which a statesman exercises in the House of Commons, a lawyer at the bar.

But how very few are the opportunities which a woman has for seeing any variety of character, or for knowing intimately the characters she does see in mankind! This is so completely acknowledged that it would be wearisome to dwell on it.

May we not then take into consideration the case of a woman living at home with her family who does not wish to marry any of the few with whom she has a superficial acquaintance? Is this likely to be such a very extraordinary case?

Now the father and mother formed their habits and modes of life, as we have said, before she had a character and inclinations at all of her own, without any reference, therefore, of course to her. Sisters differ notoriously in character from each other. Take any family. If the question were asked (and answered with sincerity) would, in most cases, any one sister like the idea of living with all the rest? Would not the answer to such a question be, in general, an acknowledgment that it was well such and such an one married, they 'could not have lived together'? But, perhaps, one or two or three remain, and of these one or two or all may be of character not disposed to adopt the life chosen by the parents to suit their own characters; may be of character finding little sympathy from any inmate of the home (not from any thing wrong in any of the party but), because of God's law of variety. Is man to make a counter law and say, they shall all be confined to the same pursuits, the same society? Why? Because it will be cruel to leave the parents; those very parents who would rejoice, probably, beyond any thing that rejoices them, in a marriage which pleased them, for this daughter who must not leave them. Did they bring her into the world to be their bounden slave as long as they live unless they can be gratified by a marriage to their taste?

Take any 'daughter at home' of the richer classes. She has her food and her lodging and 100*l.* a year. What else? There is a great deal of money spent on a carriage, but suppose she never wishes to get into it. There is money spent on a cook and giving dinners; but, perhaps, she never wants to eat them or to see the people who eat them. What has she out of the fortune but dress and food?

How intense is man's ignorance of what happiness is! How earnestly people seek the circumstances which will make impossible for them that for which the type of human nature essentially hungers and thirsts! And how eagerly are stones sought for bread! This arises much, because people really do not know what God's happiness is, and what man's capability of happiness is. Perhaps multitudes of really good people go through this life without experiencing it. Indeed, those who *do* feel it are exceptions. *Enjoyment* is felt by very many, and this prevents the want of *happiness* from being felt. Man becomes satisfied, ceases to be *dis*satisfied, without his natural food. He takes stones for bread. Some cease to be dissatisfied by smoking and drinking. Perhaps this can hardly be called *satisfaction* to those who are most eager for it. Some find satisfaction in the outward, satisfy one part of their nature so that the other is stifled and no longer cries for or even wants food. To cry for food which one wants is grievous. To cry for food, not knowing *what* food one wants, is still more so. Not to *want* the food which the type of human nature *would* want, if without it, is more so still. Yet this last is the state of by far the larger proportion of mankind, including the 'easy' classes, as we may perhaps truly call them. This, indeed, is the state which people seek and approve for themselves and others. And what a hopeless state – till some Saviour strikes a chord which reveals to man what *is* his proper food by giving him a taste of it, or a consciousness of what that taste would be; for, by God's law, it is the appetite which is to lead to food, to determine *what* food. If, then, the appetite does not exist, or if it exists for that only which is not sustaining food to man's nature, how is man ever to become the realization of his type, except through such a Saviour?

Nothing in this age is tending to reveal (unless to cases of exception which one never can tell how to calculate upon, which sometimes indeed are pressed into being, squeezed into shape, by opposition of a particular nature to the general tendency), nothing, even in the best tendencies of the age, reveals what man's proper food is.

Probably, in the course of eternity, for each man, for each woman, there is an union, an exactly adapted one. Many will be formed which will not be the exactly adapted one. Man wants variety. Man wants concentration. By this union will the latter be secured, then for the former he may go forth into the universe. He wants one fixed companionship and he wants varying companionships. Thus will he have both. Except we be as the Father, 'we shall have this treasure in earthly vessels'. Two will form one in every instance, sooner or later.

In cases in general, the excitement between the two is partly the pleasure of being an object of interest, – the hope of affection (that can scarcely be called affection which exists with so slight an acquaintance, as in many cases, or after long acquaintance, as in many others, where they remain indifferent for years, then, qualities being just the same, all at once they become devoted to each other). Partly it is the common interest, between them, of the new eventful life in prospect.

What real love is we are almost unable to say. Can it be God's plan of bringing about that man shall have intimate companion-ship, as well as infinite variety, secured in the course of exist-ence? That these *two*, when the *right two* are united, shall throw themselves fearlessly into the universe and do its work, secure of companionship and sympathy in one instance, consequently (though ready and glad to take it, when it comes in any other form), not shrinking from any temporary absence from it?

But how few 'twos' gain together that which prepares them to do the world's work! The spirit is exclusive which brings them together; it is understood that there is to be no third.

In proportion as the interests and objects of affection are exclusive, it will not last on into eternity. When two are bringing different qualities, or partly the same, to bear upon a common object, and that God's object – ought it not to be this which suggests the question, shall we physically, mentally, affec-tionately, spiritually be one? When two meet each other at work upon an object interesting to both, – should not this be their introduction to love? Perhaps it will be said that the drawing room in which they meet *is* life interesting to both. But God is not often there. And He should have a part in that which attracts them to each other. God's purpose, as to the man and woman, is to effect an union of two spirits closer than with the rest – eventually each one probably is to have a real mate. The different work to be done, in *physical* human existence, requires a physical difference, it is clear. It would not be well that every human being should perform the physical part of a mother.

There are spiritual, affectional, mental, and physical attractions. It is plain that great and even good men have had physical attractions to little and not good women. In some minds exists an attraction to great talent, without the feelings being affected. To some the affections (no other part) are attracted. *All* these attractions should meet in the two who are to be peculiarly united, but it is daily experience that it is not so. If it were, and if, though there were differences in character, there was interest for the same work, and *that good* work, then would there be a real independence for these two. They would together devote themselves to God and man, to the universe. This would secure them *all* sympathies, in the course of eternity. But they would, at each particular present, be independent in having each other's sympathy, – trusting for every other.

A married woman's life consists in superintending what she does not know how to do. (1) She goes into the kitchen and orders the dinner, and tells the cook that it was very bad the day before, but she does not know how to tell her the way to do it right. (2) She goes into the larder and store-room. She does not know how much the servants ought to use. She is certain there is waste somewhere, but she does not know where, nor how to correct it. But she does her best. She tries to say authoritatively that 'she will not have it', and to convince the family that she knows that something wrong is going on. (3) She goes into the nursery, knowing nothing about young children, where she has a nurse with whom she is much out of sorts, because the nurse actually does not like 'mistress to come into the nursery when the baby cries'. Her life is spent in imposing upon the servants, in making them believe that she knows how to do things which she has to scold them for doing badly. (4) She goes into the school-room, because she thinks it right to see 'how the children are going on with the governess'. And something different is done because she is in the room, in order that they may never *look* as if they were doing nothing. (5) She 'looks in' at the poor school, because 'they want looking after', and the master 'requires a little stir now and then'. But the master knows, privately in himself, that he knows more than she does about a school. (6) She goes into the village to visit the poor people. And what is visiting the poor? Very like visiting the rich. We ask them how many children they have, and whether they go to school, and so on. We don't go for any purpose, but as we sit in the drawing-room, merely for the chance, not because we want to say something which they want to hear, or, *vice versâ*, because they want to say something which we want to hear, but for the chance of something turning up to say. That is part of the lady's business, – to tell the poor people that they are wasteful, – that they don't make as much out of 12*s*. a week as they might, in order to be comfortable, which is very true; but *she* cannot tell them *how* to make the most of 12*s*. a week; *she* does not know.

A young married lady asked the advice of a very intelligent woman, a great many years older, as to housekeeping, and she said, 'My dear, when I married, the first thing after we settled down at home was my cook coming to ask me how I liked to have the pig cut up, – I hardly knew that pork was pig, – but I said, cut it up your own way first, and if I don't like it, I will tell you my way'. This was thought so clever (and she was a very clever woman) the mistress *taking in* the servants in this way. Probably it matters little whether the lady's pig is cut up in one way or another. But it matters very much whether her time is cut up in one way or another. This is the way her life is passed.

The business of a superior is to tell others to do what she does not know how to do herself. How different it would be if she felt a confidence in herself that she knew what was to be done and how to do it, – and to do it well! How different would

be her whole life and happiness. But now, it is all disappointment, if she is wise; ungrounded security, if she is foolish. And
so she spends her days.

PART VIII

SECTION I

It is often said that we are to stay in the religion in which we
were born, to 'abide in the calling wherein we are called'.

Were we in geography or astronomy to take one book as our
final rule, our ultimate appeal, the same thing would happen
inevitably as has happened in religion. Some things in it we
should absolutely ignore, as when we ignore that Solomon said,
'Man is like the beasts that perish'; and of other things we
should say, 'he did not mean that – he meant something else'; as
when Christ says, 'Hate your father and mother, sell all, and
follow me'. No one would cry out so much as the bibliolaters –
'what a shame!' if we were to *do* it; but they say 'he did not *mean*
it'. Could we go on with such a system in geography or
astronomy?

As much as the Roman Catholics can believe that there will
be unity and infallibility, so do we. How can the preachers of
toleration of the present day say, 'take the religion which suits
you best', any more than 'it *may* suit your mind better to believe
that the sun moves round the earth, if so, take the belief which
you find best for you'? There may be a mind which, from want
of imagination, want of cultivation, cannot be made to apprehend that the earth is not an immoveable body, but one flying
through space; and it is true, therefore to say 'there are minds
which must believe that the earth is stationary *till* they are more

cultivated'. But unity in religion there must be one day, as surely as there is unity in astronomy. There is objective truth and untruth in religion, as in astronomy, and the well-constituted mind, by the exercise of its own powers, must and will come to this unity of truth.

It is a mistake to refer us to 'private judgment'[64] – those words are dangerous, because they seem to imply that one person may judge one way, and another another, according to their 'private' views of things, according as it 'suits their own minds', as the phrase is, whereas it is the truth, as it were, which *judges* for us. The principle of 'private judgment' ought to mean (if it means anything) that we are to search earnestly with all our mights for the truth, and that *that* is to judge, not that *we* are to judge. The principle cannot be too strongly laid down that there cannot be two truths, any more than two Gods. There can be but one truth; it cannot vary to suit the minds of each. There is but one truth, and we have to find it. The Roman Catholics say, truly, there is but one truth. But some say that we are to find it in the Bible – some that we are to find it in the Bible and Church together. Comparing the churches, some say that we are to find it in the Roman Catholic church, others that we are to find it in the Church of England, and some that we are to find it in the Roman Catholic church *or* in the Church of England – they are not quite sure which. But we don't want to ask the church. We want to ask God. But God tells different people different things. So it was in astronomy. God has told Sir John Herschel a great many things which He did not tell Galileo, which it was not in Galileo's possibility to receive. Do we complain of this? We do not say that each is to take the system of astronomy which best suits his own mind. Are we not to strive to find out the truth in religion as we have been striving to find it out in astronomy? There is but one truth. Most dangerous is it to allow the belief that there may be two – that it is as our 'private judgment' judges best. God judges for us, and His truth it is which we have to find out. 'Private judgment' is not the question. It is God's 'judgment'.

There is a truth, and we must find it out. 'It is the truth for *you*', – we don't say this in medical science – we don't say 'only believe, – believe sincerely, and it does not signify what you believe – be but conscientious in your belief, that will do'. Religion is the only thing which is of so little importance that we can say this. In medical science, we say 'it is a matter of the utmost importance to health that you should discover the truth – search for it, then, with all your might; if you don't find it, there may be fatal consequences'. But in theological science, and theological science only, we do *not* say 'you must bend your whole faculties, to discover and earnestly search out the truth'. No, 'tolerance' says, 'if it be only your conscientious opinion, and if it suit the nature of your own mind, that will do'.

'But what test have we, if each man is to depend upon his own faculties?' it is said.

In sanitary science there is a test, – to make the body healthy. But this test does not exist for theological physicians, viz.: – to make the soul healthy. On the contrary. *They* are to say that the soul never can be healthy. It is as if the sanitarian were to say, 'You were born in such a state of disease that I can do nothing for you in this world. There is no hope of your ever being well. You will never get better here. Do not, therefore, expect it or strive for it. But I have to announce to you that, by some method which you cannot understand, by the death of a God a long time ago, you will be quite well in a state which comes after the time when you will be dead in this. Only believe this and you will be quite well *then;* – *here* you never can be'.

The essentials of religion are love and veneration and trust and duty. It may be that some will have less of these essentials of religion while believing one form of religion than another. Yet it will not do to say that 'that religion is true for *them*'. There is one truth, which is God's truth, and we have to find it out and to educate mankind to be capable of receiving it. But 'tolerance' says 'any religion will do which you yourself think a good thing'. Is it for me with my foolish thought to say what is a good religion? It is God's thought which I am to seek for. 'But that is the truth for you and this is the truth for me', it is said. 'If he only follows his private judgment, it is the truth for him'. It is not for him with his 'private judgment' to make a truth, – he has to find out what is God's truth. There is but one truth, which all have to find out, – there are not as many truths as there are private judgments and individual minds.

This, it is said, is to go back to the Roman Catholic Church, to 'turn back again to the only foundations of certainty, and lay once more' *in her* 'the basis of your faith'.

Rather it is to *go on* 'to the foundation of certainty, and to lay *at last* 'the basis of faith' which must be our object. It did seem no wonder, when men asked whether poor little babes were damned or not, and the Church of England said 'it was an open question', 'it did not signify, you might believe one way or another, as you chose', – it did seem no wonder that she thus sent so many earnest men, who thought that it did signify, into the Roman Catholic Church.[65]

The Roman Catholics say that the Church of England 'prevaricated in her answer'. She did not 'prevaricate'. She said, 'she did not know, – it did not signify!' The Roman Catholics say, 'ask Gregory what he would have said'. But we don't want to ask Gregory; we want to ask God.

Not through revelation do we find definite truth. Can there be anything less definite than what is called 'revelation'? or less definite than the doctrine which is to be found in it? It is not there that we can find certainty.

There are three ways as to religious truth. One is as if we said in physiological science, 'You may think for yourself, – believe conscientiously, – believe that such a system of medicine is right, – that boiling oil will cure gun-shot wounds, – that calomel will cure indigestion, – and then (it does not signify) you are safe'. Another way is to say 'there *is* a truth', and 'you will be damned if you don't believe it'. We do not say this, but 'there *is* a truth and you will find it out in time', – and it is of the very greatest importance to health that we should find it out.

But people now pique themselves upon not being startled at anything. They like to talk among one another. They make a merit of it that they 'wish to have other people's views'. They treat truth as an exercise of the intellect, not as something of the utmost importance, which is to be strained after and bought with our brow's sweat and our heart's blood. They like to 'hear people's arguments', they say. It is a titillation of the intellect, which is agreeable, – not a matter of life and death. Good men, learned men, senators, and men of action discuss together free-will, necessity, the origin of evil, God's purpose, the most momentous questions of man's destiny, and as they part to dress for dinner say laughing. 'You know *who* reasoned high –

> Of providence, foreknowledge, will, and fate,
> And found no end, in wandering mazes lost',[66]

and run off. It is a mere matter of intellectual amusement, this search into man's nature and God's nature. It would not have been so had it been a search into man's muscles and arteries.

'Unity' can only be attained through man exercising his faculties, not in *this* way, but in the way in which Archimedes and Newton and so many others set to work upon *their* sciences.

Infallibility can only be attained in the same way. Each (by exerting his own faculites) will learn of God who is infallible, the truth. The truth is discoverable, if we will bring our faculties to it as to any other truth. Is it not as infallibly true that a man must not have three or four wives, or that I am not to go into Mrs M's room and take a 5*l*. note, if I can find one, as that the earth moves round the sun? Does not all educated England believe the one as 'infallibly' as the other? Polygamy and theft are wrong as 'infallibly' as it is untrue that the earth is station-ary. Yet the Mahometan does not believe the first, nor did the Lacedæmonian[67] the second. These are discoveries as to the nature of man. These lead directly to discoveries as to the nature of God, which discoveries, when man applies his faculties to make such, instead of pinning them to a book, will be as remarkable as have been his discoveries in every other line. So, with the exercise of man's faculties, there will be 'unity'.

Suppose that, in nautical matters, we were to say 'I think *so*. You think otherwise. It would be very illiberal of me not to think that you may be right and I be right too. It is better that men should be of different opinions – let each man have his own. Let each take the opinion which suits his own mind and tolerate the other's'. Were this said in nautical matters, or were naval men to refer to a chart made in 1300, what would be the consequence? Yet thus it is in religious matters. There are two ways. The Roman Catholics say 'there must be unity', and they are right, for the want of unity results from some minds not having yet received the truth, not from there being *no* absolute truth. But they say 'there must be a church to maintain this unity and to interpret that book'. The other way is to say 'the more sects the better. Difference in religious opinions is good. Let *me* believe what I like and do *you* believe what *you* like'. This is called *liberality* or *toleration*. Religion is treated quite differently from anything else. We do not appoint a church or assembly in nautical matters, which is to be infallible. But men search and discover. The principle of searching is still unacknowledged in religious things. And as to the other way, it is simply saying that there is *no* 'truth'.

It is often wondered at that any one can be taken in by the claim to infallibility of the Church of Rome. But there is so much in saying that you are infallible. Faith can remove mountains. Faith in yourself does remove mountains. Those who speak with a tone of authority, mothers, doctors, are more than half believed for doing so. We cannot have this belief in the Church of England, because, if we were to go to her and say 'You are infallible', *she* would answer 'No, I am not'; while, if we go to the Roman Catholic Church and say, 'Mother, teach me, you are infallible', *she* answers, 'Yes, my child, I am'.

The principle of not leaving a church because you were born in it, is unintelligible. Error is error, whether you were born in it or not.

The argument is,

A church is a desirable thing,

All churches have defects.

Therefore remain in the church in which you were born,

And do not bring pain upon your family.

All churches are beset with difficulties. So is the Roman

Catholic Church – you do *not* say, 'difficulties more vital than the rest', but 'such as no one can overlook'. Is it not fair to conclude that you consider those of the Anglican Church as equal?

But most of all do we not want our God? Is he not our first want? The Roman Catholic's God is not ours. To live very closely with those who are all worshipping very fervently one God, while we are thinking about another, and that other not at all like theirs, is very painful. To have sympathy with our God, to be able to esteem Him is surely the first thing. And with the God who carries about houses in the night and opens and shuts a picture's eyes, we can have no sympathy. To live with those who are worshipping not at all fervently another God, still less like ours, because He is so far off and we are so very indifferent about him, is more painful still. The God of any church now existing is a different God from ours.

––––––––––––––––––––

PART IX

SECTION I

What is the groundwork of belief?

Many will exclaim, as if a religious belief were nothing, unless it were undoubting. To doubt is by many sincere religionists considered to sin. And, if indeed God had taken means to declare to us His nature and His purpose, so that only by wilful blindness we could doubt, to doubt *would* be to sin. That this is not the case is evident from the variety of opinions among those

who have sincerely entertained their belief. In this most important subject, this subject which is at the foundation of every
other, which is of a nature to influence every part of our being,
of our life, of our work, we are to work out the truth for
ourselves and for each other. If we were united in this search, if
we would try to live and to be, so as to come to the search in a
pure and elevated spirit, what truth might dawn upon our
hearts and our minds to bless us all!

The ground-work of belief, then, is this. With such capabilities as we have of heart and mind, with such glimpses of
knowledge as we have gathered, looking forth upon the universe
and all that it manifests, physical, intellectual, spiritual, we
discern indications which are not referable to man, nor to any of
the material beings which surround us, of benevolence, of a
benevolent spirit. The more we learn of the various sciences
which embody the laws of the universe, and the more we
understand their mutual relations tending to man's well-being,
the more our affectional nature and our intellect trace a
thought, a feeling, a purpose for well-being, for comfort, for
enjoyment in various modes of being. This cannot be denied.

At the same time, it is certain that while we perceive that
there are arrangements by which, in a healthy state of body,
there is comfort, there is liability to derangement which causes
suffering, and so throughout.

The laws which exist, if kept in a certain manner by all
mankind, would secure well-being, enjoyment. But it is an
impossibility that all mankind should so keep them.

What, then, shall we say when we look for consistency in the
character, – the purpose, – of the ruling spirit? Great power,
great benevolence, great adaptation of means to the ends of
benevolence we trace, and the more we learn the more we
trace. But we find that the inevitable ignorance of man stands
between him and the enjoyment he is capable of, besides
frequently causing intense suffering. May we not thus interpret
this difficulty? Experience shows us that mankind are capable of
making perpetual advances from ignorance to knowledge, are
capable of learning how to keep law aright (*i.e.*, so as to effect

human well-being). Sometimes, even before they are conscious of the law, they have learnt practically how to keep it aright. May we not interpret, then, God's thought to be this, viz., that mankind shall learn this law and how to keep it; that suffering and impediment to enjoyment for which humanity has capability arise from ignorance removable by humanity's efforts? One of the lessons of experience is that we cannot afford real help or benefit to others in any way, except by that which brings into activity some part of their being, or prepares for its activity. Is not this a hint to us, that it may be consistent with a perfect benevolence and wisdom to benefit us by calling our natures into activity? The cry of suffering man will be, sooner or later, man's benediction. The blissful spirit will also bless, for it will excite man to communicate, to lead on others to enjoy a being like its own.

On this ground-work of observation, reflection, and experience, do we found our belief that God is good.

- - - - - - - - - - - - - - - - - -

SECTION II

'We love Him, because He first loved us'. (1 John iv. 19.)

There is only one true ground on which to look for that love which is wanted to satisfy the divine nature in God or man. *Be* that which is true, good, wise, loving. Owe any love which you may receive to the appreciation, to the feeling called forth by truth, goodness, wisdom, love. If you owe affection to any other source, it is sure to turn into a scourge, in one way or other, at one time or other. To be loved is a natural want; but if you *cannot* be that which is truly loveable, even though you recognize what that is − if you cannot be where that is which will appreciate what there is in you of loveable, with a great magnanimity wait God's time. Man cannot wait for physical food beyond a certain time without ceasing to exist as a being of this

world. It may be that, without food, his affections will become
entirely imperceptible to others, unknown to himself. But they
cannot perish. Nothing indeed perishes. The physical framework
of man changes into other modifications of material being. But it
is ever matter, ever accordant with the laws of matter. We have
no experience of any material existence which has ever ceased
to be accordant with those laws which regulate what we mean
by *matter*. As to other modes of being, not less real – such as
thought and feeling – they also are imperishable. We recognize
them as manifested (not modified by matter) in *one* individuality;
we recognize them (modified by matter) in many individualities
forming one connected race, each individuality being influential
on every other.

Nourish yourself with love of truth, goodness, righteousness,
with reverence and admiration for wisdom, beauty, order,
wherever such attributes are made manifest. When love *to* you
springs from them, receive it, welcome it as your natural food;
but the only legitimate trying for it is by *being* that which is
fitted to attain it from the divine. You are in an attitude of
unnatural screw if you strive otherwise for it. Be wise as regards
God, and you will secure right relations as regards man, as far as
depends on yourself.

But I must vary according to the characters I am with; be
grave or gay, for instance, as suits my companionship, you say.

A real view of what *is* and a feeling consistent with it would
cause a constant flow of cheerfulness, arising from a spring too
deep for variations, *provided* the present is healthful to the
nature. But as it is God's will for man that he discover and attain
the circumstances, the organization of life, which are calculated
to call forth and exercise the divine in him, – in circumstances
not so calculated, it will not be well with him.

SECTION III

'God is Love'. (1 John iv. 16.)

It is all *one*, one unvarying principle from which spring ever-varying manifestations. The one invariable principle is indeed the spring of other invariable principles adapted to various modes of being. All, however, there is reason to believe, will prove traceable to one will – the will for the greatest degree and the highest kind of well-being (in the course of eternity) which are possible without admitting of any contradictory volitions in the mode of effecting it.

From perfect wisdom and benevolence springs the will for the various invariable co-existences and successions which are found to exist, the knowledge of which is attainable by man; and from this knowledge, which must spring from the exercise of his own nature, comes his power – his power to create, to develop, to modify. Nothing is destructible.

SECTION IV

There can be no cause for anything which exists, but that it is the will of the spirit of the universal, the righteous, the wise, the good. This spirit wills the same co-existences, the same successions through eternity. This we call law. Hence springs infinite variety. Hence springs development, evolution. There is nothing dull in the operation of invariable law. The universe varies throughout, in every part, in each present from every past. The Almighty never repeats Himself in His wonderful work. Yet His law, whence it springs, never varies. The thought, the feeling whence all springs are ever the same; the activity, His manifestation, ever varying. Is it dull to trust and love? Yet whom can we trust and love like Him, whose thought never varies, because it is always the thought of perfect love, perfect wisdom? Is it dull to work with certainty of success for every righteous wish, for those we love as well as for our poor selves? Yet what nature shall inspire such certainty as the one whose wisdom is such that in Him 'is no variableness nor shadow of turning'?

SECTION V

Oh! that again some one would cry, in a voice that might reach the human heart, 'Prepare ye the way of the Lord!'

'Woe unto Jerusalem' is a cry some read with a kind of religious feeling. We condemn those sinful Jews who crucified the tabernacle of that bright spirit. We have a sort of satisfaction in condemning them, as if thereby we were manifesting in ourselves a religious spirit; but suppose one says, Woe to London! Suppose one says, How much worse not to strive to save thousands from a crucified *spirit* than to crucify one body, thereby transferring that lofty spirit to some other reign of God's universe! Woe indeed to those who did it; their state must entail woe. But what is not entailed to multitudes by present modes of life, general even among those accounted the first of the land!

What, then, to do?

SECTION VI

Keeping to these principles – when the 'hour and the man' come, fear not to declare them and to strive to live and act them, but look to do it wisely, or the time when such truth shall be acknowledged and shall bless mankind is made more distant.

But is this time of materialism, of comfort and luxury-seeking, of conventionality, a time in which the apostle of such truth may hope that any will join him? Yes, thought and feeling are (and will be more and more) afloat, especially among women. Within half a century most decided is the change of the relations of women in society. Milton's expression of Eve's submissive devotedness to Adam is read with far different feelings now from what it was thirty years ago. What a general change there is in feeling!

Families are no longer monarchies. Household occupations are withdrawn from the middle classes. Yet, at the same time, servants educated in the best schools decline to scour. There is higher and higher mental cultivation and cultivation of the arts. Music and singing and drawing, passable thirty years ago, would not be produced now. But there is more discontent as well as more speculation. It *is* the time for a few among the speculative and discontented to listen to more enlarged views of religion and to a life consistent with these.

The word 'matter' invariably implies *limit*. The study of matter is the study of various kinds and degrees of limit, and of the development of these towards the unlimited. See the wisdom and benevolence of the Spirit of the Universe. In and through matter arise enjoyments which, without a contradiction, could not *be*, except with such a mode of existence. Some enjoyments are impossible except to the material, and these are both in themselves good, and also enhance the excellence of the spiritual being, towards which all is tending. The feeling of vigour after a cold bath is a thing with which we should be sorry to part with out of existence, and for which we thank God. This brings to our consciousness in a small matter that which we expect will prove true throughout, viz., that suffering is always to intermingle, to co-exist with enjoyment. We have not this delicious feeling of vigour, except after such a shock of cold as to make us shudder. Another truth seems to be that a wise care of the physical frame will not at all preclude great occasional efforts. An habitual care of the machine *for the purpose* of effecting its high end will *enable*, not *prevent*, its occasionally bearing great stretches, without lasting diminution of power.

And, when, having passed through the various limitations of matter, the limited merges, according to the thought of the All-wise, into that which is without limit, the unlimited thereby possesses an existence, the value of which could not otherwise have had the excellence which it possesses. For without a contradiction, thought, which has not been lived, realized, worked, exercised, cannot be, in worth, what life, reality, work, and exercise effect. And thus the Father and the Son are one, essential to each other's worth, essential to that excellence which even man thirsts to recognize in existence. Bravely then, oh man, accord with thy high calling! Be already one, in spirit, with the Unlimited to which thou art advancing. Do the hills, the woods, the tufts of heath, the active ants make the spirit of man to sing with joy? What shall it be, as limits, through work, extend themselves, and worlds and firmaments, and finally the universe, with its existence of past, present, and future, rises to our consciousness?

Cassandra[68]

'The voice of one crying in the' *crowd*, 'Prepare
ye the way of the Lord'.[69]

One often comes to be thus wandering alone in the bitternes of
life without. It might be that such an one might be tempted to
seek an escape in hope of a more congenial sphere. Yet, perhaps,
if prematurely we dismiss ourselves from this world, all may
even have to be suffered through again – the premature birth
may not contribute to the production of another being, which
must be begun again from the beginning.

Such an one longs to replunge into the happy unconscious
sleep of the rest of the race! they slumber in one another's arms
– they are not yet awake. To them evil and suffering are not, for
they are not conscious of evil. While one alone, awake and
prematurely alive to it, must wander out in silence and solitude
– such an one has awakened too early, has risen up too soon, has
rejected the companionship of the race, unlinked to any human
being. Such an one sees the evil they do not see, and yet has no
power to discover the remedy for it.

Why have women passion, intellect, moral activity – these
three – and a place in society where no one of the three can be
exercised? Men say that God punishes for complaining. No, but
men are angry with misery. They are irritated with women for
not being happy. They take it as a personal offence. To God
alone may women complain, without insulting Him!

And women, who are afraid, while in words they acknowledge

that God's work is good, to say, Thy will be *not* done
(declaring another order of society from that which He has
made), go about maudling to each other and teaching to their
daughters that 'women have no passions'. In the conventional
society, which men have made for women, and women have
accepted, they *must* have none, they *must* act the farce of
hypocrisy, the lie that they are without passion – and therefore
what else can they say to their daughters, without giving the lie
to themselves?

'Suffering, sad' female 'humanity'! What are these feelings
which they are taught to consider as disgraceful, to deny to
themselves? What form do the Chinese feet assume when
denied their proper development? If the young girls of the
'higher classes', who never commit a false step, whose justly
earned reputations were never sullied even by the stain which
the fruit of mere 'knowledge of good and evil' leaves behind,
were to speak, and say what are their thoughts employed upon,
their *thoughts*, which alone are free, what would they say?

That, with the phantom companion of their fancy, they talk
(not love, they are too innocent, too pure, too full of genius and
imagination for that, but) they talk, in fancy, of that which
interests them most; they seek a companion for their every
thought, the companion they find not in reality they seek in
fancy, or, if not that, if not absorbed in endless conversations,
they see themselves engaged with him in stirring events, circumstances which call out the interest wanting to them. Yes,
fathers, mothers, you who see your daughter proudly rejecting
all semblance of flirtation, primly engaged in the duties of the
breakfast table, you little think how her fancy compensates itself
by endless interviews and sympathies (sympathies either for
ideas or events) with the fancy's companion of the hour! And
you say, 'She is not susceptible. Women have no passion'.
Mothers, who cradle yourselves in visions about the domestic
hearth, how many of your sons and daughters are *there*, do you
think, while sitting round under your complacent maternal eye?
Were you there yourself during your own (now forgotten)
girlhood?

What are the thoughts of these young girls while one is singing Schubert, another is reading the Review; and a third is busy embroidering? Is not one fancying herself the nurse of some new friend in sickness; another engaging in romantic dangers with him, such as call out the character and afford more food for sympathy than the monotonous events of domestic society; another undergoing unheard-of trials under the observation of some one whom she has chosen as the companion of her dreams? another having a loving and loved companion in the life she is living, which many do not want to change?

And is not all this most natural, inevitable? Are they, who are too much ashamed of it to confess it even to themselves, to be blamed for that which cannot be otherwise, the causes of which stare one in the face, *if one's eyes were not closed*? Many struggle against this as a 'snare'. No Trappist ascetic watches or fasts more in the body than these do in the soul. They understand the discipline of the Thebaïd – the life long agonies to which those strong moral Mohicans subjected themselves. How cordially they could do the same, in order to escape the worse torture of wandering 'vain imaginations'. But the laws of God for moral well-being are not thus to be obeyed. We fast mentally, scourge ourselves morally, use the intellectual hair-shirt, in order to subdue that perpetual day-dreaming, which is so dangerous! We resolve 'this day month I will be free from it'; twice a day with prayer and written record of the times when we have indulged in it, we endeavour to combat it. Never, with the slightest success. By mortifying vanity we do ourselves no good. It is the want of interest in our life which produces it; by filling up that want of interest in our life we can alone remedy it. And, did we even see this, how can we make the difference? How obtain the interest which Society declares *she* does not want, and *we* cannot want?

What are novels? What is the secret of the charm of every romance that ever was written? The first thing in a good novel is to place the persons together in circumstances which naturally call out the high feelings and thoughts of the character, which afford food for sympathy between them on these points –

romantic events they are called. The second is that the heroine has *generally* no family ties (almost *invariably* no mother), or, if she has, these do not interfere with her entire independence.

These two things constitute the main charm of reading novels. Now, in as far as these are good and not spurious interests, let us see what we have to correspond with them in real life. Can high sympathies be fed upon the opera, the exhibitions, the gossip of the House of Commons, and the political caricature? If, together, man and woman approach any of the high questions of social, political, or religious life, they are said (and justly – under our present disqualifications) to be going 'too far'. That such things can be!

'Is it Thou, Lord?' And He said, 'It is I'. Let our hearts be still.

SECTION II

'Yet I would spare no pang,
    Would wish no torture less,
The more that anguish racks,
    The earlier it will bless'.[70]

Give us back our suffering, we cry to Heaven in our hearts – suffering rather than indifferentism; for out of nothing comes nothing. But out of suffering may come the cure. Better have pain than paralysis! A hundred struggle and drown in the breakers. One discovers the new world. But rather, ten times rather, die in the surf, heralding the way to that new world, than stand idly on the shore!

Passion, intellect, moral activity – these three have never been satisfied in woman. In this cold and oppressive conventional atmosphere, they cannot be satisfied. To say more on this subject would be to enter into the whole history of society, of the present state of civilization.

Look at that lizard – 'It is not hot', he says, 'I like it. The atmosphere which enervates you is life to me'. The state of society which some complain of makes others happy. Why should these complain to those? *They* do not suffer. *They* would not understand it, any more than that lizard would comprehend the sufferings of a Shetland sheep.

The progressive world is necessarily divided into two classes – those who take the best of what there is and enjoy it – those who wish for something better and try to create it. Without these two classes, the world would be badly off. They are the very conditions of progress, both the one and the other. Were there none who were discontented with what they have, the world would never reach anything better. And, through the other class, which is constantly taking the best of what the first is creating for them, a balance is secured, and that which is conquered is held fast. But with neither class must we quarrel for not possessing the privileges of the other. The laws of the nature of each make it impossible.

Is discontent a privilege?

Yes, it is a privilege to suffer for your race – a privilege not reserved to the Redeemer and the martyrs alone, but one enjoyed by numbers in every age.

The common-place life of thousands; and in that is its only interest – its only merit as a history: viz., that it *is* the type of common sufferings – the story of one who has not the courage to resist nor to submit to the civilization of her time – is this.

Poetry and imagination begin life. A child will fall on its knees on the gravel walk at the sight of a pink hawthorn in full flower, when it is by itself, to praise God for it.

Then comes intellect. It wishes to satisfy the wants which intellect creates for it. But there is a physical, not moral, impossibility of supplying the wants of the intellect in the state of civilization at which we have arrived. The stimulus, the training, the time, are all three wanting to us; or, in other words, the means and inducements are not there.

Look at the poor lives which we lead. It is a wonder that we are so good as we are, not that we are so bad. In looking round we are struck with the power of the organizations we see, not with their want of power. Now and then, it is true, we are conscious that *there* is an inferior organization, but, in general, just the contrary. Mrs A has the imagination, the poetry of a Murillo, and has sufficient power of execution to show that she might have had a great deal more. Why is she not a Murillo? From a material difficulty, not a mental one. If she has a knife and fork in her hands during three hours of the day, she cannot have a pencil or brush. Dinner is the great sacred ceremony of this day, the great sacrament. To be absent from dinner is equivalent to being ill. Nothing else will excuse us from it. Bodily incapacity is the only apology valid. If she has a pen and ink in her hands during other three hours, writing answers for the penny post; again, she cannot have her pencil, and so *ad infinitum* through life. People have no type before them in their lives, neither fathers and mothers, nor the children themselves. They look at things in detail. They say, 'It is very desirable that A, my daughter, should go to such a party, should know such a lady, should sit by such a person'. It is true. But what standard have they before them? of the nature and destination of man? The very words are rejected as pedantic. But might they not, at least, have a type in their minds that such an one might be a discoverer through her intellect, such another through her art, a third through her moral power?

Women often try one branch of intellect after another in their youth, *e.g.*, mathematics. But that, least of all, is compatible with the life of 'society'. It is impossible to follow up anything systematically. Women often long to enter some man's profession where they would find direction, competition (or rather opportunity of measuring the intellect with others), and, above all, time.

In those wise institutions, mixed as they are with many follies, which will last as long as the human race lasts, because they are adapted to the wants of the human race; those institutions which we call monasteries, and which, embracing much that is contrary to the laws of nature, are yet better adapted to the union of the life of action and that of thought than any other mode of life with which we are acquainted; in many such, four and a half hours, at least, are daily set aside for thought, rules are given for thought, training and opportunity afforded. Among us, there is *no* time appointed for this purpose, and the difficulty is that, in our social life, we must be always doubtful whether we ought not to be with somebody else or be doing something else.

Are men better off than women in this?

If one calls upon a friend in London and sees her son in the drawing-room, it strikes one as odd to find a young man sitting idling in his mother's drawing-room in the morning. For men, who are seen much in those haunts, there is no end of the epithets we have; 'knights of the carpet', 'drawing-room heroes', 'ladies' men'. But suppose we were to see a number of men in the morning sitting round a table in the drawing-room, looking at prints, doing worsted work, and reading little books, how we should laugh! A member of the House of Commons was once known to do worsted work. Of another man was said, 'His only fault is that he is too good; he drives out with his mother every day in the carriage, and if he is asked anywhere he answers that he must dine with his mother, but, if she can spare him, he will come in to tea, and he does not come'.

Now, why is it more ridiculous for a man than for a woman to do worsted work and drive out every day in the carriage? Why should we laugh if we were to see a parcel of men sitting round a drawing-room table in the morning, and think it all right if they were women?

Is man's time more valuable than woman's? or is the difference between man and woman this, that woman has confessedly nothing to do?

Women are never supposed to have any occupation of sufficient importance *not* to be interrupted, except 'suckling their fools'; and women themselves have accepted this, have written books to support it, and have trained themselves so as to consider whatever they do as *not* of such value to the world or to others, but that they can throw it up at the first 'claim of social life'. They have accustomed themselves to consider intellectual occupation as a merely selfish amusement, which it is

their 'duty' to give up for every trifler more selfish than themselves.

A young man (who was afterwards useful and known in his
day and generation) when busy reading and sent for by his
proud mother to shine in some morning visit, came; but, after it
was over, he said, 'Now, remember, this is not to happen again.
I came that you might not think me sulky, but I shall not come
again'. But for a young woman to send such a message to her
mother and sisters, how impertinent it would be! A woman of
great administrative powers said that she never undertook anything which she 'could not throw by at once, if necessary'.

How do we explain then the many cases of women who have
distinguished themselves in classics, mathematics, even in politics?

Widowhood, ill-health, or want of bread, these three explanations or excuses are supposed to justify a woman in taking up
an occupation. In some cases, no doubt, an indomitable force of
character will suffice without any of these three, but such are
rare.

But see how society fritters away the intellects of those
committed to her charge! It is said that society is necessary to
sharpen the intellect. But what do we seek society for? It does
sharpen the intellect, because it is a kind of *tour-de-force* to say
something at a pinch, – unprepared and uninterested with any
subject, to improvise something under difficulties. But what 'go
we out for to seek'? To take the chance of some one having
something to say which we want to hear? or of our finding
something to say which *they* want to hear? You have a little to
say, but not much. You often make a stipulation with some one
else, 'Come in ten minutes, for I shall not be able to find enough
to spin out longer than that'. You are not to talk of anything
very interesting, for the essence of society is to prevent any long
conversations and all *tête-à-têtes*. 'Glissez, n'appuyez pas'[71] is its
very motto. The praise of a good '*maîtresse de maison*' consists in
this, that she allows no one person to be too much absorbed in,
or too long about, a conversation. She always recalls them to
their 'duty'. People do not go into the company of their fellow-

creatures for what would seem a very sufficient reason, namely, that they have something to say to them, or something that they want to hear from them; but in the vague hope that they may find something to say.

Then as to solitary opportunities. Women never have half an hour in all their lives (excepting before or after anybody is up in the house) that they can call their own, without fear of offending or of hurting some one. Why do people sit up so late, or, more rarely, get up so early? Not because the day is not long enough, but because they have 'no time in the day to themselves'.

If we do attempt to do anything in company, what is the system of literary exercise which we pursue? Everybody reads aloud out of their own book or newspaper – or, every five minutes, something is said. And what is it to be 'read aloud to'? The most miserable exercise of the human intellect. Or rather, is it any exercise at all? It is like lying on one's back, with one's hands tied and having liquid poured down one's throat. Worse than that, because suffocation would immediately ensue and put a stop to this operation. But no suffocation would stop the other.

So much for the satisfaction of the intellect. Yet for a married woman in society, it is even worse. A married woman was heard to wish that she could break a limb that she might have a little time to herself. Many take advantage of the fear of 'infection' to do the same.

It is a thing *so* accepted among women that they have nothing to do, that one woman has not the least scruple in saying to another, 'I will come and spend the morning with you'. And you would be thought quite surly and absurd, if you were to refuse it on the plea of occupation. Nay, it is thought a mark of amiability and affection, if you are 'on such terms' that you can 'come in' 'any morning you please'.

In a country house, if there is a large party of young people, 'You will spend the morning with us', they say to the neighbours, 'we will drive together in the afternoon', 'to-morrow we will make an expedition, and we will spend the evening together'. And this is thought friendly, and spending time in a pleasant manner. So women play through life. Yet time is the most valuable of all things. If they had come every morning and afternoon and robbed us of half-a-crown we should have had redress from the police. But it is laid down, that our time is of no value. If you offer a morning visit to a professional man, and say, 'I will just stay an hour with you, if you will allow me, till so and so comes back to fetch me'; it costs him the earnings of an hour, and therefore he has a right to complain. But women have no right, because it is '*only* their time'.

Women have no means given them, whereby they *can* resist the 'claims of social life'. They are taught from their infancy upwards that it is wrong, ill-tempered, and a misunderstanding of 'woman's mission'[72] (with a great M.) if they do not allow themselves *willingly* to be interrupted at all hours. If a woman has once put in a claim to be treated as a man by some work of science or art or literature, which she can *show* as the 'fruit of her leisure', then she will be considered justified in *having* leisure (hardly, perhaps, even then). But if not, not. If she has nothing to show, she must resign herself to her fate.

SECTION III

'I like riding about this beautiful place, why don't you? I like walking about the garden, why don't you?' is the common expostulation – as if we were children, whose spirits rise during a fortnight's holidays, who think that they will last for ever – and look neither backwards nor forwards.

Society triumphs over many. They wish to regenerate the world with their institutions, with their moral philosophy, with their love. Then they sink to living from breakfast till dinner, from dinner till tea, with a little worsted work, and to looking forward to nothing but bed.

When shall we see a life full of steady enthusiasm, walking

straight to its aim, flying home, as that bird is now, against the wind – with the calmness and the confidence of one who knows the laws of God and can apply them?

What *do* we see? We see great and fine organizations deteriorating. We see girls and boys of seventeen, before whose noble ambitions, heroic dreams, and rich endowments we bow our heads, as before *God incarnate in the flesh*. But, ere they are thirty, they are withered, paralysed, extinguished. 'We have forgotten our visions', they say themselves.

The 'dreams of youth' have become a proverb. That organizations, early rich, fall far short of their promise has been repeated to satiety. But is it extraordinary that it should be so? For do we ever *utilize* this heroism? Look how it lives upon itself and perishes for lack of food. We do not know what to do with it. We had rather that it should not be there. Often we laugh at it. Always we find it troublesome. Look at the poverty of our life! Can we expect anything else but poor creatures to come out of it? Did Michael Angelo's genius fail, did Pascal's die in its bud, did Sir Isaac Newton become a common-place sort of man? In two of these cases the knife wore out the sheath. But the knife itself did not become rusty, till the body was dead or infirm.

Why cannot we *make use* of the noble rising heroisms of our own day, instead of leaving them to rust?

They have nothing to do.

Are they to be employed in sitting in the drawing-room, saying words which may as well not be said, which could be said as well if *they* were not there?

Women often strive to live by intellect. The clear, brilliant, sharp radiance of intellect's moonlight rising upon such an expanse of snow is dreary, it is true, but some love its solemn desolation, its silence, its solitude – if they are but *allowed* to live in it; if they are not perpetually baulked and disappointed. But a woman cannot live in the light of intellect. Society forbids it. Those conventional frivolities, which are called her 'duties', forbid it. Her 'domestic duties', high-sounding words, which, for the most part, are but bad habits (which she has not the courage to enfranchise herself from, the strength to break

through) forbid it. What are these duties (or bad habits)? –
Answering a multitude of letters which lead to nothing, from
her so-called friends – keeping herself up to the level of the
world that she may furnish her quota of amusement at the
breakfast-table; driving out her company in the carriage. And all
these things are exacted from her by her family which, if she is
good and affectionate, will have more influence with her than
the world.

What wonder if, wearied out, sick at heart with hope
deferred, the springs of will broken, not seeing clearly *where* her
duty lies, she abandons intellect as a vocation and takes it only,
as we use the moon, by glimpses through her tight-closed
window-shutters?

The family? It is too narrow a field for the development of an
immortal spirit, be that spirit male or female. The chances are a
thousand to one that, in that small sphere, the task for which
that immortal spirit is destined by the qualities and the gifts
which its Creator has placed within it, will not be found.

The family uses people, *not* for what they are, nor for what
they are intended to be, but for what it wants them for – for its
own uses. It thinks of them not as what God has made them,
but as the something which *it* has arranged that they shall be. If
it wants some one to sit in the drawing-room, *that* some one is
to be supplied by the family, though that member may be
destined for science, or for education, or for active superintendence by God, *i.e.*, by the gifts within.

This system dooms some minds to incurable infancy, others
to silent misery.

And family boasts that it has performed its mission well, in as
far as it has enabled the individual to say, 'I have *no* peculiar
work, nothing but what the moment brings me, nothing that I
cannot throw up at once at anybody's claim'; in as far, that is, as
it has *destroyed* the individual life. And the individual thinks that
a great victory has been accomplished, when, at last, she is able
to say that she has 'no personal desires or plans'. What is this
but throwing the gifts of God aside as worthless, and substituting for them those of the world?

Marriage is the only chance (and it is but a chance) offered to women for escape from this death; and how eagerly and how ignorantly it is embraced!

At present we live to impede each other's satisfactions; competition, domestic life, society, what is it all but this? We go somewhere where we are not wanted and where we don't want to go. What else is conventional life? *Passivity* when we want to be active. So many hours spent every day in passively doing what conventional life tells us, when we would so gladly be at work.

And is it a wonder that all individual life is extinguished?

Women dream of a great sphere of steady, not sketchy benevolence, of moral activity, for which they would fain be trained and fitted, instead of working in the dark, neither knowing nor registering whither their steps lead, whether farther from or nearer to the aim.

For how do people exercise their moral activity now? We visit, we teach, we talk, among 'the poor'; we are told, 'don't look for the fruits, cast thy bread upon the waters: for thou shalt find it after many days'. Certainly 'don't look', for you won't see. You will *not* 'find it', and then you would 'strike work'.

How different would be the heart for the work, and how different would be the success, if we learnt our work as a serious study, and followed it out steadily as a profession!

Were the physician to set to work at *his* trade, as the philanthropist does at his, how many bodies would he not spoil before he cured one! ·

We set the treatment of bodies so high above the treatment of souls, that the physician occupies a higher place in society than the schoolmaster. The governess is to have every one of God's gifts; she is to do that which the mother herself is incapable of doing; but our son must not degrade himself by marrying the governess, nor our daughter the tutor, though she might marry the medical man.

But my medical man does do something for me, it is said, my tutor has done nothing.

This is true, this is the real reason. And what a condemnation of the state of mental science it is! Low as is physical science, that of the mind is still lower.

Women long for an education to teach them *to teach*, to teach them the laws of the human mind and how to apply them – and knowing how imperfect, in the present state of the world, such an education must be, they long for experience, not patch-work experience, but experience followed up and systematized, to enable them to know what they are about and *where* they are 'casting their bread' and whether it *is* '*bread*' or a stone.

How should we learn a language if we were to give to it an hour a week? A fortnight's steady application would make more way in it than a year of such patch-work. A 'lady' can hardly go to 'her school' two days running. She cannot leave the breakfast-table – or she must be fulfilling some little frivolous 'duty', which others ought not to exact, or which might just as well be done some other time.

Dreaming always – never accomplishing; thus women live – too much ashamed of their dreams, which they think 'romantic', to tell them where they will be laughed at, even if not considered wrong.

With greater strength of purpose they might accomplish something. But if they were strong, all of them, they would not need to have their story told, for all the world would read it in the mission they have fulfilled. It is for common place, every-day characters that we tell our tale – because it is the sample of hundreds of lives (or rather deaths) of persons who cannot fight with society, or who, unsupported by the sympathies about them, give up their own destiny as not worth the fierce and continued struggle necessary to accomplish it. *One* struggle they *could* make and be free (and, in the Church of Rome, many, many, unallured by any other motive, make this one struggle to enter a convent); but the perpetual series of petty spars, with discouragements between, and doubts as to whether they are right – these wear out the very life necessary to make them.

If a man were to follow up his profession or occupation at odd times, how would he do it? Would he become skilful in that profession? It is acknowledged by women themselves that they are inferior in every occupation to men. Is it wonderful? *They* do *everything* at 'odd times'.

And if a woman's music and drawing are only used by her as an amusement (a *pass-time*, as it is called), is it wonderful that she tires of them, that she becomes disgusted with them?

In every dream of the life of intelligence or that of activity, women are accompanied by a phantom – the phantom of sympathy, guiding, lighting the way – even if they do not marry. Some few sacrifice marriage, because they must sacrifice all other life if they accept that. That man and woman have an equality of duties and rights is accepted by woman even less than by man. Behind *his* destiny woman must annihilate herself, must be only his complement. A woman dedicates herself to the vocation of her husband; she fills up and performs the subordinate parts in it. But if she has any destiny, any vocation of her own, she must renounce it, in nine cases out of ten. Some few, like Mrs Somerville,[73] Mrs Chisholm, Mrs Fry, have not done so; but these are exceptions. The fact is that woman has so seldom any vocation of her own, that it does not much signify; she has none to renounce. A man gains everything by marriage: he gains a 'helpmate', but a woman does not.

But if ever women come into contact with sickness, and crime, and poverty in masses, how the practical reality of life revives them! They are exhausted, like those who live on opium or on novels, all their lives – exhausted with feelings which lead to no action. If they see and enter into a continuous line of action, with a full and interesting life, with training constantly kept up to the occupation, occupation constantly testing the training – it is the *beau-idéal* of practical, not theoretical, education – they are re-tempered, their life is filled, they have found their work, and the means to do it.

Women, when they are young, sometimes think that an actress's life is a happy one – not for the sake of the admiration, not for the sake of the fame; but because in the morning she studies, in the evening she embodies those studies: she has the means of testing and correcting them by practice, and of resuming her studies in the morning, to improve the weak parts, remedy the failures, and in the evening try the corrections again. It is, indeed, true that, even after middle age, with such exercise of faculty, there is no end to the progress which may be made.

Some are only deterred from suicide because it is in the most distinct manner to say to God: 'I will not, I will not do as Thou wouldst have me', and because it is 'no use'.

To have no food for our heads, no food for our hearts, no food for our activity, is that nothing? If we have no food for the body, how we do cry out, how all the world hears of it, how all the newspapers talk of it, with a paragraph headed in great capital letters, DEATH FROM STARVATION! But suppose one were to put a paragraph in the 'Times', *Death of Thought from Starvation*, or *Death of Moral Activity from Starvation*, how people would stare, how they would laugh and wonder! One would think we had no heads nor hearts, by the total indifference of the public towards them. Our bodies are the only things of any consequence.

We have nothing to do which raises us, no food which agrees with us. We can never pursue any object for a single two hours, for we can never command any regular leisure or solitude; and in social or domestic life one is bound, under pain of being thought sulky, to make a remark every two minutes.

Men are on the side of society; they blow hot and cold; they say, 'Why can't you employ yourself in society?' and then, 'Why don't you talk in society?' I can pursue a connected conversation, or I can be silent; but to drop a remark, as it is called, every two minutes, how wearisome it is! It is impossible to pursue the current of one's own thoughts, because one must keep oneself ever on the alert 'to say something'; and it is impossible to say what one is thinking, because the essence of a remark is not to be a thought, but an impression. With what labour women have toiled to break down all individual and independent life, in order to fit themselves for this social and domestic existence, thinking it right! And when they have killed themselves to do it, they have awakened (too late) to think it wrong.

For, later in life, women could not make use of leisure and solitude if they had it! Like the Chinese woman, who could not make use of her feet, if she were brought into European life.

Some have an attention like a battering-ram, which, slowly brought to bear, can work upon a subject for any length of time. They can work ten hours just as well as two upon the same thing. But this age would have men like the musket, which you can load so fast that nothing but its heating in the process puts any limit to the number and frequency of times of firing, and at as many different objects as you please.

So, later in life, people cannot use their battering-ram. Their attention, like society's, goes off in a thousand different directions. They are an hour before they can fix it; and by the time it is fixed, the leisure is gone. They become incapable of consecutive or strenuous work.

What these suffer – even physically – from the want of such work no one can tell. The accumulation of nervous energy, which has had nothing to do during the day, makes them feel every night, when they go to bed, as if they were going mad; and they are obliged to lie long in bed in the morning to let it evaporate and keep it down.

At last they suffer at once from disgust of the one and incapacity for the other – from loathing of conventional idleness and powerlessness to do work when they have it. 'Now go, you have several hours,' say people, 'you have all the afternoon to yourself'. When they are all frittered away, they are to begin to work. When they are broken up into little bits, they are to hew away.

SECTION IV

Moral activity? There is scarcely such a thing possible! Everything is sketchy. The world does nothing but sketch. One Lady Bountiful sketches a school, but it never comes to a finished study; she can hardly work at it two weeks consecutively. Here and there a solitary individual, it is true, makes a really careful study – as Mrs Chisholm of emigration – as Miss Carpenter[74] of reformatory discipline. But, in general, a 'lady' has too many sketches on hand. She has a sketch of society, a sketch of her children's education, sketches of her 'charities', sketches of her reading. She is like a painter who should have five pictures in his studio at once, and giving now a stroke to one, and now a stroke to another, till he had made the whole round, should continue this routine to the end.

All life is sketchy, – the poet's verse (compare Tennyson, Milnes, and Mrs Browning[75] with Milton or even Byron: it is not the difference of genius which strikes one so much as the unfinished state of these modern sketches compared with the studies of the old masters), – the artist's picture, the author's composition – all are rough, imperfect, incomplete, even as works of art.

And how can it be otherwise? A 'leader' out of a newspaper, an article out of a review, five books read aloud in the course of an evening, such is our literature. What mind can stand three leading articles every morning as its food?

When shall we see a woman making a *study* of what she does? Married women cannot; for a man would think, if his wife undertook any great work with the intention of carrying it out, – of making anything but a sham of it – that she would 'suckle his fools and chronicle his small beer' less well for it, – that he would not have so good a dinner – that she would destroy, as it is called, his domestic life.

The intercourse of man and woman – how frivolous, how unworthy it is! Can we call *that* the true vocation of woman – her high career? Look round at the marriages which you know. The true marriage – that noble union, by which a man and woman become together the one perfect being – probably does not exist at present upon earth.

It is not surprising that husbands and wives seem so little part of one another. It is surprising that there is so much love as there is. For there is no food for it. What does it live upon – what nourishes it? Husbands and wives never seem to have anything to say to one another. What do they talk about? Not about any great religious, social, political questions or feelings. They talk about who shall come to dinner, who is to live in this lodge and who in that, about the improvement of the place, or when they shall go to London. If there are children, they form a common subject of some nourishment. But, even then, the case is oftenest thus, – the husband is to think of how they are to get on in life; the wife of bringing them up at home.

But any real communion between husband and wife – any descending into the depths of their being, and drawing out thence what they find and comparing it – do we ever dream of such a thing? Yes, we may dream of it during the season of 'passion'; but we shall not find it afterwards. We even *expect* it to go off, and lay our account that it will. If the husband has, by chance, gone into the depths of *his* being, and found anything there unorthodox, he, oftenest, conceals it carefully from his wife, – he is afraid of 'unsettling her opinions'.

What is the mystery of passion, spiritually speaking? For there *is* a passion of the Spirit. *Blind* passion, as it has most truly been called, seems to come on in man without his exactly knowing why, without his *at all* knowing why for *this* person rather than for *that*, and (whether it has been satisfied or unsatisfied) to go off again after a while, as it came, also without his knowing why.

The woman's passion is generally more lasting.

It is possible that this difference may be, because there is really more in man than in woman. There is nothing in her for him to have this intimate communion *with*. He cannot impart to her his religious beliefs, if he have any, because she would be 'shocked'. Religious men are and must be heretics now – for we must not pray, except in a 'form' of words, made beforehand – or think of God but with a pre-arranged idea.

With the man's political ideas, if they extend beyond the merest party politics, she has no sympathy.

His social ideas, if they are 'advanced', she will probably denounce without knowing why, as savouring of 'socialism' (a convenient word, which covers a multitude of new ideas and

offences). For woman is 'by birth a Tory', – has been often said
– by education a 'Tory', we mean.

Woman has nothing but her affections, – and this makes her
at once more loving and less loved.

But is it surprising that there should be so little real marriage,
when we think what the process is which leads to marriage?

Under the eyes of an always present mother and sisters (of
whom even the most refined and intellectual cannot abstain
from a jest upon the subject, who think it is their *duty* to be
anxious, to watch every germ and bud of it) the acquaintance
begins. It is fed – upon what? – the gossip of art, musical and
pictorial, the party politics of the day, the chit chat of society,
and people marry or sometimes they don't marry, discouraged
by the impossibility of knowing any more of one another than
this will furnish.

They prefer to marry in *thought*, to hold imaginary conversations with one another in idea, rather than, on such a flimsy
pretext of communion, to take the chance (*certainty* it cannot be)
of having more to say to one another in marriage.

Men and women meet now *to be idle*. Is it extraordinary that
they do not know each other, and that, in their mutual ignorance, they form no surer friendships? Did they meet to *do*
something together, then indeed they might form some real tie.

But, as it is, *they* are not there, it is only a mask which is there
–a mouth-piece of ready-made sentences about the 'topics of
the day'; and then people rail against men for choosing a woman
'for her face' – why, what else do they see?

It is very well to say 'be prudent, be careful, try to know each
other'. But how are you to know each other?

Unless a woman has lost all pride, how is it possible for her,
under the eyes of all her family, to indulge in long exclusive
conversations with a man? 'Such a thing' must not take place till
after her 'engagement'. And how is she to make an engagement,
if 'such a thing' has not taken place?

Besides, young women at home have so little to occupy and
to interest them – they have so little reason for *not* quitting their
home, that a young and independent man cannot look at a girl

without giving rise to 'expectations', if not on her own part, on
that of her family. Happy he, if he is not said to have been
'trifling with her feelings', or 'disappointing her hopes'! Under
these circumstances, how can a man, who has any pride or any
principle, become acquainted with a woman in such a manner as
to *justify* them in marrying?

There are four ways in which people marry. First, accident or
relationship has thrown them together in their childhood, and
acquaintance has grown up naturally and unconsciously.
Accordingly, in novels, it is generally cousins who marry; and
now it seems the only natural thing – the only possible way of
making an intimacy. And yet, we know that intermarriage
between relations is in direct contravention of the laws of
nature for the well-being of the race; witness the Quakers, the
Spanish grandees, the royal races, the secluded valleys of moun-
tainous countries, where madness, degeneration of race, defec-
tive organization and cretinism flourish and multiply.

The second way, and by far the most general, in which people
marry, is this. A woman, thoroughly uninterested at home, and
having formed a slight acquaintance with some accidental person, accepts him, if he 'falls in love' with her, as it is technically
called, and takes the chance. Hence the vulgar expression of
marriage being a lottery, which it most truly is, for that the *right*
two should come together has as many chances against it as
there are blanks in any lottery.

The third way is, that some person is found sufficiently
independent, sufficiently careless of the opinions of others, or
sufficiently without modesty to speculate thus: 'It is worth while
that I should become acquainted with so and so. I do not care
what his or her opinion of me is, if, *after* having become
acquainted, to do which can bear no other construction in
people's eyes than a desire of marriage, I retreat'. But there is
this to be said, that it is doubtful whether, under this unnatural
tension, which, to all susceptible characters, such a disregard of
the opinions which they care for must be, a healthy or a natural
feeling can grow up.

And now they are married – that is to say, two people have

received the licence of a man in a white surplice. But they are no more man and wife for that than Louis XIV and the Infanta of Spain, married by proxy, were man and wife. The woman who has sold herself for an establishment, in what is she superior to those we may not name?

Lastly, in a few rare, very rare, cases, such as circumstances, always provided in novels, but seldom to be met with in real life, present – whether the accident of parents' neglect, or of parents' unusual skill and wisdom, or of having no parents at all, which is generally the case in novels – or marrying out of the person's rank of life, by which the usual restraints are removed, and there is room and play left for attraction – or extraordinary events, isolation, misfortunes, which many wish for, even though their imaginations be not tainted by romance-reading; such alternatives as these give food and space for the development of character and mutual sympathies.

But a girl, if she has any pride, is so ashamed of having any thing she wishes to say out of the hearing of her own family, she thinks it must be something so very wrong, that it is ten to one, if she have the opportunity of saying it, that she will not.

And yet she is spending her life, perhaps, in dreaming of accidental means of unrestrained communion.

And then it is thought pretty to say that 'Women have no passion'. If passion is excitement in the daily social intercourse with men, women think about marriage much more than men do; it is the only event of their lives. It ought to be a sacred event, but surely not the only event in a woman's life, as it is now. Many women spend their lives in asking men to marry them, in a refined way. Yet it is true that women are seldom in love. How can they be?

How cruel are the revulsions which high-minded women suffer! There was one who loved, in connexion with great deeds, noble thoughts, devoted feelings. They met after an interval. It was at one of those crowded parties of Civilization which we call Society. His only careless passing remark was, 'The buzz to-night is like a manufactory'. Yet he loved her.

SECTION V

'L'enthousiasme et la faiblesse d'un temps où l'intelligence monte très haut, entrainée par l'imagination, et tombe très bas, écrasée par une réalité, sans poésie et sans grandeur'.[76]

Women dream till they have no longer the strength to dream; those dreams against which they so struggle, so honestly, vigorously, and conscientiously, and so in vain, yet which are their life, without which they could not have lived; those dreams go at last. All their plans and visions seem vanished, and they know not where; gone, and they cannot recall them. They do not even remember them. And they are left without the food either of reality or of hope.

Later in life, they neither desire nor dream, neither of activity, nor of love, nor of intellect. The last often survives the longest. They wish, if their experiences would benefit anybody, to give them to some one. But they never find an hour free in which to collect their thoughts, and so discouragement becomes ever deeper and deeper, and they less and less capable of undertaking anything.

It seems as if the female spirit of the world were mourning everlastingly over blessings, *not* lost, but which she has never had, and which, in her discouragement, she feels that she never will have, they are so far off.

The more complete a woman's organization, the more she will feel it, till at last there shall arise a woman, who will resume, in her own soul, all the sufferings of her race, and that woman will be the Saviour of her race.

Jesus Christ raised women above the condition of mere slaves, mere ministers to the passions of the man, raised them by his sympathy, to be ministers of God. He gave them moral activity. But the Age, the World, Humanity, must give them the means to exercise this moral activity, must give them intellectual cultivation, spheres of action.

There is perhaps no century where the woman shows so meanly as in this.* Because her education seems entirely to have parted company with her vocation; there is no longer unity between the woman as inwardly developed, and as outwardly manifested.

In the last century it was not so. In the succeeding one let us hope that it will no longer be so.

But now she is like the Archangel Michael as he stands upon Saint Angelo at Rome. She has an immense provision of wings, which seem as if they would bear her over earth and heaven; but when she tries to use them, she is petrified into stone, her feet are grown into the earth, chained to the bronze pedestal.

Nothing can well be imagined more painful than the present position of woman, unless, on the one hand, she renounces all outward activity and keeps herself within the magic sphere, the bubble of her dreams; or, on the other, surrendering all aspiration, she gives herself to her real life, soul and body. For those to whom it is possible, the latter is best, for out of activity may come thought, out of mere aspiration can come nothing.

But now – when the young imagination is so high and so developed, and reality is so narrow and conventional – there is no more parallelism between life in the thought and life in the actual than between the corpse, which lies motionless in its narrow bed, and the spirit, which, in our imagination, is at large among the stars.

The ideal life is passed in noble schemes of good consecutively followed up, of devotion to a great object, of sympathy given and received for high ideas and generous feelings. The actual life is passed in sympathy given and received for a dinner, a party, a piece of furniture, a house built or a garden laid out well, in devotion to your guests – (a too real devotion, for it implies that of all your time) – in schemes of schooling for the

---

* At almost every period of social life, we find, as it were, two under currents running different ways. There is the noble woman who dreams the following out her useful vocation; but there is also the selfish dreamer now, who is ever turning to something new, regardless of the expectations she has voluntarily excited, who is ever talking about 'making a life for herself', heedless that she is spoiling another life, undertaken, perhaps, at her own bidding. This is the ugly reverse of the medal.

poor, which you follow up perhaps in an odd quarter of an hour, between luncheon and driving out in the carriage – broth and dripping are included in the plan – and the rest of your time goes in ordering the dinner, hunting for a governess for your children, and sending pheasants and apples to your poorer relations. Is there anything in *this* life which can be called an Incarnation of the ideal life within? Is it a wonder that the unhappy woman should prefer to keep them entirely separate? not to take the bloom off her Ideal by mixing it up with her Actual; not to make her Actual still more unpalatable by trying to *inform* it with her Ideal? And then she is blamed, and her own sex unites against her, for not being content with the 'day of small things'. She is told that 'trifles make the sum of human things'; they do indeed. She is contemptuously asked, 'Would she abolish domestic life?' Men are afraid that their houses will not be so comfortable, that their wives will make themselves 'remarkable' – women, that they will make themselves distasteful to men; they write books (and very wisely) to teach themselves to dramatize 'little things', to persuade themselves that 'domestic life is their sphere' and to idealize the 'sacred hearth'. Sacred it is indeed. Sacred from the touch of their sons almost as soon as they are out of childhood – from its dulness and its tyrannous trifling *these* recoil. Sacred from the grasp of their daughters' affections, upon which it has so light a hold that they seize the first opportunity of marriage, *their* only chance of emancipation. The 'sacred hearth'; sacred to their husband's sleep, their sons' absence in the body and their daughters' in mind.

Oh! mothers, who talk about this hearth, how much do you know of your sons' real life, how much of your daughters' imaginary one? Awake, ye women, all ye that sleep, awake! If this domestic life were so very good, would your young men wander away from it, your maidens think of something else?

The time is come when women must do something more than the 'domestic hearth', which means nursing the infants, keeping a pretty house, having a good dinner and an entertaining party.

You say, 'It is true, our young men see visions, and our maidens dream dreams, but what of? Does not the woman intend to marry, and have over again what she has at home? and the man ultimately too?' Yes, but not the same; she *will* have the same, that is, if circumstances are not altered to prevent it; but her *idéal* is very different, though that *idéal* and the reality will never come together to mould each other. And it is not only the unmarried woman who dreams. The married woman also holds long imaginary conversations but too often.

SECTION VI

We live in the world, it is said, and must walk in its ways.

Was Christ called a complainer against the world? Yet all these great teachers and preachers must have had a most deep and ingrained sense, a continual gnawing feeling of the miseries and wrongs of the world. Otherwise they would not have been impelled to devote life and death to redress them. Christ, Socrates, Howard,[77] they must have had no ear for the joys, compared to that which they had for the sorrows of the world.

They acted, however, and we complain. The great reformers of the world turn into the great misanthropists, if circumstances or organisation do not permit them to act. Christ, if He had been a woman, might have been nothing but a great complainer. Peace be with the misanthropists! They have made a step in progress; the next will make them great philanthropists; they are divided but by a line.

The next Christ will perhaps be a female Christ. But do we see one woman who looks like a female Christ? or even like 'the messenger before' her 'face', to go before her and prepare the hearts and minds for her?

To this will be answered that half the inmates of Bedlam

begin in this way, by fancying that they are 'the Christ'.*

People talk about imitating Christ, and imitate Him in the little trifling formal things, such as washing the feet, saying his prayer, and so on; but if any one attempts the real imitation of Him, there are no bounds to the outcry with which the presumption of that person is condemned.

For instance, Christ was saying something to the people one day, which interested Him very much, and interested them very much; and Mary and his brothers came in the middle of it, and wanted to interrupt Him, and take Him home to dinner, very likely – (how natural that story is! does it not speak more home than any historic evidences of the Gospel's reality?), and He, instead of being angry with their interruption of Him in such an important work for some trifling thing, answers, 'Who is my mother? and who are my brethren? Whosoever shall do the will of my Father which is in heaven, the same is my brother and sister and mother'. But if *we* were to say that, we should be accused of 'destroying the family tie, of diminishing the obligation of the home duties'.

He might well say, 'Heaven and earth shall pass away, but my words shall not pass away'. His words will never pass away. If He had said, 'Tell them that I am engaged at this moment in something very important; that the instruction of the multitude ought to go before any personal ties; that I will remember to come when I have done', no one would have been impressed by His words; but how striking is that, 'Behold my mother and my brethren!'

---

* It is quite true that insanity, sensuality, and monstrous fraud have constantly assumed to be 'the Christ', *vide* the *Agapemone*[78] and the Mormons. 'Believing' a man of the name of Prince 'to be the tabernacle of God on earth', poor deluded women transfer to him all their stock in the Three per Cents. We hear of the Mormons, etc., being the 'recipients and mouth-pieces of God's Spirit'. They profess to be 'incarnations of the Deity', 'witnesses of the Almighty, solely knowing God's will, and being the medium of communicating it to man', and so forth. It does not appear to us that this blasphemy is very dangerous to the cause of true religion in general, any more than forgery is very dangerous to commerce in general. It is the universal dishonesty in religion, as in trade, which is really dangerous.

SECTION VII

The dying woman to her mourners: – 'Oh! if you knew how gladly I leave this life, how much more courage I feel to take the chance of another, than of anything I see before me in this, you would put on your wedding-clothes instead of mourning for me!'

'But', they say, 'so much talent! so many gifts! such good which you might have done!'

'The world will be put back some little time by my death', she says; 'you see I estimate my powers at least as highly as you can; but it is by the death which has taken place some years ago in me, not by the death which is about to take place now'. And so is the world put back by the death of every one who has to sacrifice the development of his or her peculiar gifts (which were meant, not for selfish gratification, but for the improvement of that world) to conventionality.

'My people were like children playing on the shore of the eighteenth century. I was their hobby-horse, their plaything; and they drove me to and fro, dear souls! never weary of the play themselves, till I, who had grown to woman's estate and to the ideas of the nineteenth century, lay down exhausted, my mind closed to hope, my heart to strength.

'Free – free – oh! divine freedom, art thou come at last? Welcome, beautiful death!'

Let neither name nor date be placed on her grave, still less the expression of regret or of admiration; but simply the words, 'I believe in God'.

VOLUME THREE

PART IV

SECTION III

_ _ _ _ _ _ _ _ _ _ _ _ _ _ _ _ _ _ _

In one sense we may say that there is no *perfection*, for perfect *thought*, perfect *feeling*, are not perfection, till manifested in activity. Thought, sentiment, activity in life dictated by thought and sentiment, these form the perfect will. But activity is development, succession of events; it is never-ending. Through fresh and fresh phases of activity, of life, the eternal purpose is being manifested. There is ever development of God's eternal purpose; there is ever attainment or preparation for attainment by work. The most desirable circumstances which any being could be in, would be circumstances willed by perfect goodness, wisdom, by Omnipotence, for the purpose of furnishing to that being means and inducement to attain perfection. Perfection attained by work, by communicating and receiving, this is the best possibility to any being. The Almighty himself would not conceive His existence righteous or satisfactory, if it were confined to willing, to contemplating, to feeling. 'My Father worketh and I work'. And by this work is all conscious being for ever being enriched, or preparing for enrichment.

Is not this the true support, if we can really feel and believe that ourselves, and all we love and care for, are really, by Almighty love and wisdom, secure of attaining God's truth, and love, and wisdom, and righteousness! On what a 'rock of ages' shall we, indeed, found our church, if we can believe this! What courage may not this inspire, even in the weary days of ignorance and error!

Without the belief in a continued identity there is really no belief in a wise and good superintendence. What is the aspect of present life, and the history of past life, without this belief? Estimate it, as you would do, if not overawed by the idea that it is God's work. Fear not to estimate God's work with such power as you have, for so only can you use the means He has given you to comprehend His nature and your own nature and destination.

We see beings forced into existence with no choice of their own; forced into an existence which most certainly they would *not* choose, if they had a choice. What battle-field is to be compared to the sufferings scattered over this world in one hour's course? – sufferings, too, generally unsoothed by any comprehension of why they exist! If there were not a sacred halo round Him, what should we say of the Being who could cause such sufferings for no ulterior benefit to the sufferer, but for future temporary benefit to some future being, who, benefiting by the experience of past ages, makes fewer mistakes?

But, in proportion as the favoured being possesses an existence valuable to himself and others, in such proportion is the inconsistency of quenching his being too.

Can the calm speculator talk of life as a 'mixture of good and evil', the 'good preponderating'? Let us well anatomize human life, before we pronounce this sentence on mankind at large. And if it cannot be truly said, then all suffering, unsatisfactory lives must surely point to a future for those identities in the will of the gracious spirit of love. Otherwise, the Omnipotent may, indeed, be said to have His hands 'bathed in blood' for ages.

But the physical laws make it incomprehensible, it is said.

Once grant that right is omnipotent, this difficulty ceases. And what is there to account for *any* co-existences, except the omnipotent will?

Is it asked, what beings will live after this life ceases? Every mode of being which admits of thought and feeling; for such modes of being require eternity for their development. No thought, no feeling, can have attained perfection, can have acted and lived perfection, in any limited period. Each individual thinking, feeling being, by the law of the Perfect, works upward, directly or indirectly, – attains to the perfect thought and feeling which comprehends all, which feels and wills all truth, – and then again sets forth to work and live, and manifest, and realize fresh phases of being, guided by the law of the all-comprehensive spirit.

Well-being consists in attainment by right exercise of true thought, feeling, and activity; of sympathy with and for one's kind; of communication to and from one's kind; of an entire trust in, and love and veneration for, a supreme being, whose will is believed to spring from a nature of perfect love, right-eousness, and wisdom; whose will is law, and whose will being law insures that all shall be well for the existences which spring from it.

It is not, indeed, for man to estimate the divine nature, but there are certain attributes of a superior power which manifest themselves in existence and in its laws. Of His attributes of love and wisdom we have, in a degree, experience and consciousness, – and by reflecting on the nature of love and wisdom, we may realize to ourselves in some degree what will be His will.

Is it possible that it will be satisfaction to Him to exist as contemplating, estimating, loving the activity which His law calls forth, but without working Himself?

Yet how, without a contradiction, can we attribute activity, work to the will which is law to the universe? The well-being of all is His will, but this well-being consists in attaining by exercise, for which His law is the means and inducement. Activity in the Being, whose will is the law of the universe, would mar His own purpose, the well-being of mankind. Yet, on the other hand, that perfect nature, can it find satisfaction without work? How shall we solve this contradiction? since it would seem inconsistent with the perfect nature either to work or not to work?

Is there anything inconsistent, contradictory in supposing this perfect spirit to will law, to will also to be the keeper of law in act, to will to Himself the satisfaction of well-being to others through His work and their work? 'My Father worketh and I work'. Would not this be the great union, the great at-onement of the Father and the Son? And if we reflect on the nature of love and wisdom and righteousness, is it absurd, or is it harmonious and consistent with such attributes, to suppose that will to be at the same time a superintending law of right, and the keeping of that law, attained by work?

With what patient endurance, with what hearty work we may go forth, if we believe that there is a will whose law secures all we can truly desire for ourselves and others, when it has been worked for aright. This will cause no slothful trust in another, for to work and to work aright is essential to each individual's success. It will give the spirit of freedom from fear in the certainty of success, if the object is pursued with a patient and earnest spirit, to which, by God's laws, it is in time insured that the right road will be found. 'Perfect love' will 'cast out fear'.

To talk of perfection without supposing it attained by the Being to whom it is attributed is a contradiction. To talk of perfection as the source of work and suffering, yet not working and suffering, is a contradiction.

The deep truths contained in those books, which, united, are called *The Book*, may well entitle it to such distinction. As religious and moral truth become revealed to us, we shall generally, perhaps, find some expression in the Bible, showing that some writer in it had a glimpse of that truth.

The spirit of righteousness, love, and wisdom is the abiding source of eternal law. The spirit of righteousness, love, and wisdom wills itself incarnated, modified by its own laws. Thus 'it is finished', fulfilled. Thus are the purposes essential to the spirit of righteousness, love, and wisdom accomplished. Thus does that spirit realize well-being to other being than its own individuality, by becoming itself the subject of its own law, while incarnating itself in varied being. Thus does the Father work in the Son. Thus does the Son work till he becomes one with the Father. Thus 'does the Father work and I work'.

'Do you, then, mean to say', may be asked, 'that God, as it

were, *divides* himself? that He exists as a perfect nature, willing law; that also He exists as an imperfect nature in other modes of being? Is not this absurd?'

In answering this, we must ask another question. What do we mean by 'God'? All we can say is, that we recognize a power superior to our own; that we recognize this power as exercised by a wise and good will. When you speak of God '*dividing* Himself', are not you, in using the word '*dividing*', referring to a material nature? I do recognize in existence the omnipotence of wisdom and goodness; or, rather, I recognize tendencies towards proving wisdom and goodness omnipotent. To man it is given in some degree to estimate the nature of wisdom and goodness. We can say, we are sure this or that would not be the will of wisdom and goodness; as we take the means we have in order to become wiser and better, we can more and more estimate what *would* be the will of wisdom and goodness. We can assuredly estimate that goodness would will happiness. We can estimate what happiness, what well-being, is. And can it be denied that this is well-being, to attain by exercise all that, in the thought of wisdom and goodness, is worthy to be attained, – to receive from and communicate to our kind, – and to pursue our course with the assurance that a super-intending power is educating us for the happiness of each and of all?

We may trace that this education is really going on. Our power of estimating the nature of wisdom and goodness is also capable of revealing to us that the perfect nature wills a perfect law of invariable co-existences and successions, which is His education of those beings whom He has so constituted, that essentially they seek their greatest satisfactions. Let it not be supposed that this is an education to selfishness; for *their* satisfactions, like His own, He has constituted to be love and wisdom.

Again, man's capability of estimating love and wisdom will reveal to him that the perfect thought, the perfect sentiment, would *will* no other interference with any mode of existence, not itself, except law, because this will would best promote the greatest degree, the highest kind of happiness.

Yet we may also distinguish that that existence would not satisfy a perfect love and wisdom, which was without other activity than will for the activity of other beings. And does not this reveal that God incarnates Himself, *i.e*, the attributes which constitute all that we know of God, wherever we find them? He wills the laws of physical existence. Are not they the limits to His nature? By knowing and keeping aright the laws which affect this material existence, does not experience prove that the divine nature, at all events, a nature corresponding to the divine, increases in power? And is it not thus revealed that God is really keeping as well as willing the law of love and wisdom, thus satisfying the desire essential to His nature for the happiness of other being than His own? For each being, in whom he thus incarnates Himself, has an identity of its own; and this identity, through His law is directly or indirectly, ever progressing till it has by exercise, by life, realized into activity His thought and sentiment.

Thus shall eternity be ever enriching eternity with fresh realizations, in successive activity, of the thought and the sentiment of which we may say,

> 'Nothing is there to come and nothing past,
> But one eternal now doth ever last'.[79]

It is said that we take for granted manifestations as proving, without other revelation, the existence of the perfect law, of a perfect nature; but, it will be asked, how do we trace this perfect law in a world where exists so much evil and suffering, so little, if any, divine happiness?

We admit that we discern tendencies, evidence only, not proof, verification. But are these tendencies, this evidence to be therefore disregarded, when they lead us to the conclusion that the process of verification extends over eternity? Mankind are, after these thousands (we know not how many) of years of existence, still in dark ignorance of the nature of the being who calls man into existence, of man's nature, of man's true destination, of God's laws which are to be kept in that one definite way which is *right*, in order to secure well being.

But the all-comprehensive all-superintending power waits while all is accomplishing itself through the law of the Father, the activity of the Son. Man has attained much; but as yet man knows not God; man knows not man; man knows not his real satisfaction, though it be essential to him to seek it; man, while unconscious of the depth of his ignorance, is alike unconscious of the height of his capability.

NOTES

[1] Samuel Johnson (1709–84), poet, dramatist, essayist, and compiler of a dictionary of the English language.

[2] John Milton (1608–74), poet and essayist, author of *Paradise Lost*; Robert South (1634–1716), Anglican divine; Isaac Watts (1674–1748), composer of hymns and religious poetry; William Law (1686–1761), author of *A Serious Call to a Devout and Holy Life* (1728).

[3] Belief in the existence of God (in contrast to atheism) that does not deny revelation (in contrast to deism).

[4] The Bible.

[5] Or Zarathustra (c. 628–551 BC), Persian founder of religious doctrine that emphasized a qualified form of monotheism.

[6] René Descartes (1596–1650), French natural philosopher; Pierre-Simon Laplace (1749–1827), French mathematician and physicist; David Hume (1711–76), Scottish philosopher and historian.

[7] F. M. A. Voltaire (1694–1778), French philosopher and writer; Edward Gibbon (1737–94), English historian.

[8] Johann Wolfgang Goethe (1749–1832) and Friedrich Schiller (1759–1805), German philosophers; John Henry Newman (1801–90), as author of several of the *Tracts for the Times*, one of the founders of the Oxford Tractarians. Newman converted to Catholicism in 1845 and became cardinal of the Holy Roman Church in 1879.

[9] James Martineau (1805–1900), Unitarian divine and younger brother of Harriet Martineau (1802–76).

[10] Hans Christian Oersted (1777–1851), Danish physicist known for work on magnetism.

[11] From Francis Bacon (1561–1626), Lord Chancellor and author of the *New Atlantis* and *Novum Organum*. 'Baconian' is associated with inductive reasoning, based on experimentation. While Nightingale desires a 'Baconian way' in religion, much of this volume negotiates between inductive reasoning from experience and deductive reasoning from faith or hypothesis.

[12] Reference to the demonstrations, most popularly advanced in Charles Lyell's *Principles of Geology* (1830–3), that the earth was not formed in one week but by a prolonged period of physical changes.

[13] August Comte (1798–1857), French philosopher who founded the 'Religion of Humanity' and who adopted the term 'positivism' for the descriptive study of material nature.

[14] The eternal becoming.

[15] A mere assertion.

[16] Slum areas of London, thought to be haunts of criminals as well as the poor.

[17] Slum neighbourhood in London. The discussion that follows is a response to English interpretations of Adolphe Quetelet's crime and suicide statistics. These interpretations argued that because statistics had shown that a certain number of events *had* occurred, that same number of events was *destined* to occur.

[18] John Calvin (1509–64), Protestant reformer who emphasized particular election and predestination.

[19] Adolphe Quetelet (1796–1874), Belgian statistician.

VOLUME TWO

[20] Severe facial neuralgia with painful spasmodic contractions.

[21] Thomas Babington Macaulay (1800–59), English historian and essayist.

[22] St Vincent de Paul (c. 1580–1660), founder of the Lazarist Fathers in 1625 and the Sisters of Charity in 1633. The Sisters of Charity was the first congregation of women devoted to the care of the sick and the poor.

[23] The 'Amazon' was a large wooden steamer-sailing ship, which was bound for Panama in January, 1852 when its engines overheated and the ship burned in the Bay of Biscay. One hundred and four passengers and crew perished out of the total of one hundred and sixty persons on board.

[24] Count Frerico Confalonieri (1785-1846), Italian revolutionary incriminated in the Piedmontese revolt (1821), sentenced to life imprisonment at Spielberg in 1824 and pardoned in 1836.

[25] Members of the Protestant denomination originated by John Wesley (1703–91) in the late 1720s and incorporated in the 1780s. Methodists emphasized the importance of personal inspiration and religious enthusiasm.

[26] Count Axel Gustafsson Oxenstjerna (1583–1654), Chancellor of King Gustav II of Sweden renowned for his abilities as a statesman.

[27] Sir Walter Scott (1771–1832), Scottish novelist and poet.

[28] Sarah Siddons (1755–1831), actress, famous for her performances at Drury Lane Theatre.

[29] Francis Jeffrey (1773–1850), Scottish critic and essayist, who founded and then edited the *Edinburgh Review*.

[30] Pauline Viardot, born Garcia (1821–1910), French singer.

[31] Pseudonym for Amandine-Aurore-Lucie Dupin (1804–76), French novelist.

[32] Robert Peel (1788–1850), prime minister from 1834–5 and from 1841–6.

[33] Friedrich Schiller (1759–1805), German philosopher.

[34] Johann Wolfgang von Goethe (1749–1832), German philosopher and novelist.

[35] Statistician.

[36] George Hudson (1800–71), nicknamed the 'Railway King' for his promotion and direction of railway companies during the 1830s and 1840s. The wealthiest and most influential railway director, Hudson was honoured with numerous testimonials and won election to Parliament in 1845. Hudson's good fortune came to an end in 1849, when he was forced to retire amid rumours of massive debt and fraud.

[37] Decorative papering.

[38] Fatigued with mental weariness or dissatisfaction.

[39] Guercino was the nickname for Francesco Barbieri (1591-1666), Italian painter. Guido was a thirteenth-century Siennese painter.

[40] Niceness is not necessarily a virtue but an amusement.

[41] Thomas Arnold (1795-1842), headmaster of Rugby and regius professor of history at Oxford from 1841. His influence was instrumental in the founding of the Oxford Movement (later called Tractarianism).

[42] Teresa of Ávila or St Teresa of Jesus (1515–82), Spanish Carmelite nun and mystic who reformed the Carmelite Order in the late sixteenth century. St Teresa was the first writer to give a scientific account of the entire life of prayer from meditation to the so-called mystic marriage.

[43] 'Evangelicalism' was used in reference to either a subset of the Anglican Church or those dissenting sects who emphasized the inspiration and authority of scripture, the depravity of humanity, justification by faith alone, and the sacraments. In 1846, the Evangelical Alliance was formed in London to link these groups so as to resist the encroachments of Catholicism and the Oxford Movement (or Tractarianism). See note 41 above.

[44] Martin Luther (1483-1546), founder of the Protestant Reformation.

[45] Baden Powell (1796-1860), liberal Anglican divine and Savilian professor of geometry at Oxford who promoted the acceptance of physical science by both the Church and the university.

[46] Mark Pattison (1813–84), Anglican divine, who reacted to Newman's 1845 conversion to Catholicism by moving from Tractarianism to liberal Anglicanism.

[47] David Cherbury (fl. 1430), Bishop of Dromore and a Carmelite friar.

[48] Ancient Egyptian dynasty (304-30 BC).

[49] John Wesley (1703–91), founder of Methodism.

[50] Another name for the Oxford Movement or Tractarianism. The movement was called 'Puseyism' after Edward Pusey (1800-1882), Anglican divine. The movement within the Church of England was founded to resist the decline of the Church and the spread of theological 'liberalism'. Tractarianism emphasized the divinity of the Church, Apostolic Succession, and the importance of the sacraments and the Book of Common Prayer. See notes 41 and 43 above.

[51] The Catholic Emancipation Act of 1829.

[52] 'I believe, because it is impossible'. Ascribed to St Augustine but founded on a passage in Tertullian's De Carne Christie.

[53] Sir William Herschel (1738–1822) and his son, Sir John Frederick

Herschel (1792–1871), both astronomers; James Mill (1773–1836) and his son, John Stuart Mill (1806–73), both philosophers.

[54] William Pitt (1708–78), first Earl of Chatham and Whig statesman. Charles James Fox (1749–1806), whig statesman both were renowned for their oratory.

[55] Nicolas Copernicus (1473–1543), Galilei Galileo (1564–1642), Johannes Kepler (1571–1630), Sir Isaac Newton (1642–1727), Pierre-Simon Laplace (1749–1827), and Sir William Herschel (1738–1822), astronomers.

[56] Sir Joshua Jebb (1793–1863), surveyor-general of convict prisons, designer and later commissioner of the Pentonville Model Prison. Lord Ashley 7th Earl of Shaftesbury (1801–85), reforming MP and president of the Ragged School Union for forty years. Ragged Schools were schools for poor children, staffed by voluntary teachers. The Ragged School Union was formed in 1844.

[57] Prince Felix (1800–52), Austrian politician and diplomat, Hapsburg minister from 1848–52 who restored imperial authority after 1848.

[58] James Blomfield Rush (d. 1849), murderer of Isaac Jermy and his son in 1849.

[59] Edward Geoffrey Smith Stanley, 14th Earl of Derby (1799–1869), British MP who, as leader of the Protectionist party, bitterly opposed repeal of the Corn Laws. Served as prime minister in 1852, 1858, and from 1866–8.

[60] Orleans King of France, 1830–48, abdicated in 1848 revolution. After a period of republic Louis Napoleon (1808–73) became Emperor in 1852.

[61] Political lobbying organization formed in 1838 to secure the repeal of the Corn Laws and to resist government interference in trade. The Laws were repealed in 1846.

[62] Followers of Islam, the religion founded by Mohammed (c. 570–629).

[63] Elizabeth Fry (1780–1845), prison reformer; Caroline Chisholm (1808–77), aided emigration efforts of English men and women.

[64] This discussion of religious 'tolerance' includes Nightingale's criticism of the resolution to the Gorham controversy. (See Introduction to this volume.)

[65] This refers to the conversions by Viscount Fielding, T. W. Allies and Henry Wilberforce following the resolution of the Gorham controversy in 1850. (See Introduction to this volume.)

[66] *Paradise Lost*, Book I, l. 555.

[67] Citizen of Sparta.

[68] In Greek mythology, Cassandra is the daughter of Priam and Hecuba. Cassandra received the gift of prophecy from Apollo, in exchange for promising to satisfy his desire for her, but when she refused, Apollo doomed Cassandra to have her prophecies ignored or disbelieved. After the Trojan War, Agamemnon took Cassandra back to Greece as his concubine. She repeatedly foretold the calamities that awaited Agamemnon's return, but he did not believe her. Both Agamemnon and Cassandra were murdered by Clytemnestra, Agamemnon's wife, as the prophetess had foreseen.

[69] Reference to Matthew 3:3, which echoes Isaiah 40:3. Nightingale substitutes 'crowd' for wilderness'.

[70] Probably from an Evangelical hymn.

[71] Remain superficial or noncommital.

[72] Reference to popular book of this title published by Sarah Lewis in 1839.

[73] Mary Somerville (1780–1872), foremost woman scientist of the day.

[74] Mary Carpenter (1807–77), philanthropist, known primarily for her promotion of reformatory schools.

[75] Alfred (Lord) Tennyson (1809–92); Richard Moncton Milnes (1809–85), later Baron Houghton; Elizabeth Barrett Browning (1806–61), contemporary poets.

[76] 'The enthusiasm and the weakness of an age in which intelligence climbs to a very high peak, swept along by the imagination and falls very low, crushed by a reality, without poetry and without grandeur'.

[77] John Howard (1726?–90), philanthropist, known primarily for prison reform.

[78] The Church of the Agapemone was founded in the village of Spaxton in 1849 by H. J. Prince. Prince claimed to be the Holy Ghost personified, but the sect was exposed as practising licentious and immoral activities.

VOLUME III

[79] *Davideis*, Book I, ll. 360–1, by Abraham Cowley (1618–67).